SO CLOSE TO THE STATE/S
THE EMERGENCE OF CANADIAN FEATURE FILM POLICY

This book examines in detail the formation of Canadian feature film policy from the 1950s to the present. It pays special attention to the role played by producers, filmmakers, and government agencies in relation to the changing production practices brought about by Canadian television.

For Canadian policy-makers, the feature film was considered to be a signifier of cultural modernity. Filmmakers' desire to experiment with a new format was subverted by a political-economic agenda intent on using the format to create cultural authenticity for a nation lagging behind its neighbour to the South. Dorland crafts a careful historical analysis based on primary sources, including government records and in-depth personal interviews with key participants. Employing Foucault's concept of governmentality, Dorland analyses the state's interest in influencing and shaping feature film production. .

A major contribution to scholarship on Canadian cinema, *So Close to the State/s* provides a revealing look at the relationship between culture and the state.

MICHAEL DORLAND is a professor in the Mass Communication Program at Carleton University.

MICHAEL DORLAND

So Close to the State/s:
The Emergence of Canadian
Feature Film Policy

UNIVERSITY OF TORONTO PRESS
Toronto Buffalo London

© University of Toronto Press Incorporated 1998
Toronto Buffalo London
Printed in Canada

ISBN 0–8020–4182–5 (cloth)
ISBN 0–8020–8043–X (paper)

Printed on acid-free paper

Canadian Cataloguing in Publication Data

Dorland, Michael, 1948–
So close to the State/s : the emergence of Canadian feature film policy

Includes bibliographical references and index.
ISBN 0-8020-4182-5 (bound)   ISBN 0-8020-8043-x (pbk.)

1. Motion picture industry – Canada – History.   2. Motion picture industry –
Canada – Government policy.   I. Title.

PN1993.5.C3D67 1998   791.43'0971   C97-932577-3

University of Toronto Press acknowledges the financial assistance to its
publishing program of the Canada Council for the Arts and the Ontario Arts
Council.

This book has been published with the help of a grant from the Humanities
and Social Sciences Federation of Canada, using funds provided by the Social
Sciences and Humanities Research Council of Canada.

Contents

Introduction

The centenary of cinema has come and gone. There was, surprisingly perhaps, little fanfare in 1996 to celebrate the anniversary. Handsome commemorative stamps were struck by various nations. Public television networks ran retrospectives of old films. In the *New York Times Magazine* the writer and filmmaker Susan Sontag published a belated obituary for the medium.[1] Given the ubiquity of moving images in contemporary life, cinema, a one-hundred-year-old technology, was just something that had happened long ago.

But the cinema whose passing Sontag and others mourned was, in fact, largely that of only one period, from the end of the Second World War until the mid-1970s. It was, in other words, the cinema of a set of historically unique circumstances, through which, in Seth Feldman's elegant phrase, 'an existentially inclined *zeitgeist* nourished the actualization of personal realities.'[2] Principal among these circumstances was the end of cinema's monopoly, particularly in Western Europe and North America, over moving images, and its displacement by a new domestic technology of image delivery, that of television. For the established film industries, notably those of the United States and of Europe, it was a time both of crisis and of opportunity. The crisis arose from the economic implications on the Hollywood film industry of the Consent Decrees of 1948 that dismantled the vertically integrated system of control by studios of production, distribution, and exhibition, and from the relentlessly downward plunge in attendance at movie theatres. As well, the shift away from studio control over distribution gave independent distributors greater play and briefly opened up new niches in international markets, affording non-Hollywood films more opportunities. For the film industries of Europe these new spaces not only encouraged an increased reliance on such resource-pooling strategies as co-production but also allowed for the appearance of a succession of 'new waves' in production aesthetics, notably as a result of lightweight cameras and portable synchronous sound-recording devices, film stocks of greater sensitivity to light, smaller crews, and the emergence of the writer-director. At about the same time, the technical and organizational changes crystallized in the writings of critics, who perceived them as manifestations of the emergence of new, 'national' styles, such as the 'French New Wave,' the 'New American Cinema,' and the like.

In the thirty-year period after the end of the Second World War, which saw first the 'de-monopolization' of cinema and then 're-monopolization' by television, possibilities for alternative practices in film production, distribution, and exhibition – in other words, for an alternative 'culture' of the cinema – opened up and, in due course, gradually closed down. These alternative spaces, however, have been *imagined* differently: for Susan Sontag and other critics of her generation, these imagined alternatives represented a form of 'cine-love' that was coterminous with cinema itself. There were other imaginings of these alternative spaces: as cinema of auteurs, experimental cinema, political cinema, cinema of emerging national sensibilities, or at times all of these combined to a greater or lesser degree. This book looks at these imaginings as they were articulated in the specific national context of Canada.

It is significant that the Canadian state would claim to be one of the feature film–producing countries of the world during the 1960s, when the transition from one hegemonic medium to another was taking place. Although several thousand feature-length films had been shot in Canada since the invention of the medium,[3] these had been produced more by accident than by design and were usually the work of non-Canadian producers during brief visits. There had been recurring attempts by Canadians to establish production firms and even studios as early as the first decades of the century, but with few exceptions these ventures were short-lived efforts or outright failures. The burden of Canadian film scholarship has been to explain why this was so, and explanations have ranged from the lack of consistent policies by the state to the accident of Canada's location alongside the northern border of the United States.

In any case, it would not be until the 1960s that the making of feature films became a continuing policy issue for agencies of the federal government with fiscal and bureaucratic implications. To be sure, the extent of the government's commitment has fluctuated considerably in the period from the 1960s to the present, but it was in that critical decade, as signalled by the allocation in 1968 of a modest $10 million for the production of Canadian-made feature-length films, that the federal state determined it would henceforth be in 'the national interest' to fund Canadian feature films. How this change in attitude came about, what kinds of pressures were brought to bear and by whom, and what determined which decisions were reached regarding ongoing and long-term changes in the international film industry, in the U.S. film industry, as well as the future of the Canadian film industry – these are some of the issues that the following narrative addresses.

As the title of this book suggests, the story is not without its ironies: Canada opted for a 'solution' to 'its' film problems that was both limited and partial. Whether there were other, better choices is a question that will be discussed in this book and will no doubt be debated elsewhere. The old joke tells about being 'as Canadian as possible under the circumstances'; this study hopes to clarify what the circumstances were. It is ironic that, given the importance of the circumstances surrounding feature film making in Canada, they have yet to be presented fully in the written record.

Accordingly, Chapter 1 reviews some of the principal problems involved in the writing of Canadian film history. The second chapter discusses the predominant role of the Canadian state in cultural development and argues that its policies are best understood through the perspective of the relationships between knowledge and policy that Michel Foucault termed 'governmentality.' Chapters 3 to 6 present the historical narrative and recount the processes by which the making of feature films became an object of state policy. Chapter 7 concludes the study with a discussion of the problems of policy formation in increasingly post-national contexts and as a result of the 'postmodern' blending of action-oriented forms of knowledge, such as scholarship and policy-making, and the risk of confusing action with analysis.

This study sees itself as a contribution to 'thick' policy analysis, undertaking through a detailed discussion of policy in a particular period to raise some of the problems affecting cultural policy-making within increasingly transnational contexts. The study does not try to be exhaustive in its treatment of the aesthetic dimensions of Canadian cinema, nor does it pretend to be definitive. However, if in clarifying the ambivalence of the historical record it helps diminish some of the wishful thinking that has animated much of the scholarship on Canadian film, it will have served its purpose.

The study initially took the form of a doctoral dissertation in the Joint PhD Program in Communication of Concordia University, the Université de Montréal, and the Université du Québec à Montréal. I would like to express my profound gratitude to the Social Sciences and Humanities Research Council of Canada for the doctoral and postdoctoral fellowships that enabled me to carry out the initial and subsequent investigations. I would also like to thank the members of my dissertation committee who have since become colleagues and friends: my former supervisor, Dr Brian Lewis, now at Simon Fraser University, Dr Maurice Charland of Concordia University and a collaborator in a forthcoming study on the rhetoric of the Canadian public sphere; and Dr Gaëtan Tremblay of the Université du Québec à Montréal, my mentor in the study of the cultural industries. Professor Peter Harcourt, my colleague at Carleton Univesity, who served as the external examiner, will always have a special place in my thoughts about Canadian cinema.

This study would literally not have been possible without the extraordinary assistance of Bernard Lutz, director of records management at the National Film Board. Jean-Claude Mahé, secretary to the Board of Governors at the NFB, kindly permitted me to consult the minutes of the board. Special thanks for access to the minutes of the Canadian Film Development Corporation is owed to Michel Montagne, director of communications at Telefilm Canada, and to Lise Corriveau, secretary to the Board of Governors, for her generosity with the photocopier. At the National Archives of Canada, archivists Anne Goddard and Michel Filion were more than helpful in their suggestions.

A special debt is owed to my colleagues in the School of Journalism and Communication at Carleton University, not only for the excellence of their own work but also for their intellectual insight and for providing an ideal environment in which to bring this study to completion. At the University of Toronto Press, the unwavering support of executive editor Virgil D. Duff made the task that much more doable. Thanks too to Margaret Williams for taking charge of the manuscript and *remerciements chaleureux* to Henri Pilon for the superb attention he brought to copy-editing. I would also like to acknowledge the helpful suggestions and careful reading of the manuscript by anonymous readers for the University of Toronto Press, the Canadian Federation of the Humanities, and the Aid to Scholarly Publications Program.

Finally, it remains to dedicate this book to a number of people: my late grandfather, Arthur G. Dorland, formerly of the History Department at the University of Western Ontario; my parents, Albert A. Dorland and

the late Janine M. Grumbach-Dorland, whose life histories introduced me
to the puzzles of history; Jean-Pierre Tadros and his former partner,
Constance Dilley, two pioneering journalists without whose devoted
work the contemporary history of Canadian cinema could never be written; my son Christopher in the continued pursuit of his dreams, with the
reminder that this project also began as a working journalist's dream fifteen years ago; and, as ever and for always, my life co-partner and colleague, Priscilla L. Walton, who inspired me to stop procrastinating.

SO CLOSE TO THE STATE/S

1

Problems of Writing Canadian Film History

Antinomies of Scholarship and Policy

Compared to the equivalent scholarship in any number of other countries[1] not only is the writing of the film history of Canada underdeveloped but also it remains entangled in conceptual difficulties largely of its own making. These difficulties have manifested themselves in the kind of film scholarship that has been produced in Canada; they have also had repercussions on the kinds of policies in support of filmmaking that have been adopted over the years by agencies of the state. The reasons for the difficulties are, of course, complex, and the pages that follow attempt to make some of them clearer. Few things take shape in a vacuum, least of all the productions of knowledge or the processes by which state agencies come to elaborate and adopt the policies to guide decisions and actions. And yet, curiously, Canadian film history – or, more precisely, the ways in which it has been written – continues to dwell within a vacuum both of scholarship and of policy.

For scholars in Canada and elsewhere the challenge posed by the Canadian example seems to be the utter heterogeneity of its cinema. At various times, it has been represented by tendencies in documentary filmmaking, in animation, or in experimental cinema. In the 1960s, with the emergence of an increasing number of Canadian-made feature-length films, the tendency was for a while labelled 'New Canadian Cinema.' As well, the varied production traditions – all identified in whole or in part as 'Canadian cinema' – emanated from a variety of institutional sites ranging from national agencies such as the National Film Board of Canada (NFB) beginning in the late 1930s to the Canada Council and the Canadian Film Development Corporation in the 1960s, to private-sector firms and independent production cooperatives. In turn, this variety of filmmaking practices has been inflected not only by the bilingual and, more recently, multicultural self-definitions of the nature of Canadian society, but also by the difficulties of translating such self-definitions into appropriate institutions.

The results of shifting practices, compounded by changing technologies of image-production, most notably from film to video, have had ramifications in such questions as the political economy of theatrical exhibition and distribution and have entailed not just the development of such para-institutional sites as film festivals, critical magazines, and journals, but also the alternative vehicles of delivery represented by broadcasting, cable, and other technologies. Recently a call for papers issued by the principal academic association representing international film scholarship for its 1997 annual meeting in Ottawa on the theme of 'Cinema(s) in Canada,' stated that 'Cinema in Canada has contours that are never simply national ... it also includes the experience of film cultures from outside Canada's national borders, notably those of the U.S. and France.'[2] In the light of such a diversity of genres, practices, institutional sites, and transnational influences, it is perhaps hardly surprising that film scholars, whether in Canada or elsewhere, have found 'the cinema in Canada' to represent a dauntingly complex object of study.

Canadian Film Studies

Cutting a path towards a better understanding of the multifaceted problematic of the cinema in Canada has been the task that Canadian film scholars took up as their own. In the 1960s and especially after the 1970s scholars began to benefit from the expansion of Canadian institutions of higher education and the creation of film studies units, initially often within English departments and eventually as largely undergraduate departments in their own right.[3] The task faced by these scholars, most of them men, was considerable, and their achievements, whether in compiling filmographies,[4] in assembling the first anthologies of critical writings on Canadian films,[5] in narrating the first substantial history of Canadian filmmaking efforts,[6] and in lobbying for film institutions, archives, and preservation practices were foundational. Their work as educators, whether with students, with cultural bureaucrats and politicians, or with radio and television audiences, was truly that of public intellectuals. But whatever else their activities consisted of, they were also an encounter with the historical imagination; above and beyond the compilation of lists and of the identification of meaningful dates and key trends, theirs was an imaginative endeavour to map out an intellectual field, then in a high degree of transnational theoretical ferment,[7] as it pertained to the Canadian case. Their work, in short, constituted an intellectual moment in which to begin to define some of the fundamental historiographical principles that underlie the study of the cinema in Canada.

It was at the beginning of this scholarly work, however, that certain conceptual choices were made that were to turn out to be regrettable. For example, the encounter with the writing of Canadian film history was a displaced form of encounter with the writing of Canadian history, itself a field of intellectual inquiry undergoing profound transformation at the time.[8] In the case of Canadian film history the encounter took the brutal form of the discovery of the power of historical amnesia. As Piers Handling remarked in an early anthology,

What struck me in assembling an anthology of this kind is the amount of film that we have produced over the decade and how little of it is ... part of our collective consciousness. Exploring Canadian film is analogous to meeting ... person[s] suffering from amnesia. Their past is no longer remembered. It has no considered relationship to their present.[9]

The initial encounter with Canadian film history thus entailed an encounter with a *displaced past* that it fell to the historical analyst to account for. But that displaced past, as Handling's co-editor for the anthology, Pierre Véronneau, would observe, although without fully drawing out the implications of his reflection, also seemed to correlate to a striking degree to the instability of 'Canadian cinema' as an object of study. Given the complex heterogeneity of Canadian cinema, where was the analyst actually to 'locate' it? As Véronneau and Handling wrote in surveying the key traits of Canadian cinema since the 1890s,

We soon discover[ed] that [Canadian cinema] never focussed on one particular [geographic] area ... It is impossible to grasp the cinema in Canada: it disappears in one area, crops up in another, moves from west to east, splits up, dies, is reborn, etc.[10]

However, rather than making these characteristics – extensive practices but no institutional memory and an extreme heterogeneity of location – starting points for a problematic of historiographical method, Canadian scholars treated them merely as problems to be disposed of. And the 'dispensation' was neatly provided by drawing on the concept of 'national cinema' from the larger field of international film scholarship.

The manoeuvre manifested itself strikingly in the first collection of proto-academic writings on Canadian cinema, *The Canadian Film Reader*, published in 1977. For its editors, Seth Feldman and Joyce Nelson, conceptualizing Canadian film clearly posed difficulties not only because of the heterogeneity of Canadian filmmaking practices but also because Canada itself presented an equivalent problem. To the extent that they understood Canada to be 'a colonized country divided by regional and linguistic barriers,' how could they consider 'a theory' of Canadian film to be possible, particularly when it was to be articulated as identifying 'essential themes' and 'central motifs'? Why should they opt for a unified theory of Canadian cinema when the surrounding political, cultural, and linguistic context was so evidently one of fragmentation, especially when they were aware that the framework they were proposing for understanding Canadian film as 'a national cinema' itself represented 'a relatively obscure if not questionable area of film study' within the terms of the discipline of film studies at the time?[11]

Feldman and Nelson gave an initial three-fold answer to this question. First, in part because their reading of film history, in particular that of 'the great national cinemas of France, Germany, Italy and Japan' as well as that of post-colonial India, seemed to confirm the correctness of such a choice. Second, film history was essentially about the intertwining of the two grand narratives of national affirmation and of decolonization. However selective, this reading of film history was not just mere bookishness; it seemed to be confirmed by actual contemporary events taking place at the time not only in filmmaking in 'nearby Quebec' or, more remotely, in Yugoslavia, but also in the events surrounding the recent struggles for the decolonization of the former European empires and of the current 'American empire' in Africa, Asia, and Latin America. Third, and most important, theorizing Canadian film as a national cinema conferred on English Canadian film scholars a more intellectually ennobling mantle than that of mere scholarship. It made them into 'nation builders,' for it presented them with a more challenging task, that of how 'to *make* a national cinema out of what we have seen.'[12]

As a way of confronting the problematic of a displaced past, the pioneers of Canadian film scholarship filled the vacuum of displacement with an idealist conception of film history.[13] The study of cinema in the

Canadian context, therefore, would consist in evaluating the degree of actualization by specific but changing film texts of an ideal-typical theory of a Canadian national cinema as defined by Canadian film scholars. Thus, the history of Canadian cinema has been that of a perpetual displacement, that, as it were, of a displaced national cinema. Measured against this standard of displacement, the resulting 'history' of Canadian cinema became more often than not one of failure, of opportunities missed, or of betrayals by an ever-expanding cast of 'traitors' that has ranged from American 'imperialism' and its avatars to various Canadian institutions, politicians, producers, and individuals.

The result was a litany of denunciation and, not surprisingly, the *beau rôle* would fall often, although not exclusively, to the scholar-critic, whose discourse remained predominantly hortatory. More than a discourse of historical scholarship, Canadian film studies has been prescriptive and moralistic.[14] As a moralistic discourse, this field of study has functioned as a mediator between the ideal of a Canadian national cinema and the representativeness of that ideal as signified by film texts and filmmakers. But attribution of canonical value would remain a prerogative of the scholar-critic, although this attribution would be subject to changes in the climate of film criticism and in the dispositions of the critics. This mediating function would, however, save Canadian film studies from becoming an exercise in critical negativity; after all, in the 'real' world of changing film practices, films did get made, filmmakers did come and go; and new practitioners and genres of practice did appear for evaluation against standards of 'Canadianness,' and afterwards to be championed or found wanting in the market place of ideas. But as to what brought about such changes, why film practices changed, and how films actually managed to get produced, Canadian film studies remained remarkably incurious about these questions. In awaiting the dawn of a better day, those who pursue Canadian film studies are perhaps blinded by the prospect that Canada will eventually achieve in its films some imagined vision of cinematic greatness and also finally cast itself free of the shackles that have since the 1920s bound the ownership of the principal movie theatre chains and the circulation of the movies that get shown to corporate representatives of a neighbouring, 'foreign' state and their local money-grubbing minions ('sleazoids' as one Canadian film professor termed them).[15] Canadian film scholars, although bitterly nostalgic, occasionally remember that in the 1960s there had occurred a sudden upsurge in Canadian feature film production and that the prospects had then seemed to offer the hope that such a day had indeed actually dawned. Now *that* had been, in Peter Harcourt's words, perhaps distantly echoing Wordsworth, 'The Beginning of a Beginning.'[16]

Non-Canadian Perspectives

Scholars looking at Canadian cinema from other national vantage points have not fared significantly better. It is ironic that the most dismissive judgments on Canadian cinema articulated by non-Canadians have often come from Australian scholars. This is doubly surprising given the many similarities between the film histories of Australia and Canada, their shared political heritage drawn from the Westminster model of parliamentary politics, and the significant interchanges between the two countries of key personnel and of ideas for similar institutional frameworks in the establishment of filmmaking institutions since the Second World War.[17] For example, Graeme Turner, one of Australia's leading students of nationalist discourse and Australian film, considers that the Canadian example continues to present a 'clear cut case of continuing colonisation.'[18] Susan Dermody and Elizabeth Jacka, in their path-breaking study of the Australian feature film industry, while agreeing that Canadian feature film production in the late 1960s underwent a revival similar to the Australian one of the 1970s, argue that it had since become 'what is now little more than an off-shore branch of Hollywood.' Although the result had empirically been 'a reasonably large body of Canadian-produced films,' nonetheless in their view the problem was that these films were 'effectively indistinguishable from the American product.'[19] In their follow-up volume, Dermody and Jacka pronounced an even harsher judgment: 'The Canadian industry seems to have internalised completely the American belief that Canada is a poor, pale copy of itself.'[20]

   Less judgmental is a significant paper published in 1993 by another Australian film scholar, Stephen Crofts. In 'Reconceptualizing National Cinema/s,' he proposed an ambitious typology of national cinemas from a world perspective. He listed seven categories of national cinemas (with the *caveat* that such categories are always analytical entities subject to permeability), and it is significant for our purposes that he could not identify a specifically 'Canadian national cinema.' Rather, Crofts identified in Canada two 'variants' of partial national cinemas: on the one hand, what he termed 'regional cinema' that in Canada was to be found in many of the feature films produced in Quebec; and on the other hand, films associated with those 'sectors of some national cinemas [that] have sought to beat Hollywood at its own game – and overwhelmingly failed.' The latter included sectors of the English-language cinemas not only of Canada but also of Britain and Australia, although in Crofts's view the feature film output of English Canada was particularly characterized by the 'bleaching out of domestic cultural specificity.'[21]

Seen from within, Canadian film scholarship, therefore, presents an *idealized* object of study. This object is a potential but always deferred Canadian national cinema, which is nonetheless partially identifiable in the analysis of shifting thematic and aesthetic practices. For instance, these have included an overwhelming presence of the geographical landscape, a construction of narrative heavily influenced by documentary techniques, and a problematic masculinity of male protagonists, not to mention identity problems of protagonists generally.[22] These traits have been identified in various film texts that have been represented at times by shorts and documentaries and at other times by feature-length narrative or experimental films. Compounding the epistemological instability of the object of study has been the discontinuities in the institutions within which these texts have been produced over the decades, including government film agencies, private firms, the national television broadcaster, and a host of additional 'arm's length' federal and provincial institutions mandated to support 'independent' film and, as of the 1980s, television production. Notwithstanding any additional extraneous factors that might impinge on the equation, the Canadian case at the very least presents a specific articulation of the interrelations between discourses about certain films and those about state policy, in other words, of an intersection between forms of knowledge and forms of power.

When it is divorced from the Canadian context, scholarship suggests a different object of study: a fragmented, partial infrastructure of production instead of an idealized Canadian cinema. Some components of this infrastructure (the Québécois cinema), have seemed to aspire to or even at times achieved a sub-national degree of coherence and resembled the 'political' cinema (the Catalan and Chicano cinemas, for example) produced by the sub-national struggles in other countries. But other components of the putative Canadian 'national cinema,' and indeed the more significant ones in their industrial and capital-intensive dimensions, have been less concerned with articulating a 'national' aesthetic than with engaging in policy-driven, 'national' industrial strategies of international economic competition in an attempt to capture a share of either the global market or of that of the established film industry of the Unites States in particular.

Where Canadian and non-Canadian scholarly accounts do intersect, despite their divergent views of what constitutes the object of study, is in their assessment that both 'strategies' have failed. Canadian film studies, despite having spent some two decades pleading for a 'distinctive' Canadian cinema, have seemingly proven incapable of convincing scholars elsewhere (except perhaps for some in France) that they have much of a valid case. Conversely, English-language scholars outside of Canada have asserted emphatically that there is a 'Canadian' cinema of some economic significance, even though there is little about it that is meaningfully 'Canadian' in the sense of a national aesthetic. Rather, it consists, in the elegant formulation of Dermody and Jacka (coined with respect to a sub-genre of Australian film), 'of a cold aesthetic of pure commercialism, of pseudo-American or mid-Atlantic placelessness'[23] that has been shared variously by elements of the British, Australian and Canadian film industries. Seemingly, then, we are left with little but another version of the old antinomy of art on the one hand and industry on the other, in which Canadian film scholarship has on the whole focused predominantly on the art to the utter neglect of the industry, while non-Canadian observers see preciously little art and a good deal of industry, regrettably largely devoted to aping current American film or TV practices. Non-Canadian scholars have also made greater headway than their Canadian colleagues in problematizing the very concept of 'national cinema'[24] that is considered so essential to Canadian film studies. As Stephen Crofts observes,

National cinematic self-definition, like *national* self-definition, likes to pride itself on its distinctiveness, on its standing apart from other(s). Such a transcendental concept of the ego repressing its other(s) urges abandonment of the self/ other model as an adequate means of thinking national cinemas. For this dualist model authorizes only two political stances: imperial aggression and defiant national chauvinism.[25]

Both accounts are partial, each leaving out, at least as regards the Canadian case, what the other sees as most worthy of attention. But it is precisely this incompleteness that provides a way forward. The predominant account in Canada, in attempting to substitute an idealized conceptual unity for the intractability of excessive fragmentation caused by transnational influences, shifting practices, and institutions in the Canadian context, has 'chauvinistically' attempted to construct a counter-narrative of Canadian cinema that prides itself on its distinctiveness. The problem with the attempt, as was seen with the account by Feldman and Nelson, is that the counter-narrative could only be possible by excluding *certain* others, namely the 'bad' others, like the American film industry or vulgar Canadian producers. But there were – there had to be – 'good' others; ideals such as 'the great national cinemas' of France and Italy but also really 'good' others, handily located in the neighbouring province of Quebec, which was involved in innovative filmmaking practices since the late 1950s. Much more problematic would be whether the Canadian state represented a 'good' or a 'bad' other.

In reducing the conceptualization of the cinema in Canada to that of a national cinema only, and in so doing hopefully eliding the difficulties of the unequal sharing of the continent with the United States, English Canadian film intellectuals staked a claim to play a role in nation-building. They wanted to be able to contribute to Canadian national development and in particular to the issues of national cultural development that had been part of a growing agenda of public debate since at least the early 1950s, especially after the publication of the report in 1951 of the Royal Commission on National Development in the Arts, Letters, and Sciences (the Massey Commission, named after its chair, then chancellor of the University of Toronto and, as of the following year, the first Canadian-born governor general of Canada).[26] But this is only to say once again that discoursing on the cinema in the Canadian context was also to enter eventually into discourse, if not conversation, with the state and its institutions. Put more bluntly, the desire on the part of film critics and practitioners, of film aficionados, and eventually of scholars – in short, of Canadian film intellectuals – to play a role on the national scene, in stressing the connections between films and 'the national interest,' was also an encounter with state power.

The Shadow of the State

That the Canadian state, or stand-ins for it, such as the Canadian Pacific Railway, played a role in supporting the production of certain kinds of films since the early years of the century is unquestionable. It is equally beyond dispute that the federal government, in the teens and again in the late 1930s, along with the province of Ontario in the 1920s, created film production agencies and a studio at Trenton, Ontario, devoted to military and industrial propaganda films, informational films for government departments, informational films addressing certain issues of social development, and occasionally documentaries dealing with topics of broad civic interest such as the coronations of British kings and queens. To the extent that this history has been reasonably well documented elsewhere, there is no need to repeat it here,[27] although some of the interpretative frameworks that have been deployed with respect to the period before 1952 will be discussed in greater detail in the next chapter.

The problem, to repeat, concerns that of the relations between Canadian film history and state policies regarding filmmaking. If the broad, descriptive contours of Canadian federal, and in some cases provincial, production policies have been relatively well established by English Canadian film scholars, this has been the case mainly for the period of time leading up to the Second War World.[28] After that, the historical record becomes fragmentary, or rather it dissolves into a series of ongoing controversies. These controversies have concerned, among other topics, the role played by the first commissioner of the NFB, John Grierson, in 'sabotaging' the Canadian film industry's alleged post-war capacity for producing feature-length films, and in turn the role played by Canadian security intelligence agencies in sabotaging the NFB; the impact of post-war currency crises on the levying of taxes by Canada on American film products; and the post-war attempt by Britain to block American film earnings there and its impact on the expectations of Canadian film producers for similar protective measures.[29]

In other words, Canadian film history of the post-war period shatters into a series of polemics that centre loosely on what might be termed 'the problem of the Canadian feature film' and its relation to Canadian state policies. Why, despite a clear commitment to support certain kinds of filmmaking in Canada, did policies seem to draw a line when it became a question of feature-length films, even if there is evidence that Canadian producers of the post-war period lobbied for the strengthening of support for production? Was the national state a friend of filmmaking in Canada or was it a foe?

Clearly, by the early 1950s a certain kind of production infrastructure, largely beholden to the state both for the legislative framework that had created the NFB and for the parliamentary allocation of its funding, had taken root in Canada. Filmmakers were primarily public servants, although there were also a select few private firms that survived less on government contract than on producing advertisements for the large American and British multinationals with branch plants in Canada, and there were as well such visionary firms as Renaissance Films in Quebec, which, as of 1944 aimed to produce wholesome features for the Catholic market. What this partial filmmaking infrastructure amounted to in economic terms is more difficult to evaluate. That it did not comprise a film industry in any greater sense than elements of a small-scale production capability is evident; that it also had few links with the other components of the industrial model for the exhibition and circulation of feature films, circuits that were largely American, sometimes British, and, in Quebec, French-owned, was patently the case.

However, as Dermody and Jacka proposed in their account of the Australian feature film revival of the 1970s, there were different routes to create a film industry, particularly in the period preceding the emergence of complex organizational structures. One approach, itself of formidable complexity, and by and large the one that developed in the United States, could be termed 'capitalistic.' It entailed centralizing organizational processes that combined capitalization of private production and exchange in order to maximize markets and profitability for the owners of the means of production and of circulation through oligopolistic control of 'entertainment' commodities. Another approach would be to view 'a film industry' not primarily as an object of economic activity but rather as the articulation of a public idea, an imaginary construct providing 'distinctiveness.' This public idea – it is above all an idea – is produced by and constituted in the form of 'talk,' whether that of journalists, filmmakers, or politicians, that of the discursive productions of institutions (reports, studies, etc.), or that of artefacts such as films. As Dermody and Jacka observed of the Australian film revival, one of the paradoxical manifestations of a film-industry-as-talk model is that the imaginary object already possesses an overdetermined and fetishistic status, even '*before* it has any claim to material existence.'[30] To be sure, the 'talk' must appear to have some grounding in a reality, however imaginary it too may be. In the Canadian context, for example, it is significant that the emergence of a policy for feature films in the early 1960s was predicated on the belief that 'a fairly effective film industry could have been established in Canada before the coming of the sound film.'[31] In this sense, for both scholarship and policy with respect to feature film production in post-colonial contexts, the talk takes the form of an historically based polemic for the 'revival' of an entity it considers it once had (or *might* have had) the capacity to produce. What allows the polemic, which assumes a collapse of an original, pre-sound film industry, to maintain itself is not the existence of a film industry per se, given that the latter is, at least temporarily, an imaginary entity produced as a signifier of national identity. It is the result instead of the persistence of elements of a film production *infrastructure* sufficiently established to be able to support the periodic emergence of formations (filmmakers, critics, etc.) that produce talk about an imaginary or potential industry. It is the survival of these production elements that makes possible the continuation of the polemic for 'the revival' of feature film production.

Whatever the empirical difficulties of assessing the size and capability of a post-war Canadian 'film industry,' there was little doubt in the minds of some critics and producers that Canada did have one, just as there was little doubt in the minds of Canadian film scholars that Canada not only had a film history worthy of sustained investigation but further that this history comprised a national cinema with a right to a place in the scholarly sun along with the study of other national cinemas. A problem was that such hopes were not very impressive so long as Canadian films merely consisted of shorts – 'of insignificant crap,' in the words of the noted French film critic André Bazin.[32] The 'revival' of the Canadian feature film in the 1960s would change all that – if the Canadian state could be persuaded to alter its long-standing, evident indifference to the importance of producing Canadian-made features.

The Economy of Talk / The Universe of Discourse

In the economy of talk that had established itself and that persisted, with ups and downs, around the problems of the cinema in Canada since the 1920s,[33] the decade of the 1950s saw three extraordinary inflations in the discursive stakes. The first was the *Massey Report*, the second, a direct result of the first, was the beginning of Canadian television, and the third, in part a result in turn of the second, was the start of the Quiet Revolution in Quebec.

The *Massey Report* (1951) was the first full-scale assessment of the policies for the cultural development of Canada and a reflection on their future orientation. As a document it was a benchmark for a number of reasons, not the least of which were its recommendations for the establishment of Canadian television, but it was especially significant because it accredited the kind of language that would be used for the discussion of cultural problems in the Canadian context and in the discourse on films in particular. In its chapter 'Films in Canada,' the *Report* observed that 'the cinema at present is not only the most potent but also the most alien of the influences shaping our Canadian life. Nearly all

Canadians go to the movies; and most movies come from Hollywood ... Hollywood refashions us in its own image.'[34]

In this and similar claims,[35] the *Report* conferred formidable power to the cultural production emanating from 'a single alien source,' the United States. Curiously, it made no effort to understand either the organizational mechanisms or the political economy of this awesome deployment of U.S. cultural power. Even more paradoxically perhaps, it recognized that, in terms of general film entertainment, 'Canadians want commercial features,' although it acknowledged at the same time that 'in this field there is practically nothing produced in Canada.' On the other hand, it had nothing but the highest praise for the films of the NFB because their documentary realism reproduced 'real' (understood oddly as 'national education and cultural enrichment') rather than 'synthetic situations'; in so doing they supposedly evoked an authentic awareness of life, as opposed to an escape from it. Expressing great fears of 'the effects of commercialization' coming from a foreign nation that 'puts its faith in the machine,' the *Report* sided with the representations made to it by organizations such as the NFB and distanced itself from those private producers who wanted the NFB's activities curtailed. Despite its recognition that Canadians wanted commercial features, the *Report* felt that the 'only truly and typically Canadian films' they should be allowed to see were those given to them by the NFB. While expressing a desire for more private production of documentaries, the *Report* concluded in the end, as Ted Magder puts it, that 'Canadian documentaries alone would have to stem the Hollywood menace.'[36]

Among the *Massey Report*'s other recommendations was an outline of the principles to steer the development of Canadian television, which began broadcasting the following year. While recognizing that this 'remarkable new form of broadcasting' had aroused great interest and enthusiasm among the general public, the *Report* was mainly struck by the unpredictable future of the new medium. 'Its history indicates that we can be certain only of its uncertain future.'[37] The development of radio in Canada since the 1930s had given rise to two different concepts of the medium: the official concept of it as a public service and considered the primary responsibility of any broadcasting organization was to the public which owned the limited number of channels; and a competing concept, promoted by the private sector, which saw commercial use as the purpose for allocating portions of the public domain. As for the *Massey Report*, it envisaged, though not without contradictions, the extension of a *single* system of public service broadcasting that would serve Canada's 'national needs.' In the view of the *Report*, 'The principal grievance of the private broadcasters is based ... on a false assumption that broadcasting in Canada is an industry. Broadcasting in Canada, in our view, is a public service directed and controlled in the public interest.'[38] Among these competing concepts of radio-television, the *Massey Report* held a rhetorical advantage in that it was consistent with the official Canadian discourse regarding radio that had taken shape since the report in 1929 of the Royal Commission on Radio Broadcasting headed by Sir John Aird. However, as to the practices in broadcasting both in radio and then in television, it was the second concept of the media, the one espoused by industry, that was rapidly overtaking the first. As Marc Raboy puts it, 'the second concept was becoming more and more strongly anchored in Canada's broadcasting reality and would, with the development of television, *completely* transform the nature of Canadian broadcasting.'[39]

Among the transformations brought about by the advent of Canadian television, perhaps none is as striking as the influence the new medium would have upon changing the world-view of Quebec society. 'One will never sufficiently stress,' André Bélanger has written, 'the influence that the coming of television had upon the *mentalités*' of Quebecers.[40] In a similar vein, Pierre Véronneau, following on the research of Gérard Laurence on the impact of French-language public affairs television, has argued that the advent of Canadian television in the French language decisively fractured the ideological monolith of traditional Québécois society.[41] Following Michel Brunet's classic enumeration of the three 'dominants' of traditional French-Canadian thought (agriculturalism, anti-statism, and Messianism), the advent of television had re-imaged the world into one that was no longer predominantly rural but urban, that was suddenly far more open to modern technologies, and that had abruptly discovered the secular discourses of modern politics and sociology.[42] Television, as Véronneau remarks, had opened up nothing less than a direct channel of communication that competed with the traditional channels of communication represented by the Church, the school, and the family, and this was particularly so for a francophone filmmaker at the NFB. One might debate the extent of the ideological power of the new medium of communication – Laurence, for example, speaks more in terms of 'dissonance' than does Véronneau, who emphasizes dissidence and resistance – but certainly profound upheavals were taking place, the beginnings of the Quiet Revolution.[43]

Throughout the 1950s, and with gathering momentum, the economy of talk concerning culture, cultural development, and the genres of cultural expression was shifting, with voices rumbling either in the press or before royal commissions and demanding more institutions, or at least institutions different from the traditional ones. Private film producers began speaking about new genres of films, commercial features, with whose production there was little experience, and they demanded from the state measures of support, even if modest, in a language that was shocking to the official discourses about national education and the tasks of civilization. Reprehensible terms that smacked of 'Americanization,' such as 'commercialization' and 'industry' were being increasingly bandied about. As well, new and unprecedented production sites, in particular a trans-Canadian television network, had come to supplement existing channels of communication. The existing channels themselves, such as the NFB, were increasingly being contested by an ever-more vociferous private sector that questioned the amounts of money allocated to the state-owned production entities. But these were still only fissures in the dominant discourse, expressions of dissonance, subterranean tectonic shifts that a far-sighted observer might have suspected constituted the opening moves in a protracted (one that is still going on) war of words and positions over fundamental political questions concerning the limits, divisions, and responsibilities of state power.

For now, the dominant discourse remained that of the federal state, to which, however, as a result of the Massey Commission, had been added a new discursive field, even if it remained far from clear exactly what the state was actually going to do with this new sphere of cultural policy. The cultural debate was represented by a still largely Arnoldian concept of high culture, but its locus had begun to shift towards the problems of 'mass culture' in the Canadian context. However little it might recognize itself in the term, Canadian broadcasting nonetheless was a mass medium; to talk about commercial filmmaking or about the radio 'industry,' regardless of how distasteful the idea was to the likes of a Vincent Massey, was also to enter on the discursive terrain of mass communications. In any event, the discourse of the state itself had breached many of these linguistic taboos in designating the cultural overflow of the American mass media as *the* enemy. Unthinkingly perhaps, the discourse of the state, by transposing long-standing insecurities concerning the territorial defence of Canadian sovereignty into the realm of cultural development policies, had opened up a new symbolic front for the culture wars of the 1960s and 1970s in which the rise of the

Canadian feature film would occupy the vanguard position. Recent scholarship has begun, however, to point to new approaches for some of these issues.[44]

Conclusion

The fragmentary infrastructure of the largely state-owned film production established in Canada as of the late teens of the twentieth century proved sufficiently durable to become the institutional centre of Canadian documentary film production until the end of the Second World War. This infrastructure, along with its often grudging clients in subsidiary private industries dealing in technical aspects of film production, proved strong enough to produce recurring waves, in the 1920s and subsequently, of public debate over the problems of filmmaking in Canada. But the role played by the Canadian state in these debates was more one of benign indifference than of anything else. All this began to change in the course of the 1950s. If film policy in the Canadian context remained, in Ted Magder's fine phrase, 'a featureless policy'[45] until the 1960s, the chapter that follows begins to explore in greater detail the transformations of featurelessness into specific traits.

2

The Canadian State and the Problem of Knowledge Formation

Governmentality

In the previous chapter it was shown that the difficulties in writing film history in the Canadian case stemmed, in part, from the instability of production genres as well as from the instability of sites of production. In other words, what *is* Canadian cinema and where was it *located*? As well, the open-endedness of both questions had given rise to a number of possible answers, including the one predominantly articulated by Canadian film studies that 'Canadian cinema' is an idealized national cinema, the narration of which consists in evaluating the extent film texts incarnate that ideal. Another way to put this might be to say that Canadian cinema, however defined, was located *in* the ideal state, and in that sense constituted an essential, but underacknowledged, dimension of statehood, or national identity. Although the actual state might have been reluctant or ambivalent in seeing matters in the same light, it was nonetheless, or so the proponents of a Canadian national cinema believed, at least open to the argument. In this sense, Canadian film studies can be seen as an *attempted* conversation with the state in the form of a discourse between intellectual or scholarly forms of knowledge and those forms of knowledge of which state power is comprised. Canadian film studies can be understood not only, as we saw earlier, as a kind of intellectual 'strategy' responding to the problems of a displaced past. It is also in the same sense, a response to a displaced 'theory' of the state, one responding to a perceived absence within the state by providing it with a theory, in Jakob Burckhardt's famous phrase, of 'the state as a work of art.'[1] In the putative conversation between these different articulations of knowledge, an immediate question might be to ask what the actual receptivity of state forms of knowledge is to such 'esthétisant' and idealistic theories of the state.

A complicating factor, as we also saw above, is that it was the 'voice' of the state itself, in the form of the *Massey Report*, that had established (or re-established, if one returns to the beginnings of the discourses about Canadian radio) the linguistic terms for the discussion of 'culture' in the Canadian context. And this language was predominantly Manichaean, with the forces of civilization pitted against the commercial threat of 'the barbaric empire' to the south,[2] and militaristic, in the sense that the 'battle' for culture in the Canadian context was seen, certainly by the Massey Commission, as a form of symbolic warfare over the future of the national cultural 'soul.' In other words, what began to emerge in the course of the 1950s was a struggle between a plurality of theories (or, perhaps more accurately, implicit theories) of the relation between the state and the public sphere, each with their own voices, modes of address, and linguistic keywords by which to speak both about and to the state. But before examining this struggle in more detail, one must first undertake a brief, preparatory theoretical detour.

An initial problem, of course, centres on the slippery words 'the state.' As a number of Canadian political scientists have argued compellingly, not only the specialized academic bodies of knowledge but also the contemporary polity at large have made little headway in adequately understanding the complexities of the state in Canadian circumstances. Gérald Bernier and Daniel Salée, for instance, have commented on the 'strange' silence of contemporary political science as regards the history of the Canadian state.[3] '[I]n this country,' political scientist Philip Resnick observes, 'writing about the state (and indeed civil society) has barely proceeded beyond square one.'[4] As we shall see below, Resnick somewhat overstates the case in the sense that, on the contrary, there has been considerable discussion of the Canadian state from *certain* perspectives. His point is rather that those perspectives have not only been limited ones and so in the end not very helpful, but it also serves as a cautionary reminder of the risks of being overly preoccupied by the mirage of *the* state, a risk amplified by the intellectual desire to play a role in 'nation building.'

To avoid the pitfalls of such temptations, the work on governmentality that was begun by Michel Foucault in the late 1970s and that has since been taken up by a number of other scholars has been enormously productive in un-thinking the state and seeing in its stead not only a fundamentally discontinuous historical as opposed to coherently conceptual entity, but also a complex, contested, and changing articulation of the practices of the techniques of governance in interaction with new fields of knowledge, particularly those of the social or human sciences, since the sixteenth century.[5]

Rather than conceiving of the state as a Nietzschean *monstre froid* impelled along by its own dynamic development from a given point of origin or, conversely, as in Marxist theories, of reducing the state to a certain number of functions such as the growth of productive forces, Foucault proposed to look at the state as 'the correlative of a certain manner of governing' that he termed variously 'governmentality,' 'governmental practice,' 'the art of government,' 'governmental reason,' etc.[6] Understanding governmentality, Foucault argued, would entail

a detailed examination not only of the history of the idea [of government], but of the procedures and means deployed to ensure, in a given society, the 'government of persons' ... the ways in which the conduct of an ensemble of individuals found itself implicated ... in the exercise of power ...[7]

As two Canadian neo-Foucauldians remind us, in a suggestive proposal for methodologies of analysis of cultural policies in Quebec, Foucault outlines not so much a general theory of the state as an historical-relational analysis of the shifting rationalities of governance. Just as governmental practices opened onto new domains of action or intervention from the sixteenth century onwards, the new domains of state knowledge took form in conjunction with emergent intellectual technologies, particularly in the social sciences, and their new vocabularies and reconfigurations of the understanding of public space.[8]

To the extent that the Foucauldian periodization of governmentality is coextensive with the colonial expansion of the Western European centralized administrative states, the model of analysis opens up rich perspectives from which to re-examine how the state in post-colonial contexts, or specifically in the historical Canadian context, has been conceptualized.[9] But given the limits of our present purposes, it will have to suffice here to remind readers of the long history in Canada of fears of military annexation by the United States and of outright attempts at carrying out the act. Against this background, which persisted well into the nineteenth century, public intellectuals provided recurring expressions of concern, not to say alarm, about the negative impact of American ideas, especially in their dissemination through newspapers and book publishing. By the late nineteenth century these concerns had hardened into what cultural historian Allan Smith has termed 'an ideology of inevitable absorption.' By the 1920s, however, and coinciding with the beginnings of Canadian state policies in broadcasting and to a lesser extent film, that ideology of inevitability had diminished, in a striking illustration of how changes in social-theoretical knowledge interact with governmental practices and policies. As Smith describes this conceptual shift,

concern with the character of the nation's cultural life entered a new phase. Critics, armed with what the social sciences were making clear about the manner in which a society's cultural environment was formed, began to argue that assimilation of the Canadian outlook to the American was not an inevitable, 'natural' phenomenon ... It derived, instead, from the exposure of Canadians to a cultural environment largely American in its composition, in its turn *the result of identifiable actions which were amenable to policy.*[10]

In this sense, discourses about Canadian cinema have historically been inscribed within the problematic of governmentality. In other words, they have, however disguised at times, been discourses of policy – attempts to dialogue with the state, but within the terms of which dialogue and which *fraction* of the state? To demonstrate this tradition of dialogue, some of the principal interpretations produced by Canadian social scientists concerning the relations between the Canadian state and filmmaking are examined next in order to emphasize the extent to which these perspectives have reinforced a limited, and ultimately paralysing, understanding of *the* state. Rather than extricating the production of cultural knowledge from the state, these forms of knowledge have only strengthened the governmentalization of the cinema in the Canadian context.

The Canadian State and Cinema: Dominant Interpretations

Interpretations of the relationship between the Canadian state and cinema fall into four principal categories: nationalist, dependent, renegotiated dependency, and alternative.

Nationalist Interpretations

The predominant interpretive framework for defining the relationship between state and cinema until well into the 1970s and even beyond was a nationalist one. This was as much the case in the analysis of policies[11] as in the writings of Canadian film historians, both in English and in French. For Peter Morris, the dean of English Canadian film historians, in his pioneering *Embattled Shadows*, the production and use of films in Canada until about 1914 'was much like that anywhere else.'[12] Canada could, Morris argues, have developed a film industry comparable, say, to that of Italy's at the beginning of the century. But 'what fundamentally distinguish[ed] Canada's film history from that of other countries' – even more so than the factor of Hollywood's economic intervention – was, first, that centralized studio production did not develop, except regionally, and, secondly and more importantly, 'that federal and provincial governments did not, in the Twenties, legislate effective protection and support for the production, distribution, or exhibition branches of the industry.'[13] (With the exception of the creation of the NFB in 1939, this situation remained largely one of laissez-faire until the 1960s and even then legislation was limited to minimal production support for features. A later attempt to legislate in the area of distribution in 1988 also failed.)

Accounting for this 'failure' leaves Morris on shakier ground. It was, he suggests, 'a failure in the Canadian [cultural] system,' explainable in part by the prevalence of regionalism as well as by a 'classical' liberal conception of the state that left entrepreneurship primarily to individual initiative. In this early work,[14] Morris opted for an 'idealist' explanation, consistent with what he and other scholars saw as distinctive of Canadian film studies. Thus he attributes the stasis of Canadian film history to what he terms 'the Canadian ethos,' a notion consistent with then current interpretations of the predominant codes and conventions of Canadian literature. The Canadian ethos can be understood as a profound passivity, not to say a form of death wish, provoked by a conflict between nature, the individual, and society, in which the individual retreats into nature as a refuge from society and social organization.[15] Implicit in such interpretations, as others who have attempted to theorize the 'Canadian imagination' have observed,[16] is not only the omnipresence of the social conformity that Frye famously identified as 'the garrison mentality,' but more specifically of a terror of the Canadian state and, as a result, the problems of theorizing it, or for our purposes of accounting for the emergence of the Canadian feature film in the 1960s.

If one of the central problems for English-Canadian film historians thus has been 'locating' either Canadian cinema or the Canadian feature, this would be less so for Québécois analysts. For them, the emergence of the Canadian feature film is easy to explain, because it is to all extents and purposes the Québécois feature film that one is talking about. As historians Lamonde and Hébert would put it in unmistakable terms: 'As a signifier of the dynamism of the cultural creativity of Quebec, the feature film in Canadian cinema is essentially a Québécois phenomenon.'[17] For film historians like Pierre Véronneau, what frames the emergence of the feature film in the 1960s is its place within the larger ideological continuum of Quebec's long historical struggle for 'national' affirmation, in which the constant of a developing nationalist consciousness intersects with the affirmation of the 'national' identity of francophone filmmakers at the NFB, in particular subsequent to its transfer to Montreal in the mid-1950s.[18] If Québécois film historians and critics have little difficulty in explaining the emergence of the Québécois feature film in the early 1960s as a manifestation of a growing Quebec nationalism – some critics will go so far as to claim that Québécois cinema 'caused' the emergence worldwide of all the new national cinemas of the 1960s[19] – they faced an historiographical problem that stemmed instead from the subsequent difficulties of explaining why this sub-nationalist emergence took place within an agency of the *federal* state.

To the extent that the emergence of so-called 'new' or modern Québécois nationalism of the 1960s depended in part on the demonization of federal institutions, and accordingly on a narrative of the various forms of oppression suffered by Quebec as a result of the governmental structures of the Canadian confederation, the emergence of innovative forms of Quebec cinema from within the primary film-producing agency of the Canadian state called for some additional explanation. The problem of the 'location' of Canadian cinema returned to haunt Québécois analysts in various ways. In one variant, Québécois cinema had unquestionably emerged in a federal agency, but that development was spontaneous, and in this sense, therefore, the Canadian state had nothing to do with it. In another, Québécois cinema had emerged in a federal agency, despite the latter, and the subsequent response of the federal state would be either to attempt to 'kill' Québécois cinema outright, or to gradually displace it by encouraging the development of further institutions of filmmaking support based instead on an industrial, commercial model of feature film making more akin to dominant Hollywood features. In yet another variant, the problem stemmed from the fact that Canada was a country colonized by the United States, and that therefore, however much it may have wanted to break the bonds of colonization, it would only unconsciously reproduce colonial relations and neither film bureaucracy administrators nor filmmakers were exempt from the vicious cycle.[20]

But even without bringing into the equation either the problem of American domination of feature film distribution and exhibition in Canada or the structures of Canadian federal institutions, Quebec film historians had difficulty as well in accounting for what had actually transpired within the NFB with regard to the emergence of feature films. Here interpretations have ranged from the frustration of filmmakers with the organizational culture of the Board, which would result in the resignations of its most significant members who would strike out on their own in an attempt to create an embryonic private sector outside governmental structures, to the 'counter-revolution' in production practices carried out by certain individuals within the upper management of the French Production unit at the NFB.[21] A final complicating factor would be that the Quebec state apparatus, except for controversial interventions in film censorship (a provincial responsibility) and the commissioning of occasional studies, would not be in any significant sense a variable in these debates until well into the 1970s. Film policy, and feature film policy in particular, remained the primary responsibility of the federal state from the 1950s until the 1970s.

In summary, nationalist explanations, while attractive to analysts writing about film in one or the other of Canada's official languages, only created more problems than they resolved, and in particular entailed additional explanations as to why 'the nation' did not behave nationalistically. Thus, interpretive frameworks shifted to focus more specifically on the Canadian state itself and the role it played in reproducing the structures of dependency.

Dependency Theory

If Canadian or Québécois film historians preferred nationalist frameworks for attempting to explain the development, or lack, of Canadian cinema, dependency theory has been the preferred explanatory framework deployed by scholars from the disciplinary perspectives of both communications and political economy. Going back at least to the pioneeering work of Harold Innis and the so-called 'Canadian' school of political economy in the 1920s, the central set of problems to be explained concerned the apparently anomalous course of Canadian economic development and the role of the state therein. However one approached it, the development of Canadian capitalism appeared abnormal: 'distorted' in one view, 'arrested' in another, 'aborted' in a third.[22] Explaining why Canadian capitalist development had not proceeded 'normally' through the developmental stages of the formation of a domestic market sufficiently large to support industrialization across a wide, as opposed to restricted, field of commodity production that would in turn provide the basis for diversified international trade, had generated a high degree of consensus among Canadian social scientists. External factors, and in particular the historical location of the Canadian economy as an integral part of the larger international, capitalist economy that had developed with the European colonial expansion of the fifteenth and sixteenth centuries, were seen to have always played a more considerable role in structuring Canadian economic development than internal factors. In brief, local factors, and these included the role of the state, had only a limited ability to control the pace of Canadian economic development. In this light, the Canadian state and the Canadian capitalist class were essentially subservient to the foreign or imperial interests of which they were, in effect, but the local representatives; at best, they could only react defensively to elements over which they had little or no control. The entire Canadian economic system, and its political and cultural superstructures, existed primarily to facilitate the adjustment to and accommodation of long-distance control from imperial centres that had shifted over the centuries from France to England and, since the early 20th century, to the United States. [23]

There were within this general view numerous controversies and analytical factions, and to the extent that these perspectives were largely Marxist or neo-Marxist it also followed by implication that only revolutionary political transformations would ever change these longstanding and deep-rooted developments. But there were less violent alternatives. On the one hand, Canadian dependency theory could be viewed as an ethical critique of modernization theory, and in this sense would be a social science equivalent to the idealism of Canadian film studies. On the other hand, after an initial preoccupation with the political economy of Canadian dependency, particularly in the late 1960s and 1970s, the focus shifted increasingly from the economics and politics of dependency to a critique of Canada's cultural dependency. One of the key initial texts of this shift in emphasis was Dallas Smythe's *Dependency Road: Communications, Capitalism, Consciousness and Canada.*[24]

Smythe, a Canadian-born former economic analyst for the Federal Communications Commission in the United States and, in his academic work, a so-called father of the political economy of communication, attempted in this book to provide a very broad analysis of the processes by which 'the capitalist system produced a country called Canada as a dependency of the United States.'[25] Ranging through discussions of the role of the mass media and popular culture, the workings of 'the audience commodity,' the rise of scientific marketing in the development of the 'consciousness industry' by big business, this fascinating but idiosyncratic study devoted three central chapters to the analysis of the media (print, motion pictures, telecommunications, and broadcasting) that had brought about Canada's 'cultural submission.' In an essay that is simultaneously intricate, simplistic, and full of interesting observations on a wide variety of topics, Smythe argued that monopoly capitalism in the United States had since the late nineteenth century developed a cluster of industries, the 'Consciousness Industry,' with the mass media of communication acting as its shock troops. The reduction of Canada to cultural submission was the result of 'a dominant, *irresistible* social formation acting on *passive* people as individuals and in their ... institutional relationships.'[26] While Smythe did attempt to argue the case for both individual and group resistance, the unidirectionality and power of the system of cultural domination radiating outwards from the United States were the key factors.

In the process of presenting this argument, including some penetrating observations concerning the profound dualities in Canadian broadcasting,[27] Smythe usefully underscored some of the intellectual liabilities of Canadian social science in thinking about the circumstances that had contributed to the inevitability of Canadian dependency. For instance, he noted a widespread tendency to confuse the presence of a state apparatus in Canada with the capacity for autonomous actions. If Canadians on the one hand overvalued the autonomy of the state apparatus, they also at the same time 'undervalue[d] their state apparatus because they so rarely use[d] it to assert Canadian needs when these needs conflict[ed] with American wishes; the history of the Canadian film, book, magazine, and radio-television broadcasting industries offer[ed] examples.'[28] As a correlative of this ambivalence, Smythe also observed, referring to the work of Harold Innis and Marshall McLuhan, that Canadian social thought showed a marked weakness for 'idealistic' categories of analysis. For example, he pointed to the privileging by Innis of the category of 'technology' as an autonomous entity unconnected to more basic human drives such as greed. In his discussion of McLuhan, Smythe considered this tendency to dematerialize social processes to have become a full-blown 'mysticism of technology,' or the erroneous idea that the medium *defines* the audience. In Smythe's view, exactly the opposite was the case: the development of media were defined by the availability and actions of the audience.[29] In placing greater emphasis on the industrial mechanics of processes of cultural domination through the consciousness industries that constituted the mass media, and in drawing attention to the underlying ambivalence of Canadian theories of the state, an ambivalence he traced back to forms of thought that were still impregnated with religious notions as opposed to 'vulgar' (because materialistic approaches in the Marxist sense), Smythe provided an innovative if eccentric analysis of Canadian dependency. It laid the basis for more detailed examinations of media policies in Canada.

It fell to a cinematographer born in India who became one of Dallas Smythe's doctoral students at Simon Fraser University to attempt to apply the Smythian model to the study of the political economy of the Canadian film industry. In *Canadian Dreams & American Control*, the book version of his 1980 PhD dissertation, Manjunath Pendakur made one of the first systematic attempts to study the roots and history of Canada's dependency vis-à-vis the film industry of the United States since the turn of the century.[30]

Approaching his topic from the perspectives of radical political economic theory, Pendakur argued that Canadian theatrical dependency on feature films made in the United States (resulting in a restricted, not to say near-impossible, capability to produce, exhibit, and distribute Canadian-made features) has to be placed in the wider context of Canada's status as a dependent capitalist state. Canada had been the chief destination of direct investment from the United States since the turn of the century and its share in the expansion of U.S. investment worldwide remained constant until well after the Second World War. The most lucrative and key sectors of the Canadian economy (oil and gas, chemicals, automobile, and electrical products, for example) were directly controlled by U.S. firms in proportions of almost 80 per cent. In the realm of the mass media in Canada, with the exception of newspapers, American firms controlled equivalently high or even higher proportions of the means of distribution and exhibition of products, of market share, and of earnings. As in the other sectors of the economy, the latter, after some taxes that remained in Canada, flowed back to the United States and were reinvested in further production, and so the ability of the Canadian-owned sectors to compete, let alone grow, except by also producing or distributing American-type materials, was constantly being undermined. In this light, the policies of the Canadian state take on the role of arbitrating between the interests of foreign and domestic capital. As Pendakur puts it:

The state assumes the role of referee of relations between various sections of capital, both foreign and domestic, and tries to resolve the often conflicting interests between them ... Canadian policies do not attempt to overthrow foreign ownership and control of the Canadian economy. They are merely aimed at restructuring the relationship between foreign and indigenous capital and between various sections of the indigenous capital in order to provide for greater participation for certain indigenous capitalists. In other words, these continuing conflicts ... remain cast in the general framework of American hegemony in Canada.[31]

Within this overall framework, Pendakur's study provides an historical account of the structures of domination that established themselves in two of the three principal sectors of the film industry in Canada since the 1920s, those of exhibition and distribution. It pays particular attention to the dialectic of competition and monopoly in these two sectors and in that of production. Pendakur draws upon organization theory to establish an understanding of Canadian market structures. Thus, degrees of buyer or seller concentration, conditions of entry, and the extent of product differentiation determine the competitive strategies and the market conduct of business rivals. In turn, market behaviour determines the size of profits, the efficiency of production, and the rate of innovation. As well, non-market factors, such as general demand, conglomeration, and industry-government relations, also influence business performance.[32]

One of the difficulties encountered by political economists in studying the Canadian case has to do with data sources. While U.S. government agencies are often a valuable source of economic information about the major American film firms, in Canada 'the cloud of secrecy surrounding company finances' presents a problem to students. To the secrecy surrounding the business activities of dominant corporations, an additional 'cloak of secrecy' is maintained by the Canadian government not only as concerns foreign investment decisions but also with respect to internal studies commissioned by state agencies.[33] In this endeavour the ingenuity of the researcher who attempts to produce reliable academic knowledge is pitted against the reluctance of the state to divulge its sources of knowledge for fear of political or other embarrassment. As has been seen above, this lack of openness exemplifies the extent to which the study of cinema in Canada pits scholarly knowledge against the forms of state power.

Ironically, perhaps, given the subtitle of the book, what Pendakur's study actually reveals is not so much the political economy of the *Canadian* film industry as the political economy of the *American* film industry in Canada, and the complex interactions between the industry, Canadian film policies, and successive attempts by Canadian capitalists to gain a purchase within the dominant structures of the American monopoly of theatrical exhibition and distribution in North America. On the one hand, the analysis of this interaction makes Pendakur's contribution invaluable to the study of the business activity of American firms and interests in Canada that Canadian film studies have been wilfully blind to. On the other hand, it is the slippage of objects that makes Pendakur's account so profoundly pessimistic. As was the case with Morris's history, Canada is again a victim, not only because of the imposition of American control of feature film circulation, but also because 'Canada's national elites, through various corporate and state institutions, actively participate in the process' of the reproduction of dependency. If the Canadian state, through its various agencies, arbitrates between powerful vested interests, it does so 'to preserve capitalism itself and keep ... intact the deeply entrenched international capital in Canada's political economy.' More bluntly still, he writes: 'The history of the Canadian feature film industry has clearly shown that as long as the Canadian vision to create a cinema is clouded by articulating it within the priorities of capital, the particular needs of Canadian filmmakers will *never* be met.'[34] It is the bleakness, not to say utter hopelessness, of such perspectives within Canadian dependency theory that would lead Gordon Laxer, among others, to comment on the 'schizophrenic character' of Canadian political economy and to argue instead for the rejection of this nightmarish vision of Canadian development in which 'Canada is stuck in a perpetual trap of resource-exporting, foreign ownership and economic and political dependence.'[35]

Renegotiating Dependency

For the generation of political economists who began publishing in the mid-1970s, 'dependency' turned out to be a far more complex phenomenon than initially imagined. The work also reflected the growing influence of British literary scholars, such as Raymond Williams and the rise of variants within British Marxist studies, such as cultural studies, both of which were more preoccupied with the analysis of the 'relative autonomy' of the cultural superstructure than with the traditional focus on economic determinations. This 'renegotiation' of the focus of classical

Marxist concerns away from political economy and towards cultural studies underpins Ted Magder's *Canada's Hollywood: The Canadian State and Feature Films*, a book produced from his doctoral work at York supervised by Leo Panitch.[36]

Although Magder sees the 'history of the cinema in Canada [as] perhaps the clearest example of ... dependent development in the sphere of cultural production,' his study of the relationship of the Canadian state and feature films is, in certain respects, a repudiation of the 'classical' dependency framework.[37] Or, if such a formulation is too strong, he recentres his analysis away from an obsessive preoccupation with the determining influence of external factors and squarely on the primacy of internal factors, particularly as they have affected the formation of state policies. Magder's critique of previous analyses, including Smythe's, is that 'they remain trapped by the most fundamental error of dependency theory in its analysis of the state, that is, the tendency to reduce the activities of the dependent state to a strict function of the dynamic forces in the imperialist core.' The state, Magder forcefully reminds his readers, does not stand above society, either as the *bête noire* of cultural dependency or as the potential saviour of national cultural development. More strongly still, he argues that Canadian cultural practices and policies do not exist 'because of some collusion on the part of American capital and the Canadian state.' If dependency is to remain relevant to understanding the development of Canadian cultural production, it must be analysed as a process of struggle and renegotiation, not as a static relation of domination. Rather than understanding feature film policy as being produced 'at the behest' of the American film industry, Magder argues that it has been determined 'by forces within Canada ... influenced by the process of dependent capitalist development.' The study of contemporary Canadian feature film policies suggests instead 'a complex and by no means uncontradictory rearrangement of the terms of dependency through which the Canadian state has facilitated the development of large-scale Canadian cultural capital integrated into the expanding international cultural marketplace.' If the result has not been an upsurge of 'truly Canadian cultural expression,' state initiatives had as of the 1960s nonetheless begun to create a Canadian feature film sector.[38]

Interestingly, the major difference between Pendakur's and Magder's approaches is not at the level of the *structures* of dependency, which remain the same for both analysts; it is at the level of the *function* of the state. For Pendakur, that function is entirely a negative one: the state is the agent of cultural *underdevelopment*. For Magder, on the other hand, that function is relatively positive: the state is an agent of dependent cultural *development*. Magder's analysis, however, at last enables Canadian dependency theory to break out of its entrapment in a vicious dialectic between external and internal forces. By situating his analytical focus squarely on internal developments and how these, more than anything else, have affected the role of the Canadian state in the formulation of feature film policies, Magder's study is the first to breach the thick encrustations of governmentality that have stifled the understanding of the relationship between the state and cinema in Canada. Prior to Magder, analyses of that relationship viewed the state either as the Leviathanic reincarnation of dependency or as the potential Messiah of 'truly Canadian' cultural forms of expression, if only that Messianic state could be persuaded to act. Magder's contribution to the study of Canadian feature film policies thus rests on a significant methodological advance, not only by emphasizing the state's mediation of the links between politics and power (classical dependency theory had already done this, if negatively), but even more importantly by emphasizing *the* state as a mediating site of *communicative* practices, that is, of the discourses within the social formation. In this perspective, not only is the state no longer *the* state, it is a complex, contradictory set of sites through which are played out not only power relations, but, as will be seen below, knowledge relations and their effects. Magder's study, it is worth repeating, breaks the object of his study, the relationship between the state and cinema, free from the framework of governmentality in which implicitly or explicity it had hitherto been contained, thus allowing for the first time the possibility of alternative analytical frameworks, to which we briefly turn.

Alternatives

Among alternative approaches proposed for the study of the cinema in Canada that are neither nationalist nor Marxist stands Ian Jarvie's meticulously researched *Hollywood's Overseas Campaign*, which analyses the triangular formation of the film trade and national policies in the North Atlantic context of Canada, the United States, and Great Britain between the 1920s and the 1950s. In this context, Canada forms one corner of a larger system, the closest so-called 'foreign' market for American film for its expansion throughout the English-speaking world. As such, in these four decades the Canadian context was distinguished by certain market characteristics that are worth emphasizing. For one, Canada, unlike Britain, was not a feature film producing country; rather it was entirely a client country, where the film 'industry' consisted mainly of exhibition and distribution. Although a predominantly rural country until well into the twentieth century, Canada's two biggest centres of population, Montreal and Toronto, generated greater box-office revenue than did all the scattered rural areas. For distribution purposes, the country was divided into territories, some of which corresponded to the provinces. The distribution exchange for each territory was in a large city from which films were moved by railway. Of the approximately eleven hundred movie theatres in Canada in the early 1920s, fewer than one quarter were consolidated into chains and centrally booked; the remainder were technically independent.[39]

The market structure in Canada, therefore, was 'a peculiar one – like a midwestern state, on a hugely magnified scale,' with a few relatively sophisticated large cities that could support premium theatres and generate the bulk of film revenue, and many small towns with only one theatre that yielded modest revenues. The extension of the American companies into the Canadian market was 'clearly ... established' by 1922, so that by 1926 American films represented 98.7 per cent of Canadian imports, replicating the market structure already familiar in other areas. As well, given the similarity of language and culture, advertising materials and campaigns could be used in Canada unaltered. The resulting strategy was

simply to dominate the market and ... to utilize the leverage of domination to prevent the emergence of rival centers of power, while permitting those not under control some sort of livelihood. The small number of American distributors and their direct links with the principal theatres and sources of revenue enabled them judiciously to buy up or indirectly control the strategic centers of distribution. Once secured, the system was maintained by zoning; clearances; first, second and subsequent runs; and by blind and block booking. None of these would have worked if there had not been a strong demand and serious lack of competitive product.[40]

In other words, resistance to the influence of the American mass medium was *not* a serious matter on commercial grounds. It was perhaps a different matter for cultural and nationalist reasons, but one that was bedevilled by a confusion of aims among nationalist elites. If, as Jarvie observes, otherwise progressive, or even radical, Canadian cultural elites all too often tended to 'become étatiste' and either vocally proclaimed their British nationalism at a time when the British connection was palpably waning or later did so in the name of a national identity different from that of Britain or the United States, they were also overly eager to impose controls on the mass media and on the products for mass audiences.[41] As Jarvie notes with some understatement, Hollywood's apparently successful business strategy of displacing locally owned distribution and exhibition interests not only secured its market and so reduced its risks, it also simultaneously created within Canada a rhetorical universe that was largely an internal construction, in which an idealist discourse of cultural sovereignty or protectionism coexisted alongside practices at odds with the nationalist discourse, apparently unaware of the contradictions between the two. As well, Hollywood had in the process also created powerful local enemies: local business rivals in theatres and distribution in a highly visible business who were well connected to the press and political elites.[42]

The resulting terrain of competing discourses has also been commented on by other analysts. British communications scholar Richard Collins, for instance, has been struck by the hold that dependency theory (an analytical framework that Jarvie, for one, does not pay much attention to) has had on the imagination of Canadian intellectuals. Collins sees this largely as a metaphorical epiphenomenon of the Canadian sociological imagination, an intellectual 'fiction conjured into existence ... by the fetishization of national economic autarchy.'[43] Like other students of Canadian culture, Collins is not insensitive to the key role such perspectives have given Canadian intellectuals in nation building (or so they imagined) and, as a result, their predilection for *étatist* policy solutions. In his 1990 book-length study of the culture of Canadian television, Collins extends the argument of the diversity of Canadian universes of discourse further, suggesting a near total incompatibility between what he terms Canada's political and anthropological cultures.[44] In other words, there is little congruence between the realms of state actions and political discourses and the symbolic cultures of what are termed 'ordinary Canadians' whose cultural universe consists of large portions of North American mass culture.

Finally, we turn very briefly not so much to another alternative theory as to the evocation of another level of explanation that has been put forth to account for the emergence of the English-Canadian feature in the 1960s. This position has been argued by Canadian cultural nationalist journalists such as Susan Crean and by Quebec film historians such as Pierre Véronneau.[45] Both writers suggest that the sudden upsurge of English-language feature films was a completely unexpected phenomenon, for which there was no preparedness, little understanding, even less policy, only great enthusiasms in certain, limited circles, and even greater hopes. How accurate such a suggestion might be will be examined in the following chapters, which look in more detail at the processes of emergence of the Canadian feature film in French and in English.

Conclusion

The strengths and the weaknesses of the kinds of theoretical models that have framed the discussion primarily of the relationship between the state and cinema in Canada have been discussed. Not only have considerable gaps continued to prevail in Canadian film history: it remains a profoundly discontinuous history, a partial history with significant dimensions still to be written, although some of its predominant traits, particularly its complex intertwinings over time with various entities within the Canadian state, are rather more focused today than they were two decades ago. It was seen also that the preferred type of explanation deployed by Canadian scholars here has been strongly deterministic (or 'tautological,' as Ian Jarvie puts it),[46] in which the actions or inactions of the state have been profoundly rooted within a predominant logic of governmentality, whether in the form of pleas for more government intervention or of appalled, if not enthralled, diagnoses of the ubiquity of 'the capitalist state,' whether in its local Canadian incarnation or from the panoptical perspectives of American 'imperialism.'

   In the end, however, as Foucault's work on governmentality teaches, it is not to theories of the state that one must look to grasp the emergence of the Canadian feature film, especially given that the theories are so often themselves implicated within the extensions of governmentality into ever-deeper reaches of the social formation. Rather, it is by understanding changing practices that one can hope to obtain a better sense of how the either totally overdetermined or completely unexpected phenomenon of the Canadian feature came about.

3

A New Policy Field, Television, and Changing Production Practices

In the perspective of the Foucauldian analysis of governmentality, governmental practices gave Canadian political culture and organization a distinct configuration. The domination of Canadian federal politics by the Liberal Party from the 1930s to 1984, except for two brief Conservative interludes, had created a strong, highly centralized and quasi-omnipresent structure of political organization. As Reg Whitaker has observed, this left extra-political organization 'weak and under-developed';[1] in other words, outside the dominant structures, there were few countervailing organizational forces. In turn, this situation had strongly reinforced the predominant institutional tendency to transform not only politics into bureaucracy but also party into state. The palpable result, as Whitaker puts it, was a 'deadening of political controversy, the silence, the greyness which clothed political life at the national level in the 1950s, were reflections of a Liberal ideal of an apolitical public life. In place of politics there was bureaucracy and technology.'[2]

This was the organizational background against which, as Philip Resnick has shown,[3] occurred the rapid take-off of the state-owned sector of the Canadian economy as it changed from a non-urban resource base to an urbanized service-oriented one. This significant transformation also coincided with an increased preoccupation within the social formation with questions of cultural production and reproduction. From 1949, with the establishment of the Massey Commission, to the institutional implementation in 1957 of one of the two major Massey recommendations, the creation of the Canada Council (the other had been the establishment of Canadian television in 1952), questions of the production and reproduction of culture became increasingly, as the decade progressed, the object of 'heavy government involvement,' in Maria

Tippett's formulation: 'Now ... recognized as an appropriate object of state attention at the highest level, cultural activity emerged – at first tentatively, then with increasing confidence – into the mainstream of the federal policy-making process.'[4] The ramifications of such extensions of governmental practices into new domains of the social formation were dramatically summarized by historian Donald Creighton: 'Canadians of the 1950's *had not yet been taught* to believe that the state was the great dispenser of social and cultural goodies and that unless the state designed and financed a literary or artistic project, its failure was virtually inevitable.'[5]

The New Horizons of Cultural Policy

In his essay on the development of Canadian cultural policy Bernard Ostry suggested that in a retrospective assessment of Prime Minister Louis St-Laurent's otherwise undistinguished years of 'comfortable power,' one speech he gave would rank high.[6] This was an address to a national conference of Canadian universities in Ottawa, convened in November 1956 to discuss the crisis in higher education. It was written by his economic adviser, former Université Laval social scientist Maurice Lamontagne. Something of an anomaly in grey Ottawa, a 'cultured politician[,] a rare bird in Ottawa's longitudes,'[7] Lamontagne, as secretary of state in the early 1960s, became the first government minister responsible for the development of Canadian policy with regard to feature film. The 1956 speech thus provides a sense of the discursive horizons within which the extension of governmentality in the cultural sphere occurred. It also presaged the terms of the discourse that governed subsequent discussions on the feature film by the state. In particular, it stated clearly that the object of policy was the reproduction within the sphere of cultural production of the predominant patterns of Canadian economic development: 'it is now time for our cultural development to parallel what has taken place in the economic field.'[8]

For St-Laurent and his speech-writer Lamontagne, Canada was experiencing in the mid-1950s the highest levels of economic prosperity in its history and one of the highest rates of industrial expansion in the world. If, as the conference of Canadian universities proposed, there was a crisis in higher education, the existence of such a crisis had revealed to the state 'that our national development suffers from a serious weakness ... our cultural progress has not kept pace with our industrial expansion.'[9]

In the economic field, Canada at the time of Confederation had consisted of 'several depressed regional economies ... more directly linked with the United States than with each other.' As a result of appropriate national policies and increasingly competitive economic relations with the United States, the economic unification 'of our territory, which seemed artificial not long ago, now appears to have been largely achieved and to have become almost natural,' resulting in a 'distinct and strong national economy' built around the realization of 'gigantic projects' through private initiative and appropriate government policies. 'This admirable accomplishment has largely taken place as a result of private initiative, but it would not have been possible without active government support.'[10]

In its current underdevelopment, however, the state of Canadian culture recalled the earlier phases of the country's economy: 'our country is comprised of several cultural regions that do not have enough interchange between one another and [yet] that are too exclusively subjected to a common influence [that originates] from outside of Canada.' This was not alarming in itself so long as exterior cultural influences were 'neither determining nor the only ones to act simultaneously upon all our regions because, then, the well-springs of our cultural life would have ceased to be [of] Canadian [provenance].' To forestall such an eventuality, 'we must resolutely get to work and attempt *to reproduce, on the cultural level, what we have achieved in the economic domain.*'[11]

On the cultural level, the state saw its role as one of providing support and encouragement to individuals and private groups in domains that were left to their own initiative, not as one attempting to control these individuals and groups. However, it was up to the state to establish the agencies necessary for culture to express itself fully. It was the duty of the state to assist and encourage private initiatives, not to attempt to overtake them, although private initiatives left to themselves could not accomplish everything. The gap between Canada's cultural and economic development resulted not from an inherent superiority of business over the arts and sciences; instead it derived in part from the fact that cultural activities were not as profitable as economic activity and, above all, from 'the fact that the State has not achieved in the cultural domain the role it has exercised at the economic level.'[12]

The address reviewed the constitutional bases for the federal government's right of intervention in certain cultural domains, seeing it as an extension of the royal prerogative in matters of taxation, the disposition of public monies, and federal transfer payments to the provinces. It demonstrated that the interventionist claims of federal cultural policy were historically based and dated back to the 1842 creation of a museum, first of a number of national cultural institutions, to be followed by the Public Archives, the National Gallery, the National Research Council, the Historic Sites and Monuments Board, the Canadian Broadcasting Corporation (CBC), the National Film Board, and the National Library. A number of federal programs designed to provide assistance to individuals and organizations in the cultural field were also reviewed. Furthermore, the policy of setting up public agencies 'deemed essential for the development and adequate expression of our cultural life' had been 'strongly supported' by the Canadian people, as attested by the Massey Commission hearings. The *Massey Report* had recommended that the fundamental principles of 'this traditional policy ... be strengthened and extended to new fields of cultural activity.'[13] The establishment of Canadian television in 1952 thus provides a concrete context in which to review the application of these principles in practice.

The Introduction of Canadian Television

The introduction of Canadian television opened up a debate as to the power of its cultural effects. For Quebec researchers, the ideological power of television meant that the new medium provided an alternative, modern channel of communications for its audience that bypassed the traditional channels of family, church, and school. One can argue over the *range* of the ideological power of the new medium, but it is empirically certain that the number of telecasts of NFB films to Quebec audiences between 1952 and 1964 was at least two and a half times as many as in any other province and over three times as many as in neighbouring Ontario.[14]

Contrary to the Québécois proponents of strong television effects, historian Paul Rutherford has argued that the impact of English Canadian television only reconfirmed what was *already* there, beginning with 'the basic structure of Canadian broadcasting ... [which] ensured that the television scene, like the radio scene before it, would be full of American messages.'[15] For Rutherford, Canadian television, despite the quasi-revolutionary hopes it had aroused at the time of its inception, would prove an ineffective instrument both for policies of Canadianization and more generally for overcoming 'existing cultural realities':

In Quebec where there remained a lively tradition of the popular arts, television was the vehicle for a brand of drama that did express something local, but in

English Canada where the tradition was feeble at best, television couldn't work any miracles.[16]

While one might further debate this point, it can certainly be strongly suggested that television had a profound impact on the practices that directly bore upon the emergence of the Canadian feature film. Before television, the possibility of seeing films either about Canada or made by Canadians, which was, more often than not, the same thing, was distinctly limited, except for the productions of the NFB. And, within the NFB, these productions were in turn limited to *certain* formats, genres, and structures.[17] 'Today,' NFB director of production Donald Mulholland wrote in a 1959 confidential report to the NFB Board of Governors, 'the National Film Board supplies almost the only reference to Canada in Canadian cinemas with its theatrical shorts ... [and] is almost the only Canadian source of film about Canada for use in schools ... With the advent of television to Canada, NFB was presented with a channel of distribution to the public which it could not ignore.'[18]

The inter-bureaucratic struggle that started in the 1940s between the CBC and the NFB over the control of television remains to be more fully documented, but it is worth noting that, as early as 1943, the NFB was supplying television outlets in the United States and Great Britain with Canadian films. In a 25,000-word submission to the Massey Commission, the NFB predicted that in Canada motion pictures would play an even greater role in television than in the United States, where a contemporary estimate showed that 25 per cent of television programming consisted of films. In its brief to the Massey Commission it outlined its readiness to expand into television by supplying its large stock of films and, more directly, by recording live TV programs on film and distributing these on circuits serving rural areas not covered by television stations. 'When television is established in Canada, it will find ready for use a very substantial program and a technical capacity which could not be developed by another organization except for a considerable period of years.'[19]

For its part, the *Massey Report* would find 'deplorable' the idea that the NFB might become simply or principally a supplier of films for television. Because the NFB would not be able to produce all the films or even genres of films the CBC would need, however attractive the idea that it do so, was assigned by the Massey Commission the role of 'principal adviser' to the CBC on film matters. The result was a dynamic of inter-bureaucratic feuding that would persist for thirty years. Within the

NFB, the 'loss' of television would, for some producers at least, make the battle for the feature film in the 1960s that much more poignant and this second crucial defeat all the more bitter.

The extent, therefore, to which the NFB had developed almost entirely within a separate film production, distribution, and exhibition economy of its own, directed as it was to an educational, volunteer, and largely rural economy, can probably not be stated too strongly. Until well into the mid-1960s the political economy of 'independent' (i.e., non-foreign-owned) cinematic distribution and exhibition in Canada would be described by N.A. Taylor, the largest independent distributor and theatre owner, as predominantly rural.[20] In this light, D.B. Jones's remark that in the eleven years between 1939 and 1950 'the Film Board did not produce a single documentary that speaks to a modern audience'[21] takes on a particular resonance. NFB producer Jacques Bobet recalls incredulously the creative fervour and technical struggles that surrounded the making of films with titles like *Udder Disease in Cows* (*Maladie du pis de la vache*).[22] With scant exaggeration one could speak of the NFB's films as a parallel cinema in Canada aimed primarily at educating schoolchildren, agriculturalists, and American tourists.[23] By the mid-1950s this parallel cinema had developed an extensive infrastructure, as NFB historian Marjorie McKay describes it, that by 1955–6 ostensibly reached a domestic audience of almost fifteen million people and a foreign audience of almost eighteen million, entirely by means of distribution 'outside the theatres and television.'[24]

To be able to access a new technology of distribution that by 1960 was within the range of 94 per cent of Canadian households and whose extraordinary expansion had 'caught on more quickly in Ontario and Quebec than in the rest of the country, in the big cities, and (by a slight edge) with French Canadians'[25] was, indeed, a channel of distribution to an *urban* (or urbanizing) audience that the NFB could not afford to ignore. But the lack of distribution of NFB films in urban centres was so preoccupying that, by early 1958, one member of the Board of Governors wondered 'whether the time has not come ... [for] legislation providing for a "quota" of Canadian films on programs in theatres.'[26]

However, in the view of the NFB the 'central and deciding' factor of its involvement with the television system – and so its connection to the general public in Canada – was its relationship to the CBC. And that relationship, as an internal report written in 1986 delicately put it, 'has not been smooth, and the public interest probably not served as well as it might have been. Since the mandate of each agency has been in conflict from the start of television forward, the piecemeal solutions developed to date have not really resolved the problem.'[27]

The NFB and French-Language Television

One part of the 'piecemeal solution' adopted consisted in the NFB functioning as a supplier of programs for the start-up of television. As Cox's 1986 review of the NFB and television from 1950 to 1984 described the situation, the NFB traditionally subsidized broadcasters during their start-up phase for English-language services, and for a longer period for French-language services, which did not have access to the huge pool of foreign English-language programming. When the TV services matured and developed their own institutional production capacity, the NFB's programming was squeezed out because it was aimed at a minority audience and so was deemed unable to compete with foreign commercial alternatives that were available at dumped prices. 'This trend could be seen even before Canadian television began.'[28]

More particularly, as of 1953–4 the NFB began producing series of films for television. By 1954–5 half of its output was destined for television, though by 1958–9 the proportion declined to one third.[29] By October 1959 ten series of varying lengths had been produced in English and nine in French, amounting to 474 films for a total running time of 225 hours, enough to fill approximately two weeks of the Canadian TV schedule.[30] These special series productions were original location documentaries and were rented to CBC, which carried them on a sustaining basis without commercial sponsorship at rates that in 1953 were negotiated at $200 per half-hour and by the 1960–1 season had been renegotiated upward to $8,000 per half-hour, representing approximately half of the production costs incurred by NFB. By comparison, rental rates for American or British series in the 1950s were approximately $2,000 per half-hour and $5,000 for American syndicated half-hour films dubbed into French.[31] In addition to such special series, the NFB also produced annual series of films for first-time showing on television in French and English, amounting to approximately thirty-six half-hours in each language under an arrangement with CBC in which the latter was granted exclusive rights for a two-year period.[32] The NFB's annual contract with CBC was cancelled in 1969 and the Radio-Canada contract continued a while longer, though Véronneau notes that there was, as of the early 1960s, a progressive 'withdrawal of the NFB from Radio-Canada's production planning: the Board would increasingly have to negotiate for each broadcast hour and more often than not was disappointed by the scheduling slots it would be allotted.'[33]

From the perspective of changing practices, the move to the production of film series for television considerably stressed the capacities of the NFB. With an output at the maximum by the mid-1950s of over one hundred original new films per year, the pace of increased production strained the NFB's production structures and necessitated organizational modifications that included increased autonomy for French Production and the first appointment of a French Canadian, Guy Roberge, as government film commissioner, the head of the NFB. Some of the strain entailed by TV series production is reflected in the dissatisfaction expressed by filmmakers Léonard Forest and Fernand Dansereau in a 1958 memorandum to Pierre Juneau:

Who would have dared ask of one individual to write and produce eight half-hours of film in the same season, of another to write seven and produce six, and of yet another to produce nine![34]

Filmmaker Marcel Carrière summed up the changing pace of production practices as follows:

When I arrived at the Board [in 1956], we produced 10-minute films, no more. One reel. Then it got longer. Twenty minutes, then thirty minutes, then an hour. And now, we're up to an hour-and-a-half, two hours. [Pierre] Perrault has made [films] up to three and four hours' long. So it was that kind of progression. It was unthinkable to imagine that we could hold an audience for more than ten minutes at a given moment with the means we had available then. We weren't making features.[35]

The point to be underscored regarding changing practices is that, while there is a formal correspondence between series of half-hour films and the feature form, in the context of NFB production that correspondence was one of 'arrested development.'[36] On the one hand, the *Passe-partout* series (fifty-two thirty-minute episodes, from October 1955 to April 1957) 'made it possible ... to increase the staffing of French-speaking filmmakers at the Board ... and to introduce some of them to scriptwriting as well as directing actors.'[37] On the other hand, *Passe-partout* proved disappointing to audiences and to artisans: the series was a hybrid, both formally and ideologically, an eclectic mix of documentaries, compilation films, and dramatic fictions (the thirty-minute format reportedly constrained dramatic development).[38] But it made possible its successor series, *Panoramique*.

Given the limitations of *Passe-partout*'s thirty-minute format, the *Panoramique* series presented from the fall of 1957 to January 1959 consisted of larger, narrative blocks or fictional 'mini-series,' as Houle and Julien put it.[39] It consisted of Bernard Devlin's four-hour saga in eight episodes of the colonization of Abitibi, *Les Brûlés*, which cost $144,010. This was followed by Louis Portugais's two-hour and four-episode, *Les 90 jours*, a drama in a trade-union context, and his five-episode *Il était une guerre*, a drama about the Second World War from a Quebec perspective, costing $62,490, which he directed.[40] The three major productions of the series were complemented by a four-episode study of oppression in the white-collar universe, *Les Mains nettes*, directed by Claude Jutra, a three-episode story about a farmer's difficulties, *Le Maître du Pérou*, directed and scripted by Fernand Dansereau, and the two-episode *Pays neuf*, in which an Abitibi mine inspector leaves his job.

Houle and Julien ascribe the considerable popularity of the *Panoramique* series to its close resemblance to contemporary *téléromans* such as *Les Plouffe*, *Le Survenant*, and *Cap aux sorciers*. But although the NFB re-edited and reissued the two shortest titles in the series as long shorts (each nearly an hour long), the four longest titles were held up for re-release by Radio-Canada. Eventually re-edited as two feature-length films, *Les Brûlés* and *Il était une guerre*, they were released through the NFB's community circuits. The results of all this experimentation, while deemed 'useful,' proved inconclusive, and plans for a follow-up series were dropped.[41]

It is in the context of the planning discussions around the proposed *Panoramique II* series for the 1958–9 television season that Véronneau situates his account of the emergence of the *aesthetic idea* of the feature form within French-language production at the NFB. For Véronneau, that emergence took the form of a tension between the continuation of a more cost-effective documentary approach to series production that was backed by the English Production units and NFB management, and an emergent dramatic tendency within the French-language unit, whose proponents argued, somewhat casuistically, that the dramatic form was actually a superior *documentary* formula for expressing the real. Thus Forest and Dansereau in a memorandum spoke of 'our belief in the validity of the dramatic formula as a 'documentary' formula, as a means of the expression of the reality ... For the 'documentarians' that we are and want to remain, dramatization is not an easy solution ... it is a peril-ous game whose umpires are honesty, justice, and truth.'[42] But such 'aesthetic' arguments would not prove convincing to the NFB's manage-ment, more concerned with costs. If *Panoramique I* proved too expensive an undertaking for the NFB alone, Radio-Canada had also expressed reservations about the production. 'When the time came to make the decisions on *Panoramique II*, the conjuncture was probably not favour-able ... [A]t the level of arguments for ... feature-length dramas ... the idea had been sown; it would, however, require five further years for the fruits to blossom.'[43] The NFB and Radio-Canada both preferred much less costly series.

As a result, the filmmakers of the embryonic French Production unit not only turned to the less costly production of series for television, such as the half-hour *Coup d'œil* series which provided the context for *Les Raquetteurs* (1958), and the *Temps présent* series which did the same for *Les Petites Sœurs* (1959), *La Lutte* (1961), and the like. More importantly, they turned to another form altogether, one that was outside television, the documentary short, which offered, as Fernand Dansereau put it, 'a new direction that truly opened the door to our own [forms] of expres-sion. Thus in Quebec we invented the direct cinema ... under the influ-ence of television and the stylistic upheavals it entailed.'[44]

The shorts of the direct cinema were, as Yves Lever points out, 'a new form of *écriture* imposed by the context and means available.'[45] This new form of *écriture* was, as filmmaker Claude Jutra described it, a 'quasi-sexual obsession' with the technical liberation brought about by the rela-tively lightweight equipment available to television crews that was the envy of NFB filmmakers.[46]

Television had brought about a much faster production rhythm and, to achieve this it was necessary to invent new technical means, such as lightweight cameras, new sound recording equipment, synchronous sound. As well, more sensitive film stock was needed to eliminate the effects of overly sophisticated lighting. Each shoot thus became a 'study session,' an informal school, where, without teachers, the 'students' experimented and taught one another a new aesthetic, with happy or unhappy results depending on the circumstances. In turn, these new shooting conditions changed the mentality of the artisans, who were granted greater mobility, making them curious to experiment with other techniques, such as *bricolage* with different camera models and length-ening film processing time to obtain unprecedented visual effects.[47]

Whatever else it was, the direct short appeared to the filmmakers con-

cerned as 'the only means available at the time to circumvent the censorship [that prevailed] at every level of the production process and, in so
doing, to bring into being a new approach to filmmaking.'[48] Marsolais is
thus undoubtedly correct in seeing, in both the direct shorts of 1958 to
1960 and, after a semi-clandestine shift as of 1963, the feature-length
film inspired by the direct shorts, the aspiration towards a new type of
communicative relationship that short-circuited (the term is Véronneau's) all the hierarchies of communication prevailing within the NFB.
These hierarchies manifested themselves at the levels of the image, of
the script, of the crew, of montage, and, beyond the confines of the NFB,
of 'the falsehoods, the ridiculousness, [and] even the grotesque [traits
that permeated] Québécois society of the 1960s.'[49]

While there were undoubtedly elements of cross-fertilization between
the NFB and CBC/Radio-Canada as a result of the former's output for
television, of the emergence of the aesthetic idea of the feature, and of
the direct form, the changes were discontinuous and in practices only. It
required several more years for an actual discourse to take shape in
Quebec that merged the idea of the feature with the form of the direct.
At the level of practices, the direct, while initially influenced by both the
style and the technology of television, was itself marginalized by the
practices brought on by the institutionalization of television. By the
early 1960s, as the televisual institution shifted from its role as a passive
consumer of footage to one of determining consumption norms, the
direct was rejected as transgressive of televisual norms. According to
Véronneau, the institutional practices of television marginalized the
direct not only by obliging the films it opted to show to conform to the
dominant models of television production, but also by forcing those
who wanted to see their work benefit from normal television exposure
to conform to current production practices.[50]

Television in English Canada and Series Production

Rutherford has argued that the coming of Canadian television reconfirmed the basic structure of Canadian broadcasting, which was English
Canada's dependence upon American programming. In this sense, CBC
(and CTV subsequently) 'never had full control of its own schedule.'[51]
As Rutherford remarks, 'When the Board of Broadcast Governors
announced late in 1959 that made-in-Canada programming must reach
a minimum of 55 per cent of the schedule, that actually reflected about
the limit of what the CBC's English service could achieve.'[52] If, in con-

trast to CBC, Radio-Canada produced about three-quarters of its programs, its greater latitude with its schedule would neither diminish the problematic nature of its relations with the NFB nor prevent it from also becoming 'the world's largest buyer of imported telefilms.'[53] As for CBC, with peak viewing hours (8 to 10 p.m.) on the network blocked out with American 'hits,' in some instances unspecified at the time of scheduling, made-in-Canada English programming aired either before or after the imported highlights. Rutherford has noted that:

The CBC produced nearly all network shows made in Canada during the 1950s. A mere 2 per cent of the shows telecast on its networks during one week in February 1958 came from 'Other Canadian Sources.' Who could compete? There wasn't a Hollywood North, and the CBC was hardly ready to encourage such, although it did work with private film companies to produce a bit of series drama at the end of the decade.[54]

An additional constraint was the fact that as late as the 1960–1 season nearly 95 per cent of the made-in-Canada programming on the English network service was live, either to air or on tape. With CBC programmers focusing their limited resources on improving informational broadcasts – the national newscast, news specials, documentaries, and assorted public affairs programs that absorbed half of the CBC's dollars for programming and left the Drama unit starved with only 13 per cent of the programming budget in 1965[55] – the development of made-in-Canada filmed television serials in English would be a function of the internationalization of American TV production.

In the United States the gradual shift that took place from live dramatic production to filmed programming in the 1950s represented 'a very real alternative to network dependence' as a result of the development of Hollywood's potential ability to supply telefilms (filmed series or serials) that could be distributed alone or in packages to the hundreds of TV stations not yet linked to the major networks.[56] In Canada, on the other hand, the centralized structure of Canadian broadcasting only increased network dependence. As Austin Weir put it,

In a curious and unintentional way, the CBC has given an indirect but important impetus to the sale of imported [tele]films. Most American organizations producing television films maintain sales representatives in Toronto or Montreal, and the CBC is the single largest buyer. If the [tele]film representative can sell the CBC without travel or other additional expenses, he is well on his way, and to accomplish this he makes every effort. To cover private stations, especially those in remote or isolated areas, is much more expensive.'[57]

Limited in their access to British television markets by a 15 per cent quota on imported programming, some U.S. film and television production companies, in the hope of qualifying as British Commonwealth production, established subsidiaries in Canada in the mid to late 1950s to begin producing made-in-Canada, half-hour comedy and adventure series.[58] Thus, for instance, Television Programs of America (TPA) set up Normandie Productions in Toronto in 1956 and, armed with a guarantee that it would be shown on the CBC, produced thirty-eight episodes of the series *Last of the Mohicans*, with American stars and direction and with Canadian equipment, crew, and supporting players. The series was sold to 150 independent stations in the United States and to networks in England, France, and Central America.[59] This venture was followed by two further series, the sitcom *Tugboat Annie* (thirty-nine thirty-minute episodes) in 1958, and an adventure series about truckers, *Cannonball* (thirty-nine thirty-minute episodes) in 1959.

The impact of these productions on the Canadian production infrastructure, particularly in Toronto, and on the trade press, daily newspapers, and monthlies, was dramatic and in sharp contrast to recent unsuccessful Toronto-based ventures in feature filmmaking. CBC-TV director Sidney Furie's independent, low-budget *A Dangerous Age* (1957) had been 'almost certainly the first Canadian film for decades to merit serious critical attention internationally,' but it was 'a flawed, first feature.'[60] Though neither it nor Furie's second feature, *A Cool Sound from Hell* (also titled *The Young and the Beat*), from 1959, received much attention in Canada, they established his reputation as a director of promise in England, for which he left in 1959. Klenman-Davidson Productions Ltd of Toronto, founded in 1957 by Norman Klenman and William Davidson, both formerly from the NFB and CBC, produced films exclusively for CBC-TV, hiring equipment and staff by the job. Early in 1958 they announced ambitious plans for expanded production and permanent personnel.[61] Their plans included sponsored documentaries and industrial films, as well as a feature, *Now That April's Here* (1958), which was based on four short stories by Morley Callaghan and was written and co-produced by Klenman-Davidson and Toronto independent producer, exhibitor, and distributor N.A. Taylor. *April* was, in the words of one newspaper critic, 'a box-office flop of the first magnitude.'[62] Their second feature, *The Ivy League Killers* (1959), was turned down as 'not good enough' by Taylor, who was described by the same critic as a lead-ing purveyor of 'cheap "B" films of the shock and shriek school.'

In 1959 Taylor, through his wife, co-produced with Meridian Films of Toronto the horror picture *The Bloody Brood*, which, according to its *Variety* review that was delicately penned by Toronto contributor Gerald Pratley, was saved by 'virile direction and deft editing [that,] ... with the convincing portrayals of the cast, prevent the entire production from collapsing into comic absurdity.'[63] The original story property was sug-gested by Hal Roach Jr, whose father was one of a number of Holly-wood theatrical film producers who had struck it rich in the telefilm business. Hal Roach Sr shifted production from feature film to TV series in 1949, placing his son in charge of the company. *Bloody Brood* producer and director Julian Roffman initially asked Roach's company to make a feature in Canada. As the *Toronto Daily Star*'s show business columnist put it in August 1959, 'The uncertainty of the feature film market is in sharp contrast with the buoyant situation of the television filming industry *where U.S. money and know-how is turning Toronto into one of the world's largest production centres.*'[64]

This statement referred to the spate of construction of studios in the previous year in anticipation of further American series. The studios included Arthur Gottlieb's Canadian Film Industries, where the TPA series was filmed, and N.A. Taylor's Toronto International Film Studios Ltd, which was intended for the production of television and feature films and which claimed, as the Taylor-owned trade publication *Canadian Film Weekly* put it, to be the 'first of its kind in Canada.'[65] As Arthur (later Sir Arthur) Chetwynd, then president of the principal lobby for the industry in Canada, the Association of Motion Picture Producers and Laboratories of Canada (AMPPLC), reported to an industry meet-ing early in 1958, when he announced that the membership of the asso-ciation had increased from thirty-five to forty-two companies: 'The technical corps of Canada's production industry is being enlarged through training under key personnel imported for American-inspired projects and a profitable trade equipment business has grown around articles [hitherto] not available in this country.'[66] As a result of the upswing in production, Chetwynd noted, television films were being made in Canada for the first time by 'parent USA companies' for Cana-dian consumption, whereas they had previously been made 'across the line' (i.e., on the U.S. side of the border), and motion picture production equipment could now also be purchased in Canada, 'whereas previ-ously all equipment had to be imported direct from the United States or other countries.' Not just equipment but also 'many of the dollars' were actually staying on this side of the border. The fact that the Americans were augmenting their crews with Canadians represented 'further training of our film technicians which will reflect on the Industry *in later years.*' Finally, as a result of this expansion in 'branch plant' television production, AMPPLC members had begun making regular contact with Canadian government officials to lobby for relief from taxes and customs duties for the importation of equipment (not all equipment was available in Canada). As Chetwynd confidently predicted, the 'future of the Industry ... appears bright.'[67]

In contrast to the enthusiasm aroused by American productions, particularly in Toronto, Canadian-made filmed drama series got off to a shaky start. Reluctant to enter into competition with private Canadian film companies, CBC apparently first experimented extensively with filmed drama with the 1957 big-budget series *Radisson* (twenty-six thirty-minute episodes in both English and French). Produced for CBC by Omega Productions in Montreal, the series was bedevilled with difficulties.[68] The production ran way over budget, costing $1.04 million, and earned back a mere $146,200 in domestic and foreign sales. It was dropped after one year.

A second joint venture in Canadian telefilm in French and English, *RCMP and Gendarmerie Royale* (thirty-nine thirty-minute episodes which aired from October 1959 to October 1960), was co-produced by Crawley-McConnell Ltd, which raised 60 per cent of production costs,[69] and with CBC and BBC each contributing 20 per cent. NFB commissioner Guy Roberge reported to the NFB's governors that the key point about the $1,365,000 cost for the thirty-nine episodes ($35,000 for each half-hour) of *RCMP*, and other such complex, big-budget productions as *Radisson*, was that, because it was doubtful these series would be released a second time after their first run on Canadian television, 'the greater part of the costs of such films *must be recovered from markets outside Canada.*'[70] The series was *not* renewed by CBC for a second season, and although it aired in Britain, Australia, and a number of other countries from Hong Kong to Uruguay, it was never picked up by the U.S. networks; some episodes were rebroadcast by CBC stations in 1965.[71]

Yet it mattered less, as Rutherford for instance argues,[72] that such a series as *RCMP* compared unfavourably to the more popular American-made *The Untouchables* in the eyes of Canadian audiences or newspaper critics, than the far more important conclusion drawn by Canadian private-sector film producers from the experience of such series production, namely that the CBC was perceived, in the words of a *Canadian Film Weekly* headline, as 'Big Brother To Our Film Makers': 'Of the $3,500,000 the Canadian Broadcasting Corp. spends annually on film production, $2,750,000 goes to private production through over 30 companies or individuals. The Government TV agency is the bulwark of private production.'[73] The perception of the government TV agency as supportive of private production was in striking contrast to their view of the government film agency. Unlike the CBC, the NFB was seen as 'a hoglike hindrance' to the sector's continued growth.[74] For the emergent private sector, the encouragement by the CBC of film production, through financial participation in and airtime for the two series, provided the private sector with production experience that correlates directly to the emergence of the feature form. On the strength of its experience with series, Crawley, for instance, announced plans for two theatrical features.[75] More importantly, the contrast between the two government agencies provided the private sector with a rationale for its own further growth by way of capital transfers from the public sector.

Statisticalization and the Beginnings of Film Policy Research

In a memorable paper on communication history, James Carey, discussing the telegraph's effects on the consciousness of time, has referred to 'statisticalization' as a correlative indicator of the penetration of the price system. For Carey, 'statisticalization' indicates the transformation of a mental world into quantity, and the distribution of quantities in space, so that the relationship between things and people becomes solely one of numbers. '*Statistics widens the market for everything and makes it more uniform and interdependent.*'[76] A similar phenomenon can be seen in the interpretations the private Canadian film industry would infer from annual summaries of the Dominion Bureau of Statistics on the growth of motion picture production in the 1950s. For instance, the DBS annual summary for 1958 showed that the volume of private Canadian film industry production in that year was 297 per cent larger than in 1952. As a 1960 confidential memorandum prepared for the NFB's Board of Governors that analysed the data would explain: 'The principal cause of this increase has, of course, been television. Television had created not only a demand for program film and film services – CBC spent $2,650,000 with the private film industry in 1957 (33% of total industry volume) – but it has also created an enormous demand for television commercials, most of which are on film.'[77]

As a result of such findings, the 1958 annual meeting of the AMPPLC announced the creation of an Industry Development Committee to act as a research department for production opportunities at home and abroad. One of its first tasks would be to look into the quota system and production funding schemes (the Eady Plan) in place in Britain, along with the equivalent measures used in Italy, France, and other countries to develop a domestic production industry.[78] Chaired by the former journalist and Australian representative in Australia of the NFB under Grierson, producer Ralph Foster of the Toronto company Meridian Films, the nine-man committee did not, initially at any rate, engage in any research of its own, but turned instead to the NFB, requesting it to gather the necessary information on existing government legislation in the development of national film industries in other countries.[79] On the one hand, such a request was not surprising, as the NFB was also an AMPPLC member; on the other hand, the work of the committee, of which the NFB was not a member, produced a brief singularly hostile to the NFB. In serving as an information-gathering facility for the committee, the NFB found itself in the paradoxical position of providing the data for arguments that would be used against it.

However, the NFB, like the members of the Industry Development Committee, appears to have had little awareness of the legislative measures adopted by other countries in the development of national film industries. As a result of this lack of information and in response both to the establishment of the IDC and to the fact that, as Pierre Juneau informed Roberge in a memo, 'In recent years there have been numerous articles in the press and in trade magazines on the subject, it is now clear that the development of a feature film industry is arousing more and more interest in Canada,'[80] at its 21 April 1958 meeting the NFB Board of Governors undertook to survey 'existing legislation in other countries concerning the development of the national film industry.'

The resulting twenty-two-page survey, 'Notes on Government Legislation Related to the Development of a National Film Industry in Various Countries,' was produced under the administrative responsibility of Pierre Juneau as executive director of the NFB, who noted, according to his covering memorandum to film commissioner Roberge, that it 'should be considered as preliminary.'[81] Paying particular attention to France, Belgium, Italy, Britain, West Germany, and the Netherlands, with briefer entries for Argentina, Brazil, Austria, Denmark, and Japan, the report covered in note form the fields of film legislation according to the following categories: institutions, importation, exhibition, revenues, money transfers, financing, and co-production. It indicated 'in a general way what some countries have done and are doing to help the development of a national film industry,' but it did not comment on the effectiveness of the legislation of each country in achieving its intended purposes. The only parallel it drew with the Canadian situation was in the entry on West Germany, whose *Länder* resembled the Canadian provinces. The report did not make any recommendations.

The information in the preliminary report however, was considered 'extremely useful' by the IDC. 'It is precisely what the doctor ordered,' wrote Ralph Foster to Juneau, concluding that 'if such countries as Sweden (34 features), Norway (14 features) and Egypt (31 features) can turn out that many major films, Canada should be able to do better than the sprinkling of third-raters so far produced.'[82] Furthermore, Foster considered that it would be useful to have 'some information on the amount of help that producers in these countries receive from their national governments,' given that the purpose of the brief of the committee was to come up with a rationale for state subsidization.

Along with such information gathering both for itself as part of its responsibility to keep the Canadian government informed on film matters and incidentally for the potentially rival, private production sector, the NFB also began to scrutinize sceptically the DBS-supported statistical claims put forward by the emergent private sector. The data suggested an *abstract* growth for which NFB executives had no equivalent personal evidence deriving from experience of working with private sector companies. An exchange of memoranda late in 1958 between E.S. Coristine, the NFB's director of administration, and Donald Mulholland, director of planning and operations, illustrates their dilemma in attempting to account for abstract statistical phenomena. The problem entailed independent efforts to verify the actual size of the private sector by trying to calculate the direct taxes paid by Canadian private motion picture companies. But this effort proved impossible, because, among other reasons, of the confidentiality of income tax data. An alternative method was to attempt to calculate the sales tax paid by individual companies, but this too proved difficult, if not impossible: Mulholland knew from experience that some private sector films 'are presented to us for educational certificates which relieve them of the payment of sales tax.' Mulholland concluded that the private companies had greatly exaggerated the growth in the number of their employees in reporting to the DBS.[83]

Similarly, in attempting to trace the reported growth in the Canadian motion picture rental equipment trade, the NFB in April 1958 sent out a

questionnaire to some twenty companies. Two companies replied by listing professional equipment, and two others indicated that they rented
amateur equipment; fourteen companies, including Crawley Films, did
not reply. It 'is safe to say,' the memo from the NFB's chief purchasing
agent to top management concluded, 'that equipment rental is in short
supply in Canada and leaves no alternative but to rent from U.S.A.,'
pointing out that this was a 'hazardous and costly undertaking.'[84]

The third impossible calculation the NFB attempted to make on the
emergent private sector concerned remittances paid by distributors to
foreign countries. After estimating, probably on the basis of data in the
Canada Yearbook, the distributors' share of total Canadian box office to be
$34,153,847 (including $28,558,433 from theatrical rentals plus $5,575,484
from TV rentals), the NFB concluded that just over $12 million of this total
could be attributed to 'the liberal figure of 20–25% ... as operating costs,
[with the result that] it would appear that about $22,000,000 is remitted to
the USA on 35mm revenue, less 10% for the withholding tax which is
allowed on USA tax returns under exchange agreement with Canada.'
Another estimated $4 million in 35mm rentals flowed out to Britain,
France, Italy, West Germany, and other countries, while most of the
rental revenue for 16mm for television (the figure was not given) was also
remitted to the United States. The conclusion drawn was that the Canadian domestic market represented about 7 per cent of the total U.S. world
market: 'Over the years that proportion appears to have remained rather
constant.'[85]

What all this might mean for government film policy was the subject
of a memorandum to Pierre Juneau sent to Roberge early in September
1958, to accompany the 'Notes on Government Legislation,' which he
recommended should be completed and 'digested somewhat' before
being passed on to the minister. At the same time, it appeared 'certain
that this whole matter' of the development of a Canadian feature film
industry 'will be brought to the Minister's attention in the near future.'[86]

For Juneau, there were three points to be considered in relation to the
Canadian situation. First, many of the legislative means detailed in the
'Notes' to help the development of a national film industry 'might be
considered, in Canada, to come under the jurisdiction of provincial governments,' if the federal government was to remain uninvolved. If, however, 'by any chance the Government wanted to consider this matter,'
which of the systems used in other countries could be adapted to the
Canadian situation? Juneau suggested the model of a film development
bank like those developed by the British National Film Finance Corpo-

ration, the German provincial government of Bavaria, and the Crédit National in France that could lend respectively 25 per cent, 42.5 per cent, or up to 65 per cent of a film's budget. He thought that perhaps the Industrial Development Bank 'would be of interest' as a model for film financing, noting that in 1957 the IDB had loaned $35 million to Canadian industries and returned a profit. Such loans, which averaged $60,000, would represent approximately 25 per cent of a film budget of $250,000, which, as Juneau pointed out, 'is more than has ever been spent on a Canadian feature film in Canada.'

But before presenting any information to the minister, Juneau recommended that 'we wait,' as there was not 'a complete picture of all the factors involved.' These factors were predominantly internal to the federal state bureaucracy and included the situation of the IDB, as well as plans within the Department of Trade and Commerce for a new section that would study means of helping small industries. External factors remained the problematic economy of the Canadian feature and the fact that 'the causes of [the] failures of Canadian feature films' were not sufficiently clear. 'Where do we go from here?' Juneau asked.[87]

The Changing International Political Economy of Film Production

The 1958 'Notes on Government Legislation,' while not able to point to any dominant pattern, nonetheless reflected the transformations that were taking place in the middle of the decade in the international political economy of feature film production. A resurgence of European filmmaking indicated the onset of a period of rearrangement in the context of the post-war dominance that the American film industry had exercised over world markets. These transformations are shown in the increase of the number of co-productions[88] (particularly between France and Italy – in 1957 France produced 127 features; 38 were in co-productions and of these 30 were with Italy); in the recommendations of the Comité d'aide du film belge (made up of film industry, parliamentary, academic, and other representatives) for a screen quota for Belgian films and the state-supported establishment of a film production fund; in the formation in West Germany of the Export-union der Deutschen Filmwertschaft similar to France's film export organization, Unifrance Film, and Italy's Unitalia; and in the establishment in 1957 of the British Film Fund agency to administer a fund to subsidize the production of British films with monies raised from a box-office levy. To understand the transformations in film production practices taking place through-

out the decade, it is important to bear in mind that European protection-
ist measures had taken their toll on the export-dependent American film
industry, which had entered a period of instability and declining profits.
Domestically, the 1948 anti-trust decrees had led it to divestment and
corporate reorganization, while the introduction of television had
sharply reduced attendance at theatres and forced a reappraisal of production strategies. The studio system of production had begun to break
down, and many theatres were closing, often for good.

By the end of the 1950s the major production interests in Hollywood
had learned to use their facilities to make television products. For the
cinema, production strategies were reoriented to emphasize the release
of fewer, bigger pictures that utilized innovations in colour and cinematography to attract audiences back to the theatre. The decline of the studio system of production, the experience of joint productions in Europe
making use of blocked earnings and local subsidies, and the risk-
aversive strategies of the distribution companies, all reinforced the
trend towards more decentralized production structures. By 1960 production in the United States hovered around two hundred films a year,
nearly half the number in the immediate post-war period. That same
year, production in each of France, Italy, and Great Britain reached
levels slightly over one-half of the U.S. total. American distributors
remained firmly in control of the world-wide film trade but they were
no longer marketing an exclusively American product.[89]

In Canada, by the spring of 1961, a front-page headline in *Canadian
Film Weekly* could report that 'USA Films' represented 'Only 43% of
Ont[ario] Total.' In the previous year there had been 'a striking increase'
on Ontario theatre screens of British, West German, Greek, and Japanese
feature films.[90] All things being equal, the decline of the American
empire was still a relative one, though perhaps worrisome enough for
Motion Picture Export Association chief Eric Johnston that he came to
Toronto to remind an industry audience that '75 per cent of Canada's
screen time goes to American films.'[91]

In an attempt to circumscribe the multinationalization of the political
economy of late 1950s feature production, Université Laval film professor François Baby termed it the emergence of a 'post-industrial cinema.'[92] For Baby, four principal strategies marked the post-industrial
cinema that had emerged as part of the continuing crisis of declining
theatrical attendance throughout the 1950s. First, the reduction of production costs shown, for example, in the reduction in the size of crews
from one hundred persons to the five to ten that characterized the

French New Wave, and in the compression of budgets from the $200,000 range in France, for instance, to the $65,000 of Chabrol's *Le Beau Serge* (1958). Second, the rise of multinational co-production as the principal means of capitalizing production. Thus France by 1966 produced twice as many features through co-production as it did strictly 'national' films. Third, related to the increase in co-production, the increased role of the national state in establishing film financing mechanisms. Fourth, the rise of super-productions that were particularly characteristic of the early 1960s U.S. cinema, for instance Zanuck's *The Longest Day* (1962).

From the perspective of changing practices, the point to be retained about the multinationalization of production financing mechanisms is that it provided the competitive international environment that made possible the extension of state policies within the domestic economy.

Conclusion

In this chapter, four sites of changing practices have been discussed against the background of the Foucauldian analysis of governmentality: an emerging cultural policy that attempted to reproduce in the cultural sphere the overall national economy; the changing nature of filmmaking practices occasioned by the introduction of television; the rise of statistical representations of the abstract growth of an emergent private production sector; and transformations in the international political economy. As a result, practices were significantly modified. On the basis of these transformations, discourses now rapidly began to assume delimitations, particularly in their interaction with state policies. It is to a detailed examination of these in the Canadian context that the discussion proceeds.

4

Reconfiguring the Public Sphere

As was suggested at the end of Chapter 1, what was fundamentally at issue in Canada throughout the 1950s was a protracted struggle, first, over positions, and then, on the basis of these positions, over words on the limits, responsibilities, and divisions of state power. As Foucault has pointed out, governmentalization can be viewed as the limitless extension of governmental rationality throughout a multiplicity of social practices. Although governmental rationality does encounter limitations to itself, such as laws, Foucault's analysis is particularly concerned with the limitations on governmentality as they developed within governmental practices, notably in the form of critiques of governmental reason that were posed by liberalism. In this perspective, the liberal critique of governmentality is thus more than a questioning of the best or least expensive means by which governmentality can achieve its effects; rather, it asks why government is necessary and does it from the perspective of the problematic of 'civil society,' in whose name liberalism seeks both the justification of government and the ends it should pursue with regard to the development of that portion of society. But rather than making the state-civil society distinction itself another universal, Foucault proposed instead to view this distinction as an *internal* limitation within the practices of governmental reason. The limitative process is therefore never definitive but instead represents, within governmental practices, a protracted, mobile negotiation between the limits of agenda and non-agenda.[1]

In a slightly different language, the emergence of a private sector discourse within the Canadian film 'industry' not only represented the beginnings of a renegotiation of the relationships between, and boundaries of, the public sector and the private sector of the economy, but it also confronted the capitalist state with the problem of the emergence of a new Canadian 'capitalist' industry. In other words, as Robert Fortner has observed, 'a new universe of discourse' had taken form in Canadian cinema and broadcasting policy of the 1950s.[2] This chapter traces the emergence of a private sector discourse within the Canadian film 'industry' so as to understand better how, and on what terms, it was initially able to mobilize the Canadian state in establishing the framework within which subsequent discussion of the Canadian feature was conducted.

The Discourse of the Private Producers

The AMPPLC Brief, October 1958–October 1959

The response to Pierre Juneau's question of where do we go from here came from the Industry Development Committee (IDC) of the Association of Motion Picture Producers and Laboratories of Canada, which tabled a draft of a brief to the Canadian government on 31 October 1958, in time for the association's executive meeting in Montreal in November. The meeting was held at a downtown hotel, although Commissioner Guy Roberge of the NFB had offered its headquarters as the venue for the meeting. As an NFB memorandum predicted, the producers' association was about 'to take a shot at the Film Board and is ashamed to do so on our premises.'[3]

The sixteen-page draft of the brief, entitled 'A Report and Recommendations Concerning the Development of the Film Industry in Canada,' urgently requested the formation of a special 'Government and Industry' committee to study the future possibilities of the film industry in Canada. It described Canadians as 'a people bent on nationhood,' but whose dreams were 'obscured by the overwhelming domination of their theatres and television screens by U.S. films and the flooding of their newsstands with U.S. publications.' It quoted the observation in the *Massey Report* that Hollywood cinema was 'the most alien of influences shaping our Canadian life.' In such a context, the draft argued that 'a stronger commercial film industry has a useful contribution to make to our national struggle' and it served notice that 'it is now an objective of our Association to increase our participation in this work' hitherto carried out exclusively by the CBC and the NFB.[4]

The draft brief – and the revisions brought to it in the year that followed before its presentation to key federal ministers in October 1959[5] – demanded the development of a policy by the state to ensure the continued growth of the private production industry. In the view of the draft brief, a policy needed to be elaborated in the following five areas: first, for the establishment of a special government and industry committee 'to study the future possibilities' of the film industry in Canada; second, by the identification of lack of investment capital as a major difficulty facing producers and the suggestion that the committee 'could discuss means of creating a production finance pool from which a producer could draw on the presentation of signed contracts guaranteeing Canadian, U.S. and British distribution'; third, by the recognition of the need for a policy at the CBC 'towards making more time available for Canadian-produced films' and, related to this, the regulation of the number of U.S.-produced commercials airing on CBC TV (the draft noted that 'in 1957, more than 25 per cent of all Canadian commercials were produced in the U.S.'); fourth, by the identification of the NFB as the major obstacle 'in the road to success on which commercial filmmakers have finally placed their feet' and, in connection with this, the clarification of future government policy vis-à-vis both CBC and NFB from the perspective of 'the film production business ... now fac[ing] the frustrating experience of being forced to compete with a body which is subsidized by our own tax dollars'; and fifth, by the development of 'the most dramatic aspect of film production anywhere in the world ... the making of theatrical entertainment features.' In regards to the last item, the drafters of the brief noted that if 'a reason' for 'our lack of success' in the making of theatrical entertainment features in the English-language field 'could be that American interests control a considerable proportion of our theatre chains,' then it seemed a more significant factor that 'apart from Canada, every country of any size has some sort of feature industry of its own'; these feature industries 'in every case,' except the American, 'have only existed with Government encouragement and statutory support.' Finally, in their demand for a government policy the drafters of the brief claimed to be consistent with 'the history of Canada' as 'a continuous march' towards nation-building, particularly as the continuum from 'the great engineering achievements ... of [the] transcontinental railways to the cultural enterprises exemplified by the Canadian Broadcasting Corp. and the National Film Board.' AMPPLC members shared 'these national ambitions and look to a future in which they shall contribute ... to the [nation-] building process.'[6]

How committed AMPPLC members actually were to the discursive content of the brief is a more debatable matter. The November 1958 meeting of the executive 'approved' the proposal for a government and industry committee, 'possibly to include' the study of the establishment of 'a production finance pool for TV series.'[7] The draft brief was returned to the IDC for revision, a process that necessitated another twelve months' work. This included engaging the research efforts of Queen's University economist David Slater and of Toronto public-relations consultant Tom Wheeler,[8] although these additions did not contribute significantly to the tenor of the brief beyond the addition of statistical appendices and the log of a sample week of CBC television programming in French. The final version of the brief was presented on 14 October 1959 to some members of the Diefenbaker Cabinet, to Dr Andrew Stewart, head of the newly created Board of Broadcast Governors (BBG), and in early November to the CBC. However, a contemporary CBC document notes that the 'AMPPLC subsequently decided to abandon its Brief and expressed a desire to "turn the page" on what had occurred before,' largely as a result of a statement by the CBC on 1 February 1961 on 'Film Production Policy' which recognized the 'importance of a vigorous film production industry in this country' and made much of the Corporation's 'consistent policy of contracting the majority of its film production to outside organizations.'[9] In this sense, the AMPPLC brief was a *strategic* document, advancing negotiating positions that could be withdrawn subsequently if, in the interim, the outcome of negotiations proved satisfactory, as they did with CBC. With the NFB, matters would be more complex.

Commenting on the draft, Don Mulholland, the NFB's director of planning and operations, observed to AMPPLC secretary-treasurer Frank Young:

> I notice that nowhere does the Brief state clearly and consistently what you want done. It protests, it complains, it calls attention to this or that situation which you feel is undesirable, but nowhere does it say, 'We therefore recommend that the following actions be taken.' If I were writing this brief, I should put in a summary page listing the actions I felt should be taken as a result of the arguments presented.[10]

Mulholland's advice was followed – the revised, twenty-five-page brief in October 1959 contained a two-page précis and a concluding chapter of recommendations. But both the draft and the brief remained ambiguous precisely in what they were trying to articulate, namely the *further* extension of governmental rationality, no longer through the agency of the NFB or, to a lesser extent, the CBC, but as the developmental framework of a budding private filmmaking sector to ensure its further growth. As the brief recognized, 'Canada gives less protection to its film industry than it does for many other industries.'[11] The difficulty in developing arguments for protectionism was that the very status of the film 'industry' itself, qua industry, was not clear. To the extent, however, that these arguments have recurred so consistently in the economy of talk surrounding the Canadian feature, four levels of the argument warrant further analysis.

1: Arguments Based on Economism

In the previous half-decade (1952–7), a change had occurred 'mainly due to the development of television.' A production 'industry' of more than fifty private companies, 'some large, some very small,' had emerged to claim a place in the sun and to search for opportunities for further growth. The future of this new 'industry' appeared promising: 'Canada now has a unique opportunity to develop a first-class film industry. It can be an industry to make a fine contribution to Canadian culture, to open new fields to Canadian artists and skilled technicians and to establish an even greater Canadian "mark" throughout the world ... The time has come for Canada to develop a robust private industry. Television and Canada's economic growth provide the circumstances which never before existed.' Furthermore, '[p]rivate industry can capture a large part of the Canadian market in competition with foreign firms *if it is given reasonable protection.*'[12] Moreover, development of a *competitive* industry was in the national interest given 'Canada's general interest in a private enterprise system.'[13]

This general interest implied that for Canada 'to have a first-class industry, there must exist a vigorous *private* film industry.' The logic of the argument quickly slipped from nationalism to economism, not only 'because private arrangements provide a climate favourable to the economical production of films,' but also because the notion of competition with foreign firms gives way to a justification for private arrangements that particularly serve 'as a competitive test, as yardstick, by which may be measured the performance of government film agencies.'[14] The argument in favour of the future development of the private film industry thus derived from its claim as economically efficient compared to the more established public-sector film agencies, especially the National Film Board: 'The private industry in 1957 employed more than 1200 [people], paid salaries and wages of about $2.7 millions, produced $8 millions of film products and services and used about $8 millions of capital equipment and facilities,' whereas 'the National Film Board employed more than 600 people, provided more than $3.5 millions of film products and used capital equipment and facilities worth about $10 millions' and furthermore paid no corporate income tax or local taxes. Particularly in light of the putative efficiency of the private sector, there was nothing inherent in filmmaking for the industry to continue to be 'a natural monopoly' or 'to such a large degree ... a state enterprise ... There is no rare commodity like [spectrum] space or radio wave channels to be conserved.'[15]

2: The Bigness-Smallness Dilemma

The difficulty with justifications derived from nationalist economism was that they tend to become unrealistically inflated. The 'reality' presented itself quite differently if read as uncertainty as to whether the emergent private industry was actually large or small and, if the latter, deserving of protection precisely because of its smallness. Visions of potential greatness aside, the problem was that '[t]he whole industry ... has been a small one.' Furthermore, the small Canadian film industry as a whole was internally divided between, on the one hand, the government or publicly owned NFB, CBC, and several provincial film production units, and, on the other hand, private industry. Despite the recent 'impressive growth' of both sectors, the private industry was increasingly 'disturbed by a number of changes which make future growth uncertain.' In a context where 'the Canadian market for films is small,' but where, in addition, TV programming had shifted from documentary shorts to dramatic filmed programs and teleseries – the latter 'almost entirely from foreign sources' – that shift meant many of the new Canadian companies that had emerged to produce commercials and documentaries for the television industry now faced competition from all sides.[16] This multifaceted competitive environment comprised: (1) U.S. and British mass-produced film dramas readily available to Canadian broadcasters as the cheapest possible program sources; (2) the 'small fraction' of dramatic products produced in Canada, of which 'less than half have been the products of the private Canadian film industry'; (3) the in-house film units that the CBC had developed for itself ('CBC appears to be getting more and more into the internal production of films for televsion, even to the point of encroaching into the field of TV commercials productions by making the majority of the "promotional clips" with their own film and animation units across the country'); and

(4) the 'major block' that was represented by the NFB which 'now contracts much less of its own and government-sponsored work to the private film industry than it has in the past' ('the National Film Board has a large annual government appropriation and capital equipment for which it does not have to pay in order to produce ... It has a large program of film-making ... The Board also acts as the agent and generally the producer of films for Federal Government Departments').[17]

3: Arguments Proposing Solutions

Beyond limiting further growth of the NFB and the CBC, the way out of these competitive dilemmas (the need for increased investment capital and for a regulatory 'system in which all Canadian television stations, public and private, would undertake to carry a certain proportion of Canadian [privately produced] filmed or videotaped material, including commercials') was to gain access to 'a market ... much larger than Canada itself.'[18] Britain in particular[19] was seen to represent such a market, given that its 14.5 per cent quota on imported TV programming did not apply to programming produced in the Commonwealth. Not only could the British 'quota system ... help enormously in providing markets for Canadian-produced films and videotapes,' but (and here the draft version was more explicit than the final brief), based on the 'beneficial' Television Programs of America experience with series production in Canada, it noted that 'We would like to see more U.S. companies working here' to take advantage of Canada's quota privileges on British television by financing the production of series in Canada which could also be marketed in the United States. Once again, the draft version is more explicit as regards the implications of such a development strategy:

Canadian made films qualify as British quota so, presumably, in any quota system introduced here, we would offer the same privilege to British films. This would imply that restrictions will aim directly at U.S. product. To offset this discrimination, there would be the extra inducement to U.S. producers to make films in Canada to qualify for both British and Canadian quotas.[20]

The revised brief acknowledged that film production in Canada by U.S. interests 'has been of value to us. It has encouraged the building of new studios and has provided employment for local producers and technicians.' The brief considered, however, that 'Canadian production by U.S. companies [wa]s only a partial answer.'[21]

The other field of development for the private Canadian industry was the feature film. While remarking that the feature business was 'endlessly complicated,' the brief noted that the existence of feature industries were above all a direct function of government encouragement and that this was the case in 'every case except the U.S. ... and now even the mighty Hollywood producers are asking government help.' The brief cursorily (and at times erroneously) surveyed government feature film policy in eight European countries as well as in Argentina, Brazil, and Japan, but it could only note that 'the Canadian Government has never taken action regarding the lack of feature production here.' Listing the imports of foreign theatrical features to Canada in 1957–8, the brief noted that 'Canada's own record of its native production' – no features in 1957, one in 1958 – was 'surely of no great pride to the Canadian film maker.'[22]

4: Arguments from History

Several sections of both the draft and the revised brief invoked historical arguments which unintentionally cast an ironic light on the claim that the Canadian film industry consisted of two principal (and presumably equal) segments, one public and the other private. In the view of the revised brief, the history of the private Canadian industry divided into two periods, *before television* and *since television*. Before television, theatrical features had constituted the principal form of film production throughout the world. Canada could not compete in this field 'because of the enormous costs and risks in small-scale production, the difficulties in obtaining distribution facilities, and the disadvantages of Canada's climate.' If a few silent films were at one time made in Canada, mainly by itinerant U.S. producers, the making of feature films stopped almost entirely after the invention of sound-recording techniques had 'raised production costs and introduced complications into outdoor location shooting.' Before the Second World War 'a state of near-paralysis' had characterized industry development.

The creation of the NFB in 1939 'lifted us from ... stagnation,' not only because of the war but because 'the Board ... contracted out work to private producers.' Although the high quality of the NFB's production would set standards in Canada and throughout the world, 'the short film did not provide the basis for a mature industry,' and the bulk of Canadian consumption of entertainment films continued to consist of imported products.

The current phase of the history of the industry had begun in 1952 with the development of television production that was largely synonymous with CBC, 'the single largest purchaser of filmed materials in the country.' Nonetheless, the brief went on to object that the 'CBC uses relatively little Canadian film and of this only a small fraction is produced by Canadian private industry.'[23]

Finally, two further historical references were invoked by both the draft and the revised brief. First, the draft in particular noted that the Canadian film industry had increasingly become 'quota conscious' and in this respect recommended support for a 'law fixing a minimum number of Canadian films to be shown on our screens [that would] force local production.' It argued furthermore that Section 61 of the Ontario Theatres Act provided a precedent 'for restricting portions of films to be of British manufacture and origin and fixing such proportions on a monthly or yearly basis.'[24] As was seen above, however, such a quota would not apply to U.S. production in Canada. Furthermore, both the draft and the final brief expressed considerable concern that a Canadian quota should contain safeguards 'to prevent ... exhibitors from being forced to show third-rate films,' a concern stemming from a reading of the historical experience of 'the first quota law in Britain [in 1927] and the infamous "Quota Quickies" which nearly wiped out Britain's chances of building a film industry.'[25] While superficially this was a plausible reading of the British experience, it is important to stress the extent to which in Canada the response since the 1920s was more one of circumventing the British quota through the encouragement of production in Canada within that quota by U.S. branch plants, whether in film or later in television production. In other words, the revised brief's reading of the impact of the quota was a strategic historical *misreading*, as a result of which a quota system would never be (and indeed never became) a credible strategy for film industry development in Canada.

Second, in discussing the Canadian government's historical inaction with respect to Canadian feature film production – despite which, as the draft boasted, 'the handful of producers has grown steadily and investment in film production facilities here reaches millions of dollars'[26] – the draft brief noted something of a precedent for Canadian government support. '[T]en years ago [the government] did consider the problem of the sums of money flowing from Canadian exhibitors to U.S. production companies'; and the result 'was the Canadian Co-Operation Project, an activity of the Motion Picture Association of America, Inc. There were hints that the Project would stimulate Canadian production, but, in its final form, it was designed to help conservation of dollar exchange in Canada and achieved a number of references to Canada on U.S. screens.'[27] The significance of this reference will be addressed below.

For all its contradictions and lacunae – or rather precisely because of them – the revised brief's definition of an emergent discourse on the Canadian feature was decisive. Not only did that definition, as will be also seen below, contribute to redefining the policy of Canadian cinema, but it established the argumentative fields in which subsequent discussion of the Canadian feature would take place. These arguments comprised four sets of dualisms within which they ranged themselves: nationalism vs. economism, bigness vs. smallness, quotas vs. external markets, and 'History' vs. history. These four argumentative fields were fundamentally ambiguous, but as such permitted the crucial elisions that made possible pseudo-economic arguments deriving from nationalism: such as the claim to be able to (re)capture the Canadian domestic market and, given the economic difficulty of such a strategy, its subsequent deflection outwards to a discourse of the strategy of entry into foreign markets as compensation for the smallness of the Canadian domestic market; and pseudo-historical arguments based on a limited and highly selective reading of the film history of other countries as well as that of Canada. In the latter case, the operative dimension of the word 'historical' became the future or past passive conditional; for instance, *if* the government would do this or that; *had* the government done this or that. The most important point, however, is that within the discursive space established by such arguments, the 'Canadian film industry'[28] thereby gained a *pseudo-reality* that existed particularly in the realm of the discursive fiction of the presupposition that such an industry actually existed. As a result of the brief, and thus its importance, the fiction of the Canadian film industry was 'transubstantiated' into a new economic entity that was within and emerging simultaneously from the space and pseudo-historical time of the economy of talk about the Canadian feature film. As N.A. Taylor predicted in his regular column in *Canadian Film Weekly* just after copies of the brief were presented to members of the Conservative government, 'Only one spark is necessary to set ablaze a whole new industry: Government subsidy.'[29] However, before proceeding to the NFB's reaction to the brief and the resulting shift in government film policy, some further discussion of the brief's reading of 'History' is necessary.

The Canadian Quota Debate in Television and Film

The enactment in the fall of 1958 of the Broadcasting Act, which created the Board of Broadcast Governors to regulate both the CBC and private broadcasters as equals, consecrated a dramatic shift 'toward the private sector, and to commercial interests.'[30] Legislatively considered complementary to the CBC from 1936 to 1958, the private broadcasting sector after 1958 became its equal. The new legislation, as federal Liberal leader Lester Pearson stated during second reading of the bill, was a move towards 'two systems, one public and [one] private, becoming more and more independent of each other.'[31] 'Between 1958 and 1963,' writes Marc Raboy, 'the system was reshaped in the image of the private sector, maximizing the potential for economic profit.'[32] Fortner has suggested, from the evidence of the increasingly aggressive discursive posture of Canadian private broadcasters in the post–*Massey Report* era, that not only was the balance between private and public sectors tilting towards the private sector as the broadcasting system was reshaped in its image, but more importantly that 'A new universe of discourse was established, one grounded in misconstruction of facts, subtle turns of phrase and redefinitions of key terms. The result was a rewriting of history, a rewriting which would justify new departures from the status quo.'[33] For Fortner, such a shift in discourse contained significant lessons for understanding the development of public policy in the Canadian context:

What happened in the case of broadcasting happens as well in all other arenas of public policy making. The interpretation of history, and the definitions of key terms, are important relevances which circumscribe the truth. Their significance increases as first-hand knowledge wanes with the passage of time and the turnover among participants in debate. The stakes get higher. These terms, relevances and interpretations of history determine what is possible and what is unthinkable. To the extent ... that history can be altered and definitions changed, new possibilities and impossibilities can be created. In the end the division between the ... possible and ... impossible are, at best, muddled, and at worst, reversed or made irrelevant.[34]

Because of the smallness of the Canadian program production industry, what was happening in broadcasting was also happening in film. Not only was the universe of discourse being rewritten, but the licensing of second stations in eight major urban centres by the BBG as of the summer of 1960 and the call for applications for a private second TV network sparked renewed activity in planning for both feature film and television production, as well as increasing corporate interlocks between the motion picture industry and private television licensees. At the centre of many of these activities was Toronto independent film producer, exhibitor, and distributor N.A. Taylor.

To illustrate the increasingly diversified nature of his operation – eight companies under Taylor Associates – Taylor in the fall of 1959 unveiled his new corporate banner in a twelve-page gold-covered booklet distributed at the 20th Century Theatres annual convention in Toronto. With about sixty theatres, 20th Century was the leading independent Canadian exhibitor circuit, and it was owned and operated by Taylor's Twinex Century Theatres. Taylor dubbed his approach a 'global concept' based 'on the inter-relationship of entertainment media today and the broader concept required of those in the motion picture industry.'[35] A Taylor company, Beaver Film Productions, had recently made commitments for 'many foreign feature motion pictures to be made in New York, London, Paris and Rome.' On closer inspection, these commitments seem to have in fact only consisted of buying Canadian and other foreign distribution rights to an upcoming Italian spectacular, *David and Goliath*. This 'coup,' which followed closely the apparently profitable release of a recent Italian spectacular, *Hercules* (1957), by another Taylor company, International Film Distributors, had placed 'Canada on the international entertainment map for the first time in its motion picture history.' Beaver Film Productions, Taylor stated, 'was drawing profits to Canada from many parts of the world and developing global business associations that can provide outlets for the films it and others plan to make in this country for theatrical distribution.' He told his audience that because 'production is coming to Canada in a big way ... we think we ought to get in on the ground floor.' Production plans included doubling (from two to four) the number of sound stages at the Taylor-owned Toronto International Film Studios, which was likely to get increased use soon: film rights to two recent Canadian novels were being negotiated by Meridian Films (co-producers of *The Bloody Brood* (1959) with Canadian distribution by Taylor Associates company, Allied Artists of Canada. (Meridian was headed by Ralph Foster, chair of the AMPPLC's Industrial Development Committee.) 'We will enter any segment of mass entertainment that is potentially profitable,' Taylor told convention delegates.[36]

In less than nine months, with the BBG decisions on second stations imminent and with talk of a private network taking on more concrete form, additional Taylor companies emerged. In the summer of 1960 Taylor-Roffman Productions Ltd was formed in Toronto along with other new firms, indicating 'a renewal of activity in the field of TV production.'[37] The new companies, located at Canadian Film Industries, a rival studio, included Caravan Television Productions Ltd, managed by radio personality Rick Campbell; Affiliated Television Productions, headed by George Richfield of New York; Dominion Motion Pictures Ltd, which had made features in the 1930s under Arthur Gottlieb who had established Canadian Film Industries in 1958, and which was now exploring series production if talks with U.S. principals proved successful (Gottlieb himself was planning three series). As well, Taylor's Toronto International Studios and Meridian Productions, 'two of Canada's top production houses,' announced plans for a $2 million videotape centre for television shows and commercials 'to stem the flow of Canadian business to USA centres and to attract USA and other producers to Canada.'[38] Taylor announced an intensive campaign to promote Canada in the United States and in Great Britain as an ideal centre for film and television production because of Commonwealth quota advantages: 'We have a selling job to do, but we have something to sell now – talent, facilities, on-location scenery, the extra markets available through the Commonwealth quota system, lower production costs – all in one spot.' With all this and with 'the big demand for entertainment and commercial material from the new Canadian television stations, Toronto must inevitably become one of the busiest production centres in the world.'[39]

The award by the BBG of the licence for Ottawa's second station to the E.L. Bushnell Television Co. brought in programs supplied by a new Taylor Associates company, NTA Telefilm (Canada) Ltd which distributed television programming, and also Britain's Granada TV. This and earlier BBG decisions on second stations had, in the view of the *Canadian Film Weekly*, 'favoured' motion picture industry people: Montreal feature film producer Paul l'Anglais and film distributor J.A. DeSève were awarded the licence for the second French-language station CFTM, or Télémétropole; Toronto film distributor Paul Nathanson was a shareholder in the Toronto licence; and Vancouver film producer Arthur Jones of Artray Film Productions (also on the AMPPLC's IDC) was awarded the Vancouver licence. As well, the television interests, CKCO-TV in Kitchener, of Famous Players, a Paramount-owned exhibition chain, had recently been allowed a power boost by the BBG.[40]

The increasing interlocking between television and film and with it the increasing presence of non-Canadian interests (such as Granada from Great Britain in Bushnell, and Associated Television, also from Britain, in CJCH-TV in Halifax) came to a head in 1961 over the proposed buy-in by ABC-Paramount of CFTO-TV, Toronto,[41] and sparked a renewed discussion of quotas but also further contributed to muddying the discussion.

In the fall of 1959 the BBG had proposed that 55 per cent 'Canadian-content' levels be phased in over a number of years, in other words a quota: not on the importation or screening of non-Canadian programming but, in a curious reversal of worldwide practice, on Canadian-made content. It was nevertheless a television screen quota, although it does not appear to have been acknowledged as such.[42] The *Canadian Film Weekly*, for instance, quoted the observation in a London *Times* article that this was 'the first time that Canada has imposed quotas in the visual field'[43] to draw attention to that fact. The *Times* article went on to underline the implications of this precedent: 'Having decided to try quotas for television in order to prevent being overwhelmed with material from the United States, the Government may listen to the producers [sic] pleas to establish quotas for feature films.'[44]

However, the reaction of the film producers to the television quota was contradictory. On the one hand, the proposal was welcomed to the degree that it would 'stimulate motion picture production in this country.' As the *Canadian Film Weekly* reported, 'Even the CBC will be affected for the $42,491,864 it spent on programs in 1958–9 produced only 51 percent Canadian content and the additional four percent will require additional expenditure.'[45] For Canadian sales managers of U.S. companies of television products, the quota meant emphasizing 'that their USA principals give consideration to the production of at least one series in Canada ... "It isn't as bad as it seems," said one [sales manager].'[46]

Objection to the TV quota came from Canadian 'independent' producers with an eye on entering television. As reported in the *Canadian Film Weekly*, Spencer Caldwell summed up the contradiction:

'As president of the Association of Motion Picture Producers and Laboratories of Canada, I'm delighted.' But as a prospective TV station operator ... Caldwell thought that the quality of programming would suffer if the 55 percent regulation becomes law. The result might be to drive viewers to USA channels.[47]

N.A. Taylor's position was spelled out in a series of columns in *Canadian Film Weekly* in the spring of 1961. As the anticipated television bonanzas of runaway U.S. production and then of new private Canadian stations and a new network failed to materialize (CTV's eight affiliates were reporting losses of over $5 million in 1961),[48] more radical proposals began circulating among the technicians, actors, and cinematographers of the production industry in Toronto. When the International Alliance of Theatrical and Stage Employees (IATSE) Local 873, Motion Picture Studio Production Technicians, under the signature of business agent William F. White, submitted a one-page letter to federal members of Parliament asking for their collaboration and action in implementing a quota system on foreign films, representatives of 'production, talent and the cinematographers' also began to gather to organize a general committee and to discuss plans.[49]

The letter of the IATSE local remarked that 'For the past two years film production in Canada has been almost nil and up to this time the small amount involved makes Canada's effort look rather insignificant. Canada is a rapidly growing country but as far as the film industry is concerned, we are being left behind.' It went on to argue that a correlation exists between high levels of film production and 'a quota system whereby a percentage of the gross box office receipts must be ploughed back to film production while others [screen quotas] stipulate that for a certain number of foreign films shown in theatres and on TV networks, a percentage must be home-produced.' The letter offered a number of countries as examples, noting, for instance, that Finland, with a population of only four million, had produced twelve features in 1960. '[W]ith every facility available for the manufacture of motion pictures,' the government of Canada was doing nothing to help production; meanwhile 'over $100,000,000 from film rentals' were leaving the country.[50]

Over four weeks beginning on 26 April, Taylor discussed the IATSE local's proposal in his 'Our Business' column in the *Canadian Film Weekly*. He polarized the issue by arguing that it involved a choice between quotas and subsidy. Acknowledging that the technicians, like the producers, were 'anxious' to see film production flourish in Canada and 'such an industry fully activated,' he noted that the concern was not shared by the government. It was 'blissfully unaware' that film was one of the principal tools in the promotion of international trade, that film represented 'a new industry which can quickly grow to employ thousands in various crafts and skills as well as earning millions in foreign currency,' and that it was an industry whose growth should be encouraged and helped in every way.

But a quota was not 'the tool' to bring this about. While some countries did have quotas to foster local production and restrictions on the importation of foreign films to save foreign currency, to encourage films produced in the native language, or to satisfy 'nationalistic sentiments [that] are so high that film production must be encouraged at any cost,' he did not consider any of these conditions applied to Canada.

For Taylor, what characterized the Canadian market for film was the smallness of its numerical returns both in dollars and in audiences: in the first place, 'potential grosses on an average film represent only about three percent of world total,' and in the second, 'our people have shown that they would shy away from – rather than flock to – Canadian produced films.' In this light, 'the cure' lay in subsidy, not quota, and through subsidy 'not only technicians but producers and the country at large can gain.'[51]

Taylor hammered away at this theme for the next several weeks, concluding the series with a vision of the benefits to be derived from the subsidized export of the fruits of Canadian talents: 'Imagine a production industry triggered by ... subsidy! It would rapidly employ thousands of many crafts and skills and quickly become of multi-million dollar magnitude.'[52]

The IATSE letter was forwarded to the office of Prime Minister Diefenbaker. He reportedly promised the 'fullest discussion of the matter' after he had gathered further information. There was no follow-up; the general committee of industry workers did not meet again. Nor, most importantly, would there be any further talk of quotas in the Canadian film industry for several years. The matter was simply absorbed within the workings of the state, to which we now return.

The NFB and Government Film Policy: Response to the Brief, 1959–61

The NFB's response to the AMPPLC brief was one of panic. A network of Canadian diplomatic missions and the NFB's own overseas offices were mobilized to gather information on production conditions in a number of countries. The information thus gathered became the basis for an almost line-by-line refutation of the brief, filling two black briefing books that were forwarded to the minister in early 1960.[53]

While we need not be extensively concerned with the minutiae of the NFB's rebuttal of the brief – its general tenor will be discussed later, two points in particular merit discussion, the one quantitative, the other 'historical.' First, the exercise pushed the NFB further along the path of statisticalization of its activities, only to come to the problematic conclusion that its own policies could not be justified 'wholly' on the grounds of economy. For instance, in attempting to calculate the expenditures it had incurred in producing TV series for the CBC between 1953 and 1959, it concluded that it had spent $1.52 million and earned $599,000, the amount paid by the CBC,[54] although upgraded rental rates per show since 1957–8 meant that it was now earning back about half its production costs. As the refutation commentary puts it,

The Board can justify sale of its television films to CBC at less than production cost because the Board's purpose is not to make films at a profit ... or even just to make films; its purpose is to reflect the life of Canada today and to provide useful information to Canadians. The showing of the Board's films on television, which reaches more Canadians than any other single medium is, in itself, important in accomplishing the Board's objectives.[55]

Economy did enter into the equation in terms of the size of the NFB's parliamentary appropriation. But given its current size (in 1958–9 it was $4,258,918),[56] the NFB could not absorb the cost of any substantially increased production for television above the current twenty documentary hours per year in a CBC schedule telecasting of about forty-five hundred hours in each language. Thus, 'half price competition' from NFB series was hardly menacing to 'the best selling efforts of the private industry' either in the 650 hours per year in both languages still available in the Talks and Public Affairs category or in the larger CBC schedule. Through calculation – and sarcasm – the NFB refuted the brief's charges that it represented unfair competition and an extravagent outlay of public funds that could more efficiently be put to use by private industry:

If the Film Board's entire production expenditure for 1958–59 ($3,259,796 – we could scarcely contract out the hidden subsidy or half the cost of Administration) were distributed equally among the 53 producers listed by DBS, it would yield each of them orders totalling $61,500 – the price of 4 of the Board's half hour television films.

If the $1,106,178 received by the Film Board in 1958–59 for all production work for other government departments were similarly distributed, it would yield $20,800 to each producer.[57]

At times, however, the NFB's contempt for the private industry and its claims could no longer be contained by sarcasm. One such outburst is worth citing at length:

The blunt facts are that the Board's experience with private producers in the production of anything but the simplest original films has not been encouraging. There are a few reliable firms but in most cases, the Board has finally had to accept a creative and technical standard of production considerably below its own standard and even that has often been achieved only with an amount of detailed guidance and instruction by the Film Board producers which almost becomes production by the Film Board itself. There have been cases of confer- . ence after conference on a script until the Film Board, in desperation, assigned the script to one of its own writers. The Film Board's producer in charge of an assigned production almost invariably spends days showing the [private] producer's editors how to lay out a sound track and then supplying half the sound effects from the Film Board library. Final mix recordings may be done two and three times until finally the whole film is brought into the Film Board's own sound department for final mix. The commentary is often re-edited and re-written by the National Film Board. The opticals have to be made by the National Film Board. Indeed, almost always, the first request we get from the successful tenderer on a contract is for use of Film Board facilities; for our lab, frequently for our sound department, for our music and effects library, optical effects department and even editing personnel as well. In several cases we have had to accept the best that a private producer can provide, pay him off and then re-record or even re-edit the film ourselves. Satisfactory and even excellent films have been made by Canadian private producers, but they are rare.[58]

It was 'partly at least, because of the inability of private producers from 1939 until well after the end of the war, to provide the quantity and quality of films required for the government information program' that the NFB had developed its own economies of continuity and volume and the government had invested in its building and facilities, an investment from which the NFB extracted 'maximum capacity' through the production of a steady volume of films made to high professional standard and keyed to the wide variety of needs of 'the state-owned system, both in Canada and abroad.' Because it was part of the state apparatus, the NFB could offer services to government departments that could not be obtained by tendering films to individual sponsors. This was most obviously the case of technical and secret training films for the Department of National Defence but, beyond the national security aspects, NFB producers working on a continuing and exclusive basis with other government departments had over the years learned to meet the needs of departments and 'devis[ed] methods and approaches for resolving its particular training and communications problems by the use of film ... Such a service could obviously not be provided if the department had to start fresh with a new producer for every film.' Furthermore, 'It is evident that most departments share this view since few departments ask the Board to tender their films to commercial producers'; as well, it was 'interesting to note the number of departments which, having once had a film made by a private producer, prefer thereafter to have its films made by the Film Board.'[59]

As the NFB grappled with refuting the charges made against it in the brief, it was increasingly clear that it operated according to an order of rationality that was not, as it would put it, '"economy" in the narrow sense.' Rather, the NFB operated under the form of governmental rationality that we termed, following Foucault, governmentalization, an unquantifiable principle of self-extension. What justified the NFB *to itself* was that it personified this principle of comprehensiveness, a voluminousness, a totality: the NFB 'enjoys a volume and continuity of production which makes possible the employment of specialists, the development of improved techniques and the efficient use of facilities and man power.' 'The entire program of the National Film Board is correlated and interrelated in a variety of ways which are possible only in a comprehensive organization like the Film Board.' In such a perspective, 'it is impossible to prove conclusively whether the National Film Board is or is not an economical way for the government to obtain and distribute its films, or whether it is more or less economical than any or all private producers ... *It is therefore not wholly on the grounds of "economy" in the narrow sense, that the Board justifies its policy.*'[60]

However, in an increasingly quantified universe of discourse, the fact that the NFB could not wholly justify its operations in numerical terms (indeed, it admitted that it 'is certainly true that the government could purchase an equal number of films of equal length to the present production of the Film Board for a much less cost') became increasingly problematic as the Board found itself as a result excluded from the new statistical universe. For, within that universe, the NFB's own computations showed constant growth by the private industry and correlatively a diminution of its own share that only confirmed the private industry's claims for greater recognition. Thus, a chart entitled 'Comparison of Relative Growth in Activities of National Film Board and Private Film Producers: 1952–1961,' initially drawn up for the black books, largely confirms the private industry's two major claims with respect to its own statistical growth as a percentage of gross revenues and to the fact that the percentage of work contracted by NFB to private industry had declined.[62]

The NFB was thus caught in a bind between, on the one hand, its discourse and, on the other, its numbers or those of the Dominion Bureau of Statistics, as a result of which its interests and those of the private producers were increasingly divergent and in contradiction. It was a contradiction that the capitalist state, in having to decide between the two, would resolve in favour of the private sector. The irony here concerned the role played by the NFB in bringing about such a choice. One illustration of the increasingly evident divergence between the interests of producers in the private sector and those of the NFB is provided by the latter's response to the brief's 'historical' reference to the Canadian Cooperation Project.[63]

The Canadian Cooperation Project, 1948–58

The brief had noted that a precedent of sorts had been set in the late 1940s when the Canadian government had supposedly contemplated blocking, among other things, the outflow of theatrical box-office remittances payable to U.S. producers. As of 1948 this had resulted in the Canadian Cooperation Project, an activity of the Motion Picture Association of America, Inc. (MPAA).

According to historian J.L. Granatstein, Canada, as a result of its historical commitment to the maintenance of Anglo–Canadian trade, found itself just after the Second World War in a financial disaster in its trade relations with the United States – to the extent of envisaging a customs union with it in order to extricate itself. With its reserves of U.S. dollars having dwindled to under half a billion by October 1947, a Canadian delegation led by Deputy Minister of Finance Clifford Clark went to Washington to present two plans for consideration.

Plan A hinged around brutal import restrictions and the banning of virtually every identifiable consumer item imported from the United States; Plan B also involved quotas but foresaw Canadian participation in the Marshall Plan and the placing of some procurement for the European recovery program in Canada. The Americans, anxious to avoid the shattering effects ... certain to be produced by Plan A, promised ... flexibility ... As a result of this quasi-promise and of discussions that followed ... Finance Minister Douglas Abbott announced the more moderate restrictions of Plan B on 17 November [1947].[64]

Imported motion picture equipment such as projectors was among the goods affected by the Emergency Foreign Exchange Conservation Act (1947). Also in November, but after passage of the act, representatives of the thirty companies that were members of the Film Producers Association of Canada met with Abbott to ask for government assistance in strengthening the Canadian private film industry and to urge Canadian government pressure on Britain to reduce the 75 per cent *ad valorem* tax on motion picture earnings exports that had recently come into effect. The idea that Canada might, like Britain, impose such a surtax or block the outflow of motion picture remittances to the United States agitated not only Canadian private producers but also Canadian exhibitors, as well as Ross McLean, Grierson's successor as government film commissioner, and finally the Motion Picture Association of America in New York, and they all lobbied for different plans. These plans varied from encouraging more Hollywood shoots in Canada (suggested by Lawson, the Canadian head of the Odeon-Rank circuit), reinvestment of four to five million dollars from Canadian earnings and U.S. distribution of the forty to fifty shorts made by the Canadian private sector for the NFB (by Ross McLean), the voluntary (i.e., non-legislated) reinvestment of part of U.S. earnings in Canada (by the Canadian Motion Picture Distributors Association), and, as of January 1948, the Canadian Cooperation Project itself (by the MPAA).[65]

As Véronneau has remarked, the Canadian Cooperation Project 'remains one of the great mystifications of Canadian film history,' not only because of the public relations spin successfully given to it at the time, but particularly because of the mythological status it holds in nationalist film historiography. The NFB's backgrounder on the project, produced as part of the materials generated to refute the brief, is fascinating in several respects. The first is because of the continuing uncertainty it reflected over the extent of remittances taken out of Canada annually by American distributors, supposedly the issue at the heart of the Canadian Cooperation Project debate. The NFB's paper gave four estimates of what this amount *might* have been in the late 1940s: an estimate of $12 million by one of the representatives of the U.S. motion picture industry in Canada'; an estimate of $17 million by unidentified 'other sources'; an estimate by J.J. Fitzgibbons, president of the U.S.-owned exhibition chain Famous Players Canadian Corp. of 'about $12 million a year'; and a later calculation by unidentified 'government economists' of 'between $5 and $8 million.'[67] Whatever the amount, 'the Motion Picture Association of America was *extremely disturbed at the possibility* of government interference with *its* distribution in Canada.' Remarkably, the NFB paper states that: 'the logic of the [MPAA] move was quite clear. They decided that if they could help the government to get at least as much if not more dollars brought into the country, the Canadian government would not undertake any restrictions.'[68]

As outlined by Eric Johnston, MPAA president, the Canadian Cooperation Project proposed 'to help present Canada's current problems to the people of the United States and to speed up the flow of United States dollars to Canada' by: (1) production of a film on Canada's trade-dollar problems; (2) more complete newsreel coverage of Canada; (3) short films about Canada to be produced and distributed; (4) consideration of NFB releases for theatrical distribution in the United States; (5) use of Canadian sequences in features; (6) radio recordings presenting Canada's problems by Hollywood stars; and (7) more careful selection of films shown in Canada. The NFB paper notes the Canadian government accepted the MPAA offer, which included also appointing a Canadian to Hollywood to work with the major studios and hiring Maclaren Advertising, based in Toronto but with offices across Canada, to assist American producers and moreover 'offered considerable assistance through other government departments, such as the NFB, Travel Bureau, National Revenue (Customs), etc.' It noted as well that Johnston had pointed out in his original proposal that 'if the Canadian Cooperation Project could help Canada increase her tourist trade by as little as 5%, the increase in U.S. dollars from this source would more than offset what the American distributors were taking out of the country.'[69]

The NFB's satisfaction with the project, although never directly stated, stemmed especially from the role it afforded the Board in the extension of governmental rationality. To start, it was one of the Canadian government agencies cooperating with the MPAA on the project. For another thing, it was former NFB staff member Stuart Legg who produced for Paramount the first film, *Neighbour to the North*, on Canada's trade-dollar problem to be made under the aegis of the project. Thirdly, in the context of the project, 'Canadian government offices in the United States held frequent screenings of films produced under this Project and *also NFB films.'* Finally, as of 1949 administrative responsibility for the project was transferred to the NFB itself.[70]

As the NFB's paper on the Canadian Cooperation Project stated in its conclusion, attitudes towards its success or failure were a matter of

'points of view.' From the perspective of the MPAA, the Canadian state
and its agencies, such as the NFB, were implicated since the war in what
Peter Morris called *'the illusion'* of widespread distribution of NFB films
in U.S. theatres; the project allowed 'more information about Canada
[to] reach ... the screens of the United States and Canada's tourist trade
showed a substantial increase.'[71] On the other hand, if, as a number of
Canadian private film producers believed, the project 'was instituted
mainly to encourage film production in Canada by American producers
in cooperation with Canadian studios, labs and producers,' then it was
'a dismal failure.'[72]

A Shifting Policy Field, 1960–2

If the NFB, in its detailed, point-by-point response to the brief, was vigorous in its denials and protestations, its general response was, surprisingly, somewhat more sympathetic. By January 1960 it had boiled
down the brief into six propositions. These were: (1) that CBC tender
all major film productions to Canadian film companies – a proposition
rejected by CBC; (2) that NFB assign production of more government
sponsored films to Canadian film companies – the proposition was
rejected by NFB on the grounds that the private film industry, largely
a by-product of television, did not need its business (given the immi-
nence of new private television stations and Canadian-content requirements, private industry faced an expanding television market in
which the NFB was not a significant factor); (3) that the government
increase tariffs to encourage the production of Canadian commercials
in Canada – the NFB 'recommend[ed] that sympathetic study be given
this proposition'; (4) that 'a reasonable proportion of theatre screen
time be reserved for the showing of Canadian-produced feature films'
– the NFB 'did not recommend the establishment of a quota in Canadian theatres for Canadian produced feature films at the present time,
because the Canadian feature film industry is not sufficiently established as yet to provide feature films in adequate volume and quality
to meet a quota'; (5) that the government put in place a method of
financial assistance to Canadian-owned companies producing entertainment films for theatres and television – the NFB recommended the
establishment of an interdepartmental committee 'to examine the
advisability and possible methods' of providing financial assistance
'towards the production in Canada of feature films and possibly films
for television'; and (6) that tariffs be increased and government film

agencies instructed to encourage the growth of Canadian motion picture laboratories – the NFB 'is of the opinion that present tariffs ... provide adequate protection.'[73]

In outline, the NFB's recommendations presented all the structures, with one exception, of the policy field in which Canadian feature film development would be framed. These recommendations are worth insisting on if only to underscore both the narrowness of the policy field of Canadian feature development and the earliness of its definition. Thus, the emerging field of feature film development policy was delineated by its increasing separation from television, a separation that was intensified by the failure of the BBG's 'grand design' for private TV[74] and, related to this, of Canadian content regulation, of the absence of a made-in-Canada advertising policy, and of the development within CBC of a separate film production capability. In turn, the separation further reinforced the dependent character of film industry development and in particular its dependence on the state: no quota meant that the direction and the dynamic of development were externally oriented and subsidy driven. Finally, the character of a film 'industry' as an object of talk was reinforced; now it would be designed by an interdepartmental committee mandated to study a 'possible' course of development, one that was more imaginary than real. Implicit in the NFB's recommendations, then, was precisely such a course of development: isolated, dependent, and discursive.

The NFB's recommendations were revised, though largely unmodified, in October 1960 in preparation for a 2 November meeting between Ellen L. Fairclough, minister of citizenship and immigration in the Diefenbaker Cabinet and as such responsible for the NFB, and representatives of the AMPPLC to discuss the contents of the brief. At the meeting, Fairclough stated in seemingly unequivocal terms that feature film development, unlike broadcasting, was not a matter under federal authority at that time:

Please, do not misunderstand me. My Government is conscious of the desirability of having more Canadian material on television, newsstands and in the cinemas. The recent appointment of a Royal Commission on Publications – presided by Mr Grattan O'Leary – indicates that we are conscious of the problem.[75]

'At the present time,' she continued, 'I do not see the Federal Government setting up a financial assistance scheme to producers of feature entertainment films.' In part, the government's position of non-involvement was constitutional: 'I wonder if the Federal Government has authority to decide what shall or shall not be shown in the cinemas ... in terms of ... foreign content in cinema programs. Insofar as I may be aware, matters relating to what is shown in the cinemas in Canada have, to this day, been handled by the provinces.' She repeatedly suggested that the producers turn to the provincial levels of government as 'the possible avenue of assistance' for feature film development. It followed, therefore, that the brief's suggestion of a quota system to secure distribution for Canadian films was premature: 'Have we as yet in Canada,' the minister wondered, 'feature films in adequate number and quality to meet a quota? It seems to me that part of the solution of your problems, at present, could be found in private arrangements between producers and distributors, both here and abroad.'[76]

What is particularly striking about this meeting is its anomalous status within a policy context that was shifting towards the opposite of what Fairclough had said to AMPPLC representatives, namely, *greater* federal involvement in the development of a feature film industry. Within less than two months, the Conservative government would abruptly triple the 5 per cent withholding tax it levied on theatrical remittances flowing out of Canada, the first such increase 'in years' as the *Canadian Film Weekly* pointed out, noting that 'It would appear that the USA ... is the major victim of Ottawa's step.'[77]

At the centre of the shift in policy was the NFB itself, in the person of its chairman, Guy Roberge. In the year since the AMPPLC brief had first been presented to Fairclough, Roberge had been pushing for the establishment of a working committee of senior departmental representatives to study it.[78] He returned to the idea of such an interdepartmental planning group repeatedly.[79] The NFB's Board of Governors had met informally with N.A. Taylor late in 1959 and a member had suggested more such informal meetings. As we have seen, government subsidies, not quotas, for Taylor were the preferred mechanism for the development of a feature film industry in Canada. As long as the AMPPLC brief recommended a quota, further government involvement in the development of the industry was apparently precluded. It is likely that Fairclough's meeting in November with AMPPLC representatives was meant to convey that message to the producers' association; admittedly the evidence for this is not conclusive, but shortly afterwards Roberge informed members of the NFB that 'consideration of the Association's brief as far as the Board is concerned' was terminated.[80] In addition, in a memorandum to Fairclough concerning IATSE Local 873's February

1961 circular letter calling for a quota, Roberge referred her 'to your correspondence with the Hon. the Minister of Finance at the time you examined the AMPPLC brief':

Mr [Donald] Fleming was then reluctant to single out the film industry for a special treatment which would have involved *both* the setting up of a loan or subsidy system to film producers and the adoption of specific restrictive or protective measures such as an import quota system to hold back some of the monies earned in Canada by foreign films.[81]

As Taylor had argued in the debate opposing quotas and subsidies, these were either/or options, but as we shall see shortly they were still the object of bureaucratic contemplation.

By early 1962, following a trip to London and Paris and talks with government film officials in the two countries, Roberge concluded that he had found the mechanism for developing a feature film industry in Canada.[82] In a handwritten, restricted memorandum to Fairclough dated 14 February 1962, Roberge put forward for the government's consideration the case for 'the advisability of making inter-governmental agreements which would facilitate the association of Canadian and British and Canadian and French productions.'

My conversations in London and Paris have made it quite clear ... it could very well be in the national interest for Canada to seek some kind of agreement ... which would facilitate the production of theatrical feature films and entertainment films in Canada as well as their distribution in these foreign countries.[83]

After explaining the mechanism of co-production to the Minister, Roberge reiterated that an 'association with Great Britain or France could very well provide an impetus to the entertainment or feature film industry here, *an industry which otherwise could continue to find it very difficult, if not impossible, to develop.*'[84]

The proposal, he noted, was 'not tied to establishment of a federal financial assistance scheme nor to the imposition of a special levy at the box-office level, proceeds of which would be divided between Canadian films and films co-produced under an international agreement,' options apparently still being envisioned somewhere within the state bureaucracy although both the NFB and the 'industry' were by this point unmistakably more in favour of subsidies. 'Even a modest sized investment in the feature film industry' by the state, he concluded, 'would represent at least an additional five to seven million dollars per year' to the gross income of the industry.[85]

The minister's initial response to the memorandum was to take it under advisement. Then, at the 56th meeting of the Board of Governors of the NFB, held in Montreal on 19 May 1962, Roberge reported that the minister, after consultation with the departments of External Affairs and of Trade and Commerce, had forwarded a recommendation to Cabinet for the formation of an interdepartmental subcommittee:

On behalf of the Government of Canada, the National Film Board in committee and association with the Department of Trade and Commerce and the Department of External Affairs, be authorized to approach formally and through official channels the British Government and the Government of France in order to explore the possibility of inter-governmental agreements being reached.[86]

With Cabinet's approval of the minister's recommendation on 28 May, the shift in government policy was formalized. This decision was the first step by the government of Canada towards entering the economy of private sector feature film development. The latter now became a field of state policy, to which it has maintained a commitment ever since, and the object of deliberation within the state. The specifics of this discussion are examined in the next chapter.

5

Discoursing on Cinema within the State

The preceding chapter showed how the discourse of an emergent private sector in film production took shape within the changing logic of governmentalization, as a result of which the concerns of private film producers rapidly became the object of a new field of government policy. This is not to say that the state simply took on as its own the interests of the private producers. Rather, in response to the discourse of the private producers, a separate state discursive formation developed surrounding the Canadian feature. However, what distinguished the state discourse from the one of the producers was that, with its links to the state apparatus which has the power to create institutions, it constituted what Franklin terms a 'discourse of power.'[1]

The extension of governmental rationality that delimited this new policy field and the resulting discursive formation within the state derived its developmental justification from changes in the international environment of film production: as Roberge remarked, without the state's intervention in developing closer association with the film industries of Britain and France, the Canadian film industry would 'continue to find it very difficult, if not impossible to develop.'[2] But Canadian governmentality also stemmed from a perception of the international environment as one in which competition between states (and film industries) was in fact so limited as to be its opposite: it was not competition but collaboration, through which the stronger film industries of Europe and the United States would directly assist in the establishment of the Canadian industry. In this perspective, the principal function of the Canadian state in feature film policy was to further collaboration and, indeed, as of 1968, to institutionalize it in the policies of the Canadian Film Development Corporation (CFDC).

However, governmentalization, it will be recalled, is as much a process of limitation as it is of the extension of governmental rationality, particularly in the sense of redefining the limits of the public sphere in response to the emergence of new private actors within capitalist contexts. In the Canadian case, the process of internal delimitation entailed, notably, the detachment of the developing policy field of the Canadian feature film from the aegis of the NFB by the reinforcement of the feature film 'industry' as a would-be economic entity. This paradoxical task of extension and limitation was the responsibility of the state discursive formation whose institutionalization of the feature film within the economy of talk is traced in the current chapter up to the establishment of the CFDC.

The Limitation of the NFB, 1962–3

With the challenge posed by the AMPPLC brief to its hegemonic position within Canadian filmmaking apparently averted – deflected outwards into the international sphere of the negotiation of co-production treaties – the NFB appeared, by the early years of the 1960s, advantageously positioned to influence decisively the development of the new policy field it had been instrumental in establishing. And to do so to such an extent that the NFB seemed to have become the driving force behind what might even prove to be a 'distinctively Canadian' approach to the feature film. At least, this was how it seemed to a number of contemporary journalists by the fall of 1963.

In the first of a four-part series on the full-blown emergence of a revitalized NFB, tellingly entitled 'Our faceless giant stirs restlessly,' *Toronto Telegram* entertainment journalist Sid Adilman rhetorically painted a sharp contrast between the 'old' and the 'new' NFB. From the 'dully functional' buildings of its Montreal headquarters, where it was 'largely ignored' by its neighbours, a response on their part that was 'deadly typical' of that occasioned by the cinema of short films and documentaries it produced, which even NFB senior executives and top producers admitted privately were 'stodgy, stagey, flat, toothless and sometimes vacuous,' came evidence that 'the heart of Canada's puny film industry' had undergone a dramatic change in recent months. 'Quietly and painfully, maturity came. Now the NFB is emerging full blown.'[3]

For Adilman, the sudden transformation of the NFB was the result of a number of significant new developments. First, the NFB had 'launched the first English-speaking full-length feature film *The Dry-landers* [1963] playing to jam-packed movie crowds throughout western Canada,' and it had also released 'its first full-length [French-language] feature film, *Pour la suite du monde* [1963] on French-Canadian TV.'[4] Second, the first co-production 'pact' with France had been signed at Montreal on 11 October 1963. Third, ongoing technical experiments with lightweight cameras and cableless sound equipment would, Adilman predicted, 'revolutionize the documentary industry.' Fourth, bookings of NFB films in 'Canadian movie houses' had increased by 12 per cent over 1961. As a result of these developments, 'the NFB stands on the threshold of its 25th birthday [1964] happily stunned by the successes of the past months.'[5]

Two other contemporary journalistic accounts confirm Adilman's perception of a changed NFB. An unsigned article in *Variety*, dated 21 August 1963, announcing plans for the first film to be produced in Canada under the France-Canada co-production treaty,[6] noted that 'Canada's film production industry which until now seemed to be in a state of perpetual infancy ... has entered an historic phase.' The 'historic phase' comprised two aspects: the co-production treaty with France which, in the writer's view, was 'unique' because it permitted 'joint venture participation with producers – using private capital – from countries other than the two signatories,' and the decision by the NFB 'to expand its operations into the field of feature films.' According to *Variety*, Roberge had announced 'Revolutionary changes in Canada's film-making policies' at the first competitive Canadian Film Festival held alongside the Fourth Montreal International Film Festival in August.

What it all appears to add up to is a realization on the part of Canadian film officials that if feature production is to get anywhere in this country, the government will have to play the big part in offering encouragement with technical assistance (by the NFB) and a ready-made distribution formula as provided by the new treaty ... Now, according to Roberge, there is the possibility of Canada being able to get going in full-length commercial theatre films, to provide a product that will have a fighting chance on the world markets.[7]

Whereas the *Variety* article envisioned the NFB in a supporting role as part of a changing governmental framework that would provide greater encouragement and 'a ready-made distribution formula' through co-productions or joint ventures for the private production of features in

Canada, a third contemporary press account attributed to the Board a
more central position. Reporting on press conferences held by Roberge
in Vancouver and Swift Current as part of the release of *The Drylanders*,
Vancouver Sun movie columnist Les Wedman proclaimed the birth of a
taxpayer-supported film industry led by the NFB:

Forget the pipedreams of promoters and the piddling efforts of penny-pinching
producers in the past to start a movie industry in Canada. There's a Canadian
movie industry getting underway, all right, but it's you, the taxpayer, who's
helping launch it, because at long last the NFB has decided to do what should
have been done ages ago. And that's make feature films about Canada and in
Canada.[8]

Wedman paraphrased Roberge as stating 'that these two films [*Drylanders* and *Pour la suite du monde*] could be the start of full-length feature
filmmaking in Canada.' His report continued:

The NFB, [Roberge] said, has been standing by waiting for private companies
and individuals to make a solid go of a Canadian movie industry. They haven't
done it. The board, reluctant to move into features for fear of criticism that it was
interfering in free enterprise, has proceeded quietly to make two features without raising a cry of 'wasting the taxpayers' money.' Hollywood no longer domi-
nates the Canadian market. There is a growing demand for 'Canadian identity'
and a shortage of films for theatres. So the NFB is entering to fill the gap.
Roberge made it clear that 'we are not in the entertainment business ... we
are not thinking of making musicals and comedies. We don't intend to displace
Hollywood. This is foolish. We want only time on our own screens to show
Canadian films.'

What these various accounts underlined, each in a different way, was
just how much ambiguity surrounded both the emerging Canadian feature film and the policies making it possible. Adilman, for instance, in
entitling the second part of his series 'Will BB [Brigitte Bardot] join the
NFB?,' raised the question of how a feature capability at the NFB would
fit into the international industry. For Wedman, this was no problem:
American companies would simply distribute Canadian-made features.
'[T]he future for Canadian feature films – especially since Columbia Pictures has agreed to distribute the NFB movies – looks rosy.'[9] The *Variety*
article indirectly pointed out a major ambiguity in the Canada–France
co-production treaty: other than technical assistance by the NFB,

Canada, unlike France, did not offer access to a pool of capital as an inducement to producers, although opening the treaty to joint ventures by outside (presumably U.S.) producers who could contribute capitalization might be a way around this limitation. While everyone tended enthusiastically to welcome, and to exaggerate, the potential *industrial* implications of the NFB's shift to feature production, only the piece by Wedman, and then only en passant, made any reference to the actual practices involved in making the productions, as opposed to dreaming about their potential. 'The work of finishing *The Drylanders* was spread over three years so that the $200,000 it cost could be taken from NFB annual allocations and profits without inflating the budget in any one year.' In the light of such a detail, the NFB's initial involvement in features appeared a somewhat less than revolutionary development and more an indication of tolerance of *some* experimentation with a film form to which its commitment would be at best occasional. As Roberge reported to the Board of Governors of the NFB in what was, in effect, to become NFB policy for features: 'since feature film production was expensive it was unlikely that with its present day budget the NFB could become heavily involved.'[10]

In fact, the NFB was increasingly entangled in the contradiction stemming from its dual position as, on the one hand, the government film production agency and, on the other, the principal adviser to the government in matters of film policy. In a context where the gap between the two positions was widening, as the latter in particular shifted in response to an increasing preoccupation with commercial feature film production, maintaining the divergent orientations within the responsibility of the one institution was becoming untenable.

While newspaper accounts presented him in the guise of the champion of an approach centred on the NFB to feature production, Roberge by the fall of 1963, and with the approval of his Board of Governors, was eliciting from the Liberal government elected in April a commitment similar to that given by the preceding government, but with a difference of emphasis. Although couched in language that was largely similar to what he used in February 1962 with Fairclough, the memorandum Roberge wrote on 11 September 1963 to the secretary of state (a newly created ministerial position that was held by J.W. Pickersgill until the spring of 1964 when Maurice Lamontagne took it over) was more emphatic about the role of the state in the development of a domestic film industry: 'I have reached the conclusion that ... without government financial assistance a feature film industry is not possible. I therefore submit that the government should now consider whether it is prepared to support the development of this industry.'[11] In stating that 'if we do not take action now, the opportunity to get a feature film industry in Canada may well be missed for another generation,' it could be argued that Roberge was advising the government in matters of film policy on behalf of the creative community of 'talented individuals,' the 'writers, artists and film-makers across the country ... and members of the film industry' who were all manifesting 'a very great interest at the moment in feature films.' But, 'as in many other fields,' these creators might decide 'to realize their hopes outside the country' if decisive government action on their behalf were not forthcoming.[12]

Roberge's memorandum recommended two policy measures: the establishment of a film industry development revolving fund and the adoption by the Industrial Development Bank of a special set of regulations 'on the basis of which *bona fide* Canadian film producers would obtain loans under conditions specially applicable to the motion picture business.' The latter was necessitated, in Roberge's view, by the 'very specialised' nature of motion picture financing and by the fact that 'Canadian banks have no tradition in this kind of lending,' in which the financial institution lends up to 65 per cent of a film's budget against advance distribution guarantees.

It was never, or so the main protagonists claimed, the intention to make the NFB the central institutional structure of a developing feature film industry in Canada. Both Roberge and Juneau in in-depth personal interviews emphatically denied that it had anything more than a formal interest in the structuring of the industry. Moreover, the NFB could not envisage greater investment in feature production for two reasons: ideologically, in the sense of conceiving of features as only a limited aspect of a more general range of filmmaking activities for the government, and economically, because without substantial budgetary increments the NFB, given the prevailing conception of its role in filmmaking, did not have the resources to undertake more than the occasional feature. If it had a role to play as part of the institutional framework within which a Canadian feature-film industry might develop, the NFB envisioned that framework as neutral in its effects upon the kinds of films that would emerge. In its view, also, the content of Canadian features was the entirely separate matter of the interaction of filmmakers and the public.[13]

However, for Jacques Bobet, one of the NFB producers under whose immediate responsibility a number of the first French-language features were produced as of 1963–4 (*Le Chat dans le sac* in 1964, *La Vie heureuse de Léopold Z* in 1965, though some shooting had begun in late 1963), the form and content of a Canadian feature cinema were indissolubly linked, and the role of the NFB was central to both. In an open letter addressed to Roberge as government film commissioner (and published just prior to Roberge's resignation in the spring of 1966), Bobet linked the institutional future of the NFB to the extent of its commitment to what had for him by then unmistakably become 'the main current of Canadian cinema ... the feature film.'[14] As he pointed out, this was not the co-production of feature films by a number of international partners including Canadian producers, but more specifically the upsurge of what was 'truly the Canadian feature film, that is, simply, the birth and development of a NATIONAL cinema. Everything indicates that Canadian cinema is experiencing a moment of intensifying national identity ... with which the NFB must collaborate with all its might.' Such a commitment did not mean the occasional production of one or two features; on the contrary, it meant that 'if, in French Canada alone, ten films can be produced with sufficient cultural dignity to truly represent a people both to itself and to foreign eyes, the NFB must be able to produce six [of these] and sponsor at least two more under the table.'[15] Bobet predicted that if the NFB placed itself outside the current of the production of feature films and if it did not forcefully and continually participate in the development of a 'great Canadian cinema,' it stood to lose everything, including its 'traditional mission' of government film production: 'all that will be left of the Board – in the end, this is very clear and very simple – will be a deserted and forgotten warehouse.' For Bobet, the choice facing the NFB was clear and from the vantage of 1966 it had been so since at least 1963–4, if not implicitly since the post-war loss of the medium of television to the CBC: 'If the Board had at one time stupidly failed to become the State Television, it must not now fail to *become the State Cinema*.'[16]

Both Roberge's memorandum to Pickersgill in 1963 and Bobet's open letter to Roberge in 1966 represent attempts to delimit the domestic role of the state and the NFB in the development of a Canadian film industry. Bobet's letter suggests one extreme of the extension of government rationality into the feature form of an NFB-developed state cinema, while Roberge's memorandum provides a median point (a commitment 'in principle' of state support in the form of an NFB-administered loan fund). The response to Roberge's memorandum indicated a third possibility which, instead of being an *extension* of government rationality (which would have been the development of a state cinema), attempted to delimit that extension to a very precisely circumscribed domain: to the establishment of a government committee, on which the NFB would be represented, to discuss *possible* scenarios for the development of a film industry in Canada. In other words, the response aimed at a delimitation *within* the state of a discursive space in which to circumscribe both the role of the NFB and the orientation of feature film development. This space was thus both extensive and delimitative and entailed splitting the policy field into three parts: the role of the administrative state, the role of the NFB, and the role of the development of the film industry, in which the role of the administrative state would now be primary. The precise problem to be dealt with was how to *reduce* the NFB through the *increased* role of the administrative state in the development of the film industry. The leverage for this was provided by Lamontagne's concept of 'cultural development,' as will be seen below.

In effect, the response by Pickersgill and the Liberal Cabinet to Roberge's memorandum replicated the one by the Diefenbaker Cabinet to Roberge's memorandum of February 1962 to Fairclough. But this time, instead of an interdepartmental committee to explore the state-to-state possibility of co-production agreements, the same mechanism was turned inwards, within the Canadian state itself. In a memorandum dated 9 December 1963 to Cabinet, which it approved on 12 December, Pickersgill recommended that 'an interdepartmental committee be set up to consider the possible development of feature film production in Canada' and that it should specifically 'explore ways and means of assisting financially and otherwise such development,' 'examine proposals which may be put forward,' and make appropriate recommendations to Cabinet. Furthermore, he recommended that the proposed committee should consist of one representative from each of the major economic ministries – Finance, External Affairs, and Industry, Trade, and Commerce – one representative from the Bank of Canada, and of one representative from the National Film Board, and that it should be chaired by the government film commissioner.[17]

The Interdepartmental Committee on the Possible Development of Feature Film Production in Canada, 1964–5

The work of the Interdepartmental Committee on the Possible Development of Feature Film Production in Canada has received little detailed examination in the scholarship of Canadian film policy.[18] And yet, it provides a complete microcosm of the economy of talk of the Canadian feature. In the course of its twenty-five meetings between January 1964 and December 1965 the committee heard testimony from the principal figures in the Canadian film industry, received briefs and submissions from the craft and professional associations active in Canadian filmmaking, commissioned four studies on aspects of the Canadian film industry and international film legislation, including a major study of the problem of feature film distribution in Canada, engaged two European consultants, and submitted two reports to the Pearson Cabinet. In the course of its deliberations, the Canadian feature assumed its fully elaborated discursive form, the course of the policy for Canadian film industry development was set definitively both in the language to be used about it and the kinds of institutions established for its development, and the NFB, increasingly marginalized by its accelerating loss of influence over film policy, was plunged into a crisis over its orientation from which it never recovered.[19]

The work of the committee fell into two periods, an initial four months (January–April 1964), at the end of which a first report to Cabinet was submitted, and a second round of meetings (October 1964–July 1965) following a Cabinet request for further studies, which closed with a second and final report to Cabinet, though the committee continued to meet in Ottawa, usually once a week on Tuesday afternoons, until 21 December 1965.

Chaired by Roberge, the committee was initially composed of deputy ministers from each of the departments enumerated in the Cabinet decision. Under-Secretary of State G.G.E. Steele was added to the committee to represent the secretary of state. The secretary of the committee was Gordon Sheppard, also from the Department of the Secretary of State. As special assistant to Lamontagne, Sheppard, a filmmaker, was the author in 1965–6 of the four-volume *Special Report on the Cultural Policy and Activities of the Government of Canada*.[20] Michael D. Spencer, who became the CFDC's first executive director, was the representative of the NFB. The representative from the Department of Industry, Trade, and Commerce initially and later for the Department of Finance was Simon S. Reisman, who would later be the chief negotiator for Canada for the 1988 Canada–United States Free Trade Agreement.

At the committee's first meeting on 13 January 1964, Roberge opened with a brief account of the background that had led to its establishment. Three significant moments were singled out: the 1959 AMPPLC brief, the 1963 co-production treaty with France, and Roberge's September

1963 memorandum to Pickersgill. However, the chief item of business at this first meeting was deciding when the committee should sit.[21]

At the second meeting, on 21 January, the committee got down to business. Should the effect of the developing film industry primarily be economic (for instance, to help the balance of payments and to stimulate employment) or cultural (such as to enhance Canada's prestige abroad and to assist biculturalism domestically)? *The consensus was that the film industry should be primarily economic* with ancillary cultural effects,' though the committee noted that the cultural effects 'might be quite important.'[22] A conclusion such as this might well be expected of a committee made up largely of representatives of economic ministries, but because the economic orientation was so pronounced, something far more fundamental was at issue. Most significantly, in terms of the language within which the Canadian feature was institutionalized as an object of policy, the economic status of the film industry established the feature film as a symbolic, 'economic' entity within a discourse of power. As Franklin has argued, a discourse of power involves an order of valuation in which six levels of equivalency intersect: the form of value itself, its rationality, its monetary form, its power and dominance within the economy, the social order of which it has constituted, and the social order its managers have constructed.[23] Accordingly, though the committee would on occasion pay lip-service to cultural aspects of the development of Canadian feature films, that concern was secondary by far to the order of valuations subsumed within its economic significance.

The committee identified five questions it deemed central to its deliberations: (1) was it possible for a feature film industry to start up without government help? (2) should the role of government be that of 'pump-primer' to an industry that could become a potential source of income, or should its role be that of a provider of temporary aid? (3) was it worthwhile to start such an industry? (4) what evidence was there that such an industry would be viable? and (5) 'what is a Canadian film?'[24]

The committee defined its principal task as determining 'how the Canadian film industry could mesh with international trends while retaining a national identity,' though how to ensure the latter was neither clear nor essential. At the fourth meeting, on 11 February, Roberge was asked how Canadian feature films would get distribution in Canada and abroad. He replied that 'he was confident distributors in Canada would want to cooperate. Moreover, many of the big international distributors in New York, with offices in Canada, would likely understand the importance of assisting Canadian features to get distribution abroad. He cited the case of Jutra's *À Tout prendre* [1963] which Columbia had agreed to distribute internationally in both English and French.' At its sixth meeting on 4 March, the committee interviewed Canadian producers, beginning with the ubiquitous Toronto exhibitor, distributor, and producer N.A. Taylor, followed by Ottawa producer 'Budge' Crawley, and at subsequent meetings film director Don Haldane (*The Drylanders*), who appeared as president of the Screen Actors' Guild of Canada, and filmmakers Claude Jutra and Guy L. Côté, respectively president and secretary of the Association professionnelle des cinéastes (APC). No minutes of these in camera meetings were kept. By late February, the committee had produced a draft of its initial report to Cabinet that, along with an addendum, was accepted by the committee at its tenth meeting on 17 April for submission.

The committee's initial report was significant in several respects. Not only was it the most sustained piece of writing about Canadian feature production since the AMPPLC brief, but it also provided an overview of the transition of Canadian feature development as it became a problem of knowledge within an emerging policy field that was increasingly organized according to economic categories. The status of the policy-object was becoming clearer: it was to enhance the output and employment capacity of an industrial or economic entity, although it was still discussed interchangeably with the development of Canadian features or of a Canadian feature film industry or of both. But, because the object of the policy was clearer, it was increasingly and obviously the embodiment of an instrumental *ratio* that was not only, from the perspective of the state, economic (i.e., knowable in terms of economic categories) but also historical. Thus, it stated that it 'is not altogether unreasonable to suppose that a fairly effective film industry could have been established in Canada before the coming of the sound film in the late nineteen-twenties.'[25]

Despite economic historicization of the policy object, there were still enormous gaps in knowledge. The report did not, or could not, account for why an industry with such potential had proved unable to negotiate the changeover to sound technology, why 'no more than two or three feature films have been produced per year,' since the Second World War or why 'their success, both financial and artistic, has been limited.' The report only noted that the 'private film industry ... largely turned its attention to industrial[s,] ... documentary films and, since 1952 ... commercial advertising shorts for television.'

A dialectic of knowledge and ignorance resulted. On the one hand, for the first time within the economy of talk of the Canadian feature, it became possible to derive a statement about the economic basis of the 'industry': 'Almost all the films produced by the Canadian private film industry today are ... industrial, training and public relations short films and television commercials' and this, it said, was because 'TV commercials and industrial films involve the producer in no risk ... since the sponsor has paid the film's cost before any screenings take place.'[26] On the other hand, how such a risk-aversive 'industry' of short-film producers had shifted to risk-intensive feature-length production, the report could not explain. It could only reiterate pseudo-economic 'facts,' such as the familiar DBS statistical aggregates of gross income growth and fluctuating estimates of remittances paid to foreign distributors – here $20 million, an amount some $7 million lower than Roberge's estimate in his September 1963 memorandum. The absence of exact information, however, made possible speculative leaps. If, in recent years, private producers had approached government seeking information on assistance to film production, it was only 'in the last six months' that the government itself

has been made aware of film projects to the value of $3–4 million in advanced planning stages which will be undertaken if additional financing can be obtained ... These film projects involve individual budgets ranging from $75,000 to $900,000, and are supported by Canadian film producers ... If a substantial number of these projects could be brought to a successful completion and receive widespread distribution in Canada and abroad, the feature film business could be given a good start. The result would be that the gross revenue of the industry would be quite substantially increased and there would be more employment of Canadian technicians and film makers, as well as actors, writers and musicians. Furthermore some part of the money which is now expended abroad in rentals of foreign films would be saved ... and paid instead to Canadian producers ... In addition, it is expected that successful Canadian films would earn money abroad.[27]

This was a chimera created by hearsay; there was, in fact, no basis for assessing the validity of establishing a feature film industry in Canada. Instead, the report derived the grounds from recent changes in the international industry. It was thus a change in the international division of film labour that justified the development of a film industry in Canada. 'Hollywood once the source of the majority of successful films in all countries is now no longer the film capital of the world,' because, in the last decade, feature film production had become 'an international industry.' Not only were more American producers working abroad, but film producers from outside the United States were finding markets on the North American continent. As fewer films were being produced in the United States as a result of the reduced audience caused by television, distributors and exhibitors had increasingly turned to foreign productions. 'The conclusion may be drawn therefore that the diversification of the feature film industry into new types of production, the wide screen spectacular, the foreign film and the film designed for the more discriminating audience' now afforded possibilities for two types of Canadian-made production: 'the kind of film which receives good distribution in the Art houses in Europe and the U.S.,' and the 'fairly low budget' second features in a double-bill program 'which could be made here as well.'[28]

An alternation of fragments of knowledge with non sequiturs characterized the report as a whole. After observing that the 'big cinema' chains in Canada were controlled from abroad, and so 'might be inclined to give priority to their own production,' it was simply assumed that 'any future Canadian feature film industry should be well supported by the cinemas in its own country.'[29] In any event, the 'challenge for the Canadian producer is that, since his home market is not large enough to provide him with adequate finance for his film (in contrast to countries like France and the UK ...) he must produce the kind of picture which will do well everywhere, including Canada.' The report's discussion of the role of government in assisting film industries centred narrowly on examining funding and assistance schemes in France (the Fonds de développement de l'industrie cinématographique), in Great Britain (the Eady assistance scheme and the National Film Finance Corporation), and in Sweden. Although the report made the observation that the use of quotas for the dual purposes of cultivating local industry and preventing American domination of a 'significant mass medium of communication' was 'not unrelated' to the thinking that had caused Canada to establish the CBC in the 1930s, nothing further was inferred from it.

The report concluded that if the Canadian feature film industry was to be established on a regular and developing basis, it would have to meet two requirements: be aimed at developing Canadian talents and providing facilities and employment for scriptwriters, directors, actors, cameramen, etc.; and 'develop along lines which would be in accordance with international trends.' The example cited was the production by Crawley Films of *The Luck of Ginger Coffey* (1964), written by an Irishman, directed by an American, produced by a Canadian, and with British leads and a British director of photography, 'but all other services provided in Canada.'[30]

Existing technical and creative facilities in Canada were deemed sufficient for more productions such as *The Luck of Ginger Coffey*. '[T]here are film directors who have graduated from private industry or the NFB and now have feature film experience, including Pierre Patry, [René] Bonnière, Claude Jutra, Michel Brault, Julian Roffman,'[31] 'at least two' directors of photography whose work was up to standard for features, 'some' editors and designers, and 'many fine actors and actresses.' What, then, were the obstacles to a Canadian feature film industry? In the view of the report, there were two main interlocked problems: distribution and finance. 'To get a film financed one must have a distribution contract, to get a distribution contract one presumably should have some experience in feature film production.' To compound the problems, Canada was 'a free market for films' with no controls on the importation or exhibition of films (the report did not explicitly advocate any), Canadian banks did not specialize in lending for film production, and although a co-production agreement existed between France and Canada, 'French producers ... have expressed the view that there should be some public assistance for Canada to counterbalance their own state aid.'[32]

Of all the difficulties, the most pressing was that of finance, the sources of which (grants, loans, or subsidies, or indirectly through quotas) still remained unclear. Even more problematic, 'particularly in the developmental stages of the industry,' was the fact 'that through various arrangements, the majority of important Canadian distribution and exhibition channels are controlled from abroad,' which 'compound[ed] the difficulty for Canadian producers.' Significantly, the 'Committee felt ... that in the first instance it would appear advisable to rely on *moral suasion* to obtain good distribution and exhibition of Canadian feature films in Canada.'[33] Cabinet's response to the committee report was not made known until 4 August, the day before Secretary of State Lamontagne, at the official celebrations of the NFB's 25th anniversary, made the first public announcement of the government's intention to seek authority from Parliament to establish a loan fund for feature films. Cabinet approved 'in principle' the recommendations of the secretary of state that a loan fund be established as outlined by the committee, that the committee prepare specific recommendations for the fund's administration and on the terms of the loans, that the committee investigate 'the distribution problems faced by Canadian films both in Canada and abroad' and make recommendations 'to improve the present situation,' and that the committee be authorized to hire two special consultants to prepare 'preliminary studies on the various factors affecting the production and distribution of Canadian feature films.'[34]

The Committee's Studies of Canadian Feature Film Production and Distribution (1965)

The Interdepartmental Committee resumed sitting on 8 October. As the minutes of the eleventh meeting put it, the 'Government has decided there should be a Canadian feature film industry.' The committee returned to work with a discussion of the economic benefits to Canada of a feature film industry. Such benefits were assumed to be four-fold in their positive effects on employment, both in the film industry itself and in ancillary industries, on the Canadian balance of payments, on tourism, and on foreign trade. It agreed that while the impact of a film industry on the last two categories of economic activity were 'more difficult to measure,' these were, in fact, the most important of the four categories, particularly tourism.[35]

At the committee's twelfth meeting on 5 November, a discussion arose as to 'whether the committee shall produce a non-economic appraisal of the value of the feature film industry.' The committee concluded that this was unnecessary 'because the government had already affirmed the desirability of this industry for non-economic reasons.' In other words, while it had the authority to undertake non-economic appraisals, the committee opted not to do so because, as far as it was concerned, the matter was closed. Instead, its task was to delimit the economic characteristics of the new industry that had been pronounced into being by the state. In such a perspective, as Franklin remarks, 'discourse ... develops in the form of the language of economics.'[36]

The Production Studies: Spencer (1965) and Cadieux (1965)

In January 1965 the Interdepartmental Committee engaged two production consultants 'to provide as far as possible a realistic assessment of the country's potential in the feature film production field.'[37] Michael Spencer, Roberge's director of planning and the NFB's representative to the committee, prepared a report on 'Canadian Feature Film Production in the English language,' which was dated 6 April 1965, and Fernand Cadieux, a close collaborator of Pierre Juneau, an undated report on 'French-speaking Canada.'

Spencer's report drew its information from three sources, confidential questionnaires submitted to producers and would-be producers, briefs submitted by craft groups and unions, and confidential information provided by Canadian banks, insurance companies, and other financial sources. It covered a range of topics, beginning with producers. The sixteen producers who provided information ranged 'from individuals with few assets except their personal enthusiasm to companies with considerable creative, technical and financial resources.'[38] All except Crawley Films Ltd in Ottawa and Lew Parry Film Productions in Vancouver were located in Toronto, and all were in agreement with the study's 'basic premise that Canada has the technical resources and talent for a feature film industry and that government has a part to play in bringing it into being.'

For Spencer, the producers divided readily into two categories: established companies and independent producers. '[W]ith sufficient resources to maintain a significant flow of either television commercials, or industrial and documentary films,' five of the seven established companies had plans for twelve feature films in the half-million-dollar budget range. However, they all 'expect[ed]' to make distribution deals in advance, they could all raise the production money from chartered banks because they were given distribution guarantees, and they all intended to aim their films at the international market, as a result of which 'non-Canadian content' in such films would be high.[38]

The other production companies that were surveyed were 'independent producers with limited resources.' Usually recently incorporated, they had little or no organizational profile, and their production experience was synonymous with the individual work of their principals. Their production plans included fourteen features for an average budget of $225,000, 'a little low,' Spencer noted, 'for film of international stature,' but 'these producers are more concerned with achieving some success in the Canadian market first.' These producers had received 'completely negative reactions from distributors and from bankers,' though their faith in Canadian content, talent, and resources, which was shared by the unions and associations, was greater than among the larger producers: 'low budget producers had more confidence in Canadian creative resources.'

It is from this group or from other producers like them who will get into feature film production as the market and opportunities improve, that many of the feature film-makers will develop for the Canadian industry of the future.[39]

However, although it repeatedly mentioned that large and small producers differed in their assessments in every respect – primary markets and existing technical or creative facilities – the study minimized these differences by attempting to elaborate a consensus in which the perspective of the large producers was dominant. Observing, for example, that low-budget producers felt confident Toronto and, to a slightly lesser extent, Vancouver offered all the necessary facilities for low-budget 'black and white, 35mm feature production,' the study concluded that it is 'likely therefore that, except for highly sophisticated special effects, large studio interiors and 35mm colour processing, all the necessary facilities exist even for high-budget productions.' High-budget, professional quality, international standards, these were the norms that informed the Spencer study and to which the Canadian industry had to be made to conform.[40]

The Interdepartmental Committee discussed Spencer's report at its eighteenth meeting on 27 April, when it was recorded that the feature film fund legislation was 'listed as 18th in the "C" category of the legislative priority list.'[41] Because of the low legislative priority, the committee felt it 'need not rush its report' to Cabinet; it was not submitted until July. Discussion of the Spencer report by the committee revealed that government actions – in the form of talk about possible action – had already become a significant factor in the governmentalization of the Canadian feature film. For one thing, big-budget (group 'A') producers had indicated to Spencer that they had no difficulty raising production money and so were neither primarily interested in the Canadian market nor impressed with the quality of Canadian technical facilities or creative talents. Nevertheless, in the committee's view these producers fell within the policy field because their 'main production difficulty was not money but distribution.'[42] For another, the 'B' group of producers, who could get into production only with government financial help, had 'paused in their feature film production plans to await the government scheme.'[43] For the committee, the entire field of Canadian feature film production was now under the responsibility of the coordinative policy of the administrative state.

Cadieux's study, despite placing emphasis on a more sociological approach to the emergence of feature filmmaking in Quebec and on a more pronounced experimental role for the state in feature film development, also illustrated the extent to which the committee was engaged in an economic discourse of development for the Canadian feature. For Cadieux, Canada, in particular its 'French-speaking segment,' was in the throes of a cultural crisis that had far less to do with the economy than with 'a rising generation which hopes to find' in feature film 'a means of expression' first and only secondarily 'employment and a source of revenue.'[44]

The 'tremendous enthusiasm with which so many new talents [are] enter[ing] the motion picture field despite repeated economic disappointments' was 'psycho-social rather than economic.' For Cadieux, the repeated requests for the establishment of a motion picture industry stemmed from socio-psychological motivations, and in Quebec these motivations were particularly to be found among an 'expanding "class" of artists, comedians and film-makers who want to express themselves in feature films' that was undergoing a process of professionalization and that was 'less concerned about market outlets than about expressing itself.'[45]

This conclusion emerged from Cadieux's interviews 'with all the known production companies, all individuals reputed to be producers and the official agencies representing film makers.' Like Spencer, Cadieux grouped his respondents into old (those established for over three years) and new (those established since 1962) companies, but unlike Spencer he included two more categories, individual filmmakers and associations. The 'old' companies (e.g., Omega, Onyx, and Van der Water Films, all in business between three and fifteen years), produced documentaries, commercials, and TV serials, and so, although 'with the greatest financial resources[,] had not made any feature length films.'[46] Instead, it was the eight new companies, as little as two months old (Orbafilm) and up to the three-year maximum for the category (Claude Jutra's Cassiopée), that 'with more limited resources have produced 9 [feature] films over a period of three years, have seven films under production, and plans for 19 others.' Moreover, this proliferation of feature activity and plans had taken place under the most unfavourable economic conditions:

The new companies, particularly those using the co-operative system [e.g., Coopératio], are sufficiently eager to produce feature length films ... under highly unfavourable conditions, i.e., insufficient capital and equipment, lack of adequate administrative organization, no distribution contracts, and inadequate permanent staff ...

This concerted effort can be taken as the basic investment through which the embryo of a feature-length film industry was created in Quebec. Despite the desire and willingness of the participants ... this effort cannot be maintained on a continuing basis and the industry is doomed to remain at the stage of a craft, unless there is a substantial investment in order to establish a strong industrial basis.[47]

As an industrial sector, the film 'industry' was 'still a craft' undergoing 'a period of apprenticeship during which many people are trying to find a new social role.' In this context, in which social roles were multiplying, improvisation and conflict were 'inevitable' and specialization had not yet been established. Feature filmmaking remained an 'adventure' and thus older companies were disinclined to engage in features until 'economic advantages are assured.' For Cadieux, the role of the state in such a context was to be 'on an experimental basis,' and he recommended that it should be reassessed after a three-year period.[48]

Cadieux met with the committee on 28 April to present his report. While the discussion largely focused on details about making feature films in the Montreal area and on the justification Cadieux gave for a proposal for an experimental film fund with 100 per cent state support, the first question he was asked is profoundly revealing. As the minutes of the eighteenth meeting put it:

Mr. Cadieux was asked whether Canada was really too late in trying to enter the feature film production field. Mr. Cadieux replied that it is difficult for a country or a society to escape from the complexity of the modern world and one of the aspects of that complexity today is feature film making both as a cultural expression and as a means of employment for young creative people. In one way, government financial help to a nascent film industry might be considered as risk capital invested in the youth of the country.[49]

Firestone's Distribution Study (1965)

The capstone of the work of the Interdepartmental Committee was the voluminous, two-part study, *Film Distribution, Practices, Problems and Prospects*, undertaken between late 1964 and October 1965 by University of Ottawa economist Otto John Firestone.[50] Although never published, the study represented the most comprehensive attempt undertaken until then to 'crunch' the facets of exhibition, distribution, production in the Canadian private film industry into rational greater form as an economic object. The enterprise was hazardous, not only because it was 'difficult to find in Canada a more complex field to build a new industry than the film business,'[51] but also because key data, such as the yearly outflow of remittances stemming from U.S. control of Canadian film distribution were, as Firestone informed the Interdepartmental Committee, 'a most elusive set of figures.'[52] Accordingly, he recommended that the introduction of a government aid program include a 'statistical reporting system so as to obtain a more comprehensive overall view of the film production and distribution business in Canada and the place which an expanding Canadian film industry will play in this sector of economic activity.'[53]

His study dealt with the problem of insufficient data by establishing as broad a consensus of opinion as possible and, where necessary, indicating discrepancies in the information gathered. In preparing the study, Firestone consulted with independent French-language distributors in Montreal, with professional associations of filmmakers such as the APC, with the cross-section of the Canadian film industry represented by the Motion Picture Council of Canada, with the Directors' Guild of Canada (DGC), and with Canadian representatives of the U.S. Majors, represented by the Canadian Motion Picture Distributors Association, as well as with representatives of their head offices and of the Motion Picture Association of America in New York City. Firestone was advised on business aspects of Canadian independent distribution and exhibition by N.A. Taylor and his partner David Griesdorf, while Guy Côté of the APC advised on technical aspects. Michael Spencer of the Interdepartmental Committee acted as liaison officer and made available copies of the briefs received by the committee; proposals on aspects of distribution were reported in the study. Firestone's work is thus widely reflective of the 'common sense' of the industry, particularly of distributors.

The premise of the study and of the policy options it would explore was that 'the key approach in any Government program to establish a viable film industry in Canada must be ... that this country is creating an export industry like nickel which in the case of medium budget films must export something like 90 per cent of its output if it is to prosper.'[54] However, developing an export industry involved more than creating a favourable climate for individual initiative at home and providing financial assistance to help an infant industry get on its feet. What was needed was a legal framework of broad international arrangements to facilitate the successful marketing of the films Canadians would produce, either on their own or in conjunction with other foreign producers and distributors in co-production or other partnership arrangements. It was thus necessary to take 'a much broader approach,' namely, to confront 'the question of industry integration on a North American scale' and to parallel recent continental policies between Canada and the United States with respect to oil and motor cars.[55] A similar export-oriented approach was recommended for developing French-language film production in Canada through 'the establishment of [greater] links between Canadian producers and European producer-distributors.'[56]

But, unlike its proven oil resources and growing markets for minerals and natural gas and its well-established automobile industry, the film industry in Canada had little to offer world markets. In fact, the exhibition of Canadian films had been declining up to 1963; production was 'almost non-existent ... except for a few heroic efforts on the part of individual producers plus a small number of feature films produced more recently by the National Film Board'; 'about 80 per cent of the total film distribution business done in Canada' was by U.S.-controlled companies; and 'there does not appear at this time to be an international demand for Canadian feature films.'[57]

On the other hand, Canada did remit in excess of $20 million annually to U.S. film producers and distributors and was said to be the fifth largest foreign market for U.S. film products. Firestone told the Interdepartmental Committee that in his view Canada was in fact probably the second or third largest market for feature films produced by the United States,[58] that Canadian and U.S. film producers and distributors had close business and organizational ties, and that 'the U.S. is also taking out large sums out of Canada in the form of rentals for films shown on television ... [and] participation in [ownership] of Canadian [commercial] television stations.'[59] From these interconnections, it followed not only that 'U.S. distributors must play their proper part in the distribution of Canadian produced feature films,' but also that the successful marketing of feature films produced in Canada required 'direct assistance from the American film industry.'[60]

The key issue for 'a Government wishing to aid in the development of a feature industry' was 'deciding which avenue to follow in pursuing the objective of maximizing returns from a Canadian produced film.'[61] The options for distribution were two: television or theatres. It was possible, in the view of the study, 'for the Canadian feature film-maker to bypass

Canadian theatrical outlets,' and so the problem of U.S. control of distribution, and to 'exhibit their products primarily on Canadian television,'[61]
with production costs underwritten by CBC and the private TV 'networks.' 'Thus, TV networks could take the place of film showings in first-
run locations, with theatre showing possibly relegated to re-run presentation ... if shown at all.' But, if the distribution route to be taken was in
the theatres, the policy implications of the U.S. control of theatres and
film distribution in Canada had to be confronted. This the study undertook, particularly in a chapter entitled 'Government Measures.'

Among the broad range of measures discussed in the chapter (loans,
subsidies, production advances, income tax remission, accelerated capital cost allowances, grants and awards, a public inquiry into restrictive
trade practices in film distribution, the use of quotas as a means of last
resort, and the establishment of a Canadian film registry officer, a film
development corporation, and a film industry development committee)
one in particular will be discussed here because it redefined the place of
the U.S. film industry in the policy development of the Canadian one.

In effect, Firestone proposed that Canadian feature film development
be formally structured by means of an agreement between Canada and
the United States for a common market in feature film production, as
well as one between Canada and Western Europe.

In the case of the United States, arrangements might be worked out for major
American companies to participate in Canadian film productions and to handle
international distribution of such films to the extent of 10 per cent of U.S. film
earnings in Canada over a five-year period. The framework was to be a Canada–
U.S. Film Agreement, another sequel to the 'continental approach' (motor car
agreement and oil policy).[62]

Such a plan was not far removed from, if broader than, the principle of
international co-production. Second, it had the tacit support of Canadian producers and distributors for whom

no adequate arrangements can be worked out for distributing Canadian produced films on a commercial basis unless such films are exhibited not only successfully at home but also have full access to world markets including the U.S.
with such access being made available through international film distributing
facilities, especially those at the disposal of American major companies in the
case of English language films, and possibly well established European firms in
the case of French language films.[63]

The representatives of the Canadian film industry consulted by Firestone were prepared to join into such a form and with the Interdepartmental Committee's support to negotiate their continued access to the Canadian domestic market, a market that, in the received wisdom of the industry, was in any event too small to guarantee the commercial success of Canadian-produced films. However, in Firestone's view, 'considering the size of Canada in terms of population and gross national product this country represents one of the major markets of the world in terms of film distribution.'[64] In exchange they would receive guaranteed access to U.S. and world markets through an association with the major film firms in the United States. Accordingly, Firestone, with the approval of the Interdepartmental Committee, broached the question of a Canada–United States film agreement with the major American companies at a meeting in 1965 in New York arranged by N.A. Taylor.[65]

The problem was that, unlike the Canadians, the Americans were not interested in formal rationalization of a 'continental approach' to the production of feature films. As Firestone reported to the committee at its nineteenth meeting on 25 May, he 'had discovered that American distributors were not interested in co-operating with each other, even on such an obviously useful thing ... Mr [Griffith] Johnson [president] of the MPAA had said that it was very difficult to get the ten majors together to do anything co-operatively. This is an industry of individualists.'[66] An unidentified U.S. film industry executive commented on the proposed Canada–U.S. Film Agreement: 'So far as I know, Canadian oil is just as good as American oil and Canadian cars are just as good as American cars but if Canadian films are going to be handled on the same basis as oil and cars, it scares the hell out of me.'[67]

As Firestone reported in part 2 of his study, which he submitted in October 1965, months after the Interdepartmental Committee had made its final report to Cabinet, the American film companies preferred 'voluntary arrangements' between themselves and Canadian producers rather than the legal framework of the proposed film agreement with its entrenchment of what were viewed as 'compulsory features.' Indeed, they proposed a countermodel of the kind of voluntary arrangement that could be concluded between private American film companies and the Canadian government, the 1948 Canadian Cooperation Project.[68]

In Firestone's view, while the Canadian Cooperation Project was 'a useful example' of voluntary arrangements it was a limited one to the

extent that it had only used Canadian scenery as a backdrop for shooting film and did not use enough Canadian personnel and capital facilities: 'A Canadian film industry cannot be built up by using Canadian
scenary [sic]. It must involve the employment of artists, authors, musi-
cians, producers, directors and technical personnel. It is people and their
ideas that create new and lasting values, and not reproductions of
nature on a screen.' Accordingly, while such voluntary arrangements
were useful, 'any direct arrangements between the Canadian Government and individual film companies' would have to 'make quite clear ...
what would be expected from American film producers and distributors
in participating in the development of a film industry in Canada.'[69]

Comprehensive government assistance, by transferring 'part of the
risk ... from the private sector to the public sector,' could absorb some of
the costs of film production, but it would not significantly reduce overall costs. Given, first, that nationalizing U.S.-controlled distribution
firms was not only 'contrary to established Canadian policies and traditions' but also impractical because 'American motion pictures are likely
to remain the main source of film showing in Canada ... [and] this is
what the Canadian public wants,' and, second, that an import quota system, if it is to be considered at all, should be ... a means of last resort ...
a more rational alternative ... would [be to] accept the assurance
given by American controlled film distributors operating in Canada
that Canadian made films would be given every opportunity for adequate distribution and exhibition in Canada.'[70] Furthermore, given that
'most experienced producers and distributors canvassed expressed the
view that little harm and possibly greater benefits may accrue from
allowing foreign investors [up to 50 per cent] ... participation in Canadian film ventures ... during the infant industry phase, which may last
between 5 and 10 years,' future Canadian feature film production in
that period stood the best chance if it consisted of 'internationally
oriented films.'[71]

Canadian feature films are most likely to succeed as commercial ventures if they
combine proven success formulae with a freshness of approach relying on top
stars and first-class producers with world-wide reputations, assisted by and
associated with Canadian artists, professional and technical personnel. This
would contribute importantly to such Canadian film-makers to grow in stat-
ure and experience over time. A varity [sic] of arrangements, including co-
production, partnership, joint distribution and financing arrangements, etc.,
would serve such objectives.[72]

The two 'massive' volumes that comprised part 1 of the report were attached to the Interdepartmental Committee's second, and final, report to Cabinet on 28 July 1965. The size of the Firestone study, as Spencer puts it, 'caused some concern at the Privy Council Office. "You can't expect ministers to read all that stuff," one officer remarked. In fact, the final memorandum was not too different from the first one I had drafted three years before.'[73]

Recommendations of the Interdepartmental Committee

It almost seemed that the Interdepartmental Committee took completely literally Firestone's observation that the question was not whether government assistance should be forthcoming, 'but in what form, under what conditions and to what extent.' The main outlines of the committee's recommendations were drawn by May–June 1965. Though the committee had commissioned a fourth report, Guy Côté, 'A Survey of film legislation in several European countries with particular reference to National Feature Film Production and including statistical data for 1963' submitted on 6 April, which raised some interesting questions with respect to national film policies, as far as the committee was concerned there was no question about the rationale for government assistance. Only the form, conditions, and extent remained to be settled. In early June it held meetings with its two overseas consultants, Jean-Claude Batz of the Université Libre de Bruxelles, and John Terry, managing director of the British National Film Finance Corporation, which largely concentrated on pragmatic details: how much money should be involved in the fund, how long should it be established for, and how many films might it fund?[74]

The committee's final report to Cabinet consisted largely of a reiteration of its earlier views, views that were now empirically 'confirmed' by the reports and studies undertaken for the committee whose findings the report summarized in six paragraphs. Thus, from the Firestone study was drawn some data on distribution in Canada, the emphasis on the high risk nature of film production, and the need for substantial help from foreign producers through co- and joint-production to build a Canadian film industry. From the study by Cadieux the report concluded that cinema was an industry in which a nation's artists expressed themselves, and from Côté's that the purpose of state support of feature film industries was to maintain national production of films, with the resulting equation of the production by Canadian private companies with national production.[75]

The committee recommended the establishment of 'a Canadian film development corporation,' subject to review after five years, 'to promote the overall development of the feature film industry in Canada' by providing financial assistance, fostering creative, technical, and managerial skills, and advising and assisting those engaged in feature film production. The corporation would be empowered to invest in individual Canadian films; it would enjoy wide discretion in its choice of projects but its decisions would be based on 'the commercial potential and ... intrinsic merit' of the films, assessed on the basis of scripts and distribution guarantees. The corporation would have some flexibility with respect to Canadian ownership and content. Headed by a board of five to seven members appointed by the government, one member being the government film commissioner, the corporate structure would be as simple as possible: an executive director, secretary, treasurer, comptroller, legal advisers, and film production and budget specialists. A broadly representative film industry advisory group would be appointed on the corporation's recommendation. For investment purposes, a revolving fund of $8.5 million would be established from consolidated revenue and an additional $1.5 million would be appropriated for the initial five years for making awards and grants. Lastly, the 'co-operation of major distribution companies is a necessity for the development of the industry and Canadian feature films must be given fair and equitable treatment in distribution and exhibition, particularly in Canada.'

It is, however, difficult to prejudge the attitude which the major distributors will take toward Canadian productions. This can only be determined after Canadian producers have made a number of films and have established a proven record. Little or no evidence exists at the moment to show that there would be a negative attitude on the part of foreign-controlled distribution companies.[76]

Lamontagne's Policy Framework for Feature Film Development, 1964–5

The emergence of an industrial discourse for the development of feature films was paralleled in the speeches of Secretary of State Maurice Lamontagne. Two speeches in particular, one at the time of the establishment of the Interdepartmental Committee, the other subsequent to its recommendations, are evidence of the displacement of what was initially a discourse about cultural development by one of industrial development. As well, the displacement paralleled the transition of institutionalization from the old institution embodied in the NFB to the new one that would be established with the Canadian Film Development Corporation.

At the official celebration of the NFB's twenty-fifth anniversary on 5 August 1964, Lamontagne repeated much of the substance of the 1956 speech he had written for then Prime Minister Louis St-Laurent. This, it will be recalled, was a rationale for the policy of state intervention in the domain of cultural production to redress the disequilibrium between Canada's economic growth and the poverty and isolation of Canadian cultural life. The anniversary was an occasion for bringing the same framework to bear upon the problem of feature film production.

In his 1964 speech, Lamontagne considered it 'essential ... that a country with a high standard of living like ours should try to create an atmosphere in which motion pictures, radio, television, the theatre and music will provide means of expression for creative Canadians, and sources of intellectual enrichment for the public at large.' Particularly 'in cultural matters, a country cannot live continually by borrowing its material from others. It must set up itself the institutions it needs.' The NFB was the institution through which 'we now have a place in the [international] film world ... [I]n one field of the arts at least, we have succeeded in doing something good.'[77]

The NFB's shorts were by no means a minor cinematic genre, but another film form, the feature-length film, had emerged; as a form of artistic creation, it 'presents a mode of expression that is both seductive ... and highly efficacious.'

It is in cinema today that ... we find [all] the great questions, the anguish, the problems, as well as the successes of man. A nation that does not have a feature film [capability] finds itself deprived of one of the most important [modern] means of expression.[78]

The problem was that 'we cannot be ... happy about the present state of the Canadian film industry.'

Unlike most other countries with similar problems and similar professional talents, we seem to have been unable to bring forth a film industry in Canada which could find its inspiration in a Canadian setting and produce and distribute a Canadian-made product to place alongside the production of the National Film Board.[79]

Accordingly, the function of the state was to create a film industry and the NFB was henceforth to be subordinated to that development, particularly to the extent that 'one of the functions of the NFB would be to assist ... in the development of a Canadian film industry.' While Lamontagne went on to announce the government's intention of asking Parliament for authority to establish a loan fund for the production of Canadian feature films of high quality, it was the tripartite involvement of government, the NFB, and industry in that development that he emphasized.[80]

Just over a year later, in a speech on 13 October 1965 to the Canadian Conference of the Arts, an arts policy lobby group, Lamontagne gave an account of the work and recommendations of the Interdepartmental Committee and 'a broad outline of the film policy which the federal government intends to implement ... to help this vital new industry.'[81]

He was candid about what had been concluded so far. Both the proposed Canadian Film Development Corporation 'and the producers which it will assist will be expected to work with and through established distributors to arrange for the widest possible distribution of the films in Canada and abroad.' While some countries imposed import controls to protect their domestic industry, the Canadian state preferred 'a reasonable share of the domestic and foreign markets through measures of encouragement and international co-operation.'

We can now hope to have the co-operation of American film companies in our effort to build a film industry in Canada. There are great advantages indeed in developing an industry which will cater to the North American market. We have developed ... recently successful techniques in sharing our markets in other areas for the greater good of Canadians and Americans alike. In the field of feature films, we have now a kind of common market which goes only one way. We must try to make it two ways.

As a result of this co-operation and these joint ventures which, we hope, will develop not only with American but also with French, British and other producers, we expect that Canadian films will have free access to foreign markets just as foreign films now have free access to the Canadian market.[82]

On the basis of the Interdepartmental Committee's final report, Lamontagne on 12 August 1965 recommended to Cabinet the establishment of a Canadian film development corporation. At the Cabinet committee meeting which considered film policy, 'some suspicion' was expressed as to 'how the National Film Board will be involved.' As Ernie Steele, Interdepartmental Committee member and under-secretary of state, said in a memorandum to Lamontagne about the meeting, 'it is important from the point of view of policy to create a clear distinction in the public mind' between the new Canadian Film Development Corporation and the NFB. The minister, Steele advised, 'might wish to [re]consider whether the lead [on CFDC legislation] should be given by Guy Roberge,' who had written to the Department of Justice about drafting the legislation for what would become the Canadian Film Development Corporation Act.[83] However, by the time the bill was formally introduced to the House of Commons on 20 June 1966, Lamontagne was out of office and Roberge too had resigned as government film commissioner to accept a posting in London with the Quebec government.[84]

With the act finally passed in February 1967, Michael Spencer, who became the first executive director for the CFDC when it was set up in February 1968, sent a memorandum to Steele: 'You know the Canadian Private Film Industry has always been a bit of a Cinderella – left at home to brush dusty Television Commercials and Industrial Films into the corner – while its glamorous sister the National Film Board goes to the ball and brings back all the international prizes.' But now, with the passage of the CFDC Act, development of Canadian feature films would be framed by 'a law to assist a Canadian film industry [into which] we tried to build ... the best we could find in other countries.' Spencer hoped that 'with our ten million dollars ... our ... Cinderella will expand into a $50,000,000 lusty starlet and start making her mark on Canadian screens.' The credit for Cinderella's transformation, however, rested with the NFB and with Roberge in particular:

On the whole ... the private producers owe much to the efforts which the NFB has made over the years on their behalf. It was this agency, after all, which suggested first that something should be done to build a feature industry in the private sector. It was under the chairmanship of Guy Roberge, the former Film Commissioner, that all the home-work was done which led to the creation of the Film Development Corporation.[85]

With the establishment of the CFDC, the task of severing the NFB from the economy of talk of the Canadian feature film was accomplished. Henceforth, Cinderella was on her own, left to develop the

Canadian feature as a private industry subject to the vicissitudes of the market place under the supervision of the administrative state. The following chapter considers whether there were alternative strategies and, if so, what they proposed.

6

Filmmakers, Critics, and the Problem of the Critical Voice

As was seen in the previous chapter, the development of a policy on feature films, in particular in the continental or transnational framework given to it by the discourse of the administrative state, was broadly consensual. It was a consensus, however, that was especially attentive to the views of the established producers and distributors. As well, as was evident in the two studies by francophones, Côté and Cadieux, commissioned by the Interdepartmental Committee, different conceptions of the role of the state were possible but they did not have a noticeable impact on either the committee's deliberations or its recommendations. One reason is that these notions would have necessitated a more extensive role for the state, which went against the logic of governmentality as delimitation, particularly in the expanded role that would have been given to a state agency such as the NFB. A related reason might be that alternative emphases stemmed from a different order of valuation in which the feature film derived its value more from 'cultural' than 'economic' characteristics. In this present chapter, this difference of emphasis in approaching feature films is examined to determine whether the value ascribed to the feature-style film elaborated by the direct filmmakers at the NFB might have formed the basis for alternative policies in feature film development. How that difference gained discursive form in Quebec will be looked at particularly closely. In short, the question of alternatives within the film industry to the commercial discourse that was institutionalized in the economy of talk about the Canadian feature is our concern here, although the term 'film industry' will be understood in a broad sense to include other developing sites of talk, such as film festivals and film criticism.

The Association Professionnelle des Cinéastes, 1963–4

Cadieux had reported to the Interdepartmental Committee that the film industry in Quebec was still at the stage of an unstable craft industry in which specialization of functions had not yet developed. This may have been so of the division of labour generally, but certain groups had at an early date developed specific organizational characteristics that reflected a process of professionalization. The most notable was the Association professionnelle des cinéastes, a professional association established in the spring 1963 as a result of the work of a provisional committee created in fall 1962 by seven francophone filmmakers at the NFB. Not only was the APC the first self-proclaimed 'truly cinematographic' association in Quebec, it went on to define its specificity as an association of French-speaking professionals within a branch of production in its statutes as 'the artistic creation of films.'[1] Although the APC would become increasingly conscious of itself as a corporate entity, the phase did not reflect a defensive corporatism. On the contrary, as Véronneau puts it:

Those involved brought to their activities wide-ranging perspectives; broad, generous, utopian ideals. They had a vision of their craft, of their professional status, of the significance of their art, and beyond their corporate objectives they aimed for something much larger, the establishment of a national cinematography that conceived of itself ... at that time ... as part of, and benefiting from, the support of the Canadian state.[2]

The membership of the APC rapidly grew by 1964 to just over one hundred persons, which represented, as its briefs noted, almost all the French-speaking filmmakers in Canada. Half of the members worked at the NFB; a majority of the members worked in the short-film form. The bulk of the APC's efforts, especially in that year, consisted in lobbying the state for the establishment of a feature film industry. This took the form of the production of four major briefs addressed alternatively, and often in identical language, to the Canadian or Quebec governments.[3] To the APC, it mattered less which state acted, as long as *the* state did so. As the APC's brief to the Quebec government in March 1964 put it, 'It is up to the state to plan the cinema industry in such a way that the film-maker can have freedom to create and to show his works to the public, otherwise all the speeches on the virtues of freedom will be only words thrown to the wind.'[4]

In certain respects, the APC briefs differed from the formulations we have encountered so far. Their briefs gave greater emphasis to 'the monopolistic structure of distribution and exhibition of [feature] films in Canada.'[5] For the industry, as a U.S.-controlled monopolistic structure, 'the prime motive in determining Canadian film programming is not necessarily to obtain a maximum profit for theatres in Canada ... it is to attain maximum profits for the American producers and distributors.'[6] It followed not only that 'this system is not interested in creating a Canadian competition' – the brief noted that, not surprisingly, '[w]e do not know of a single instance where the profits or credits amassed by the American distribution companies have been used to finance a Canadian film' – but also that 'the highly integrated character of the American film distribution [system] in Canada' produced 'tragic cultural consequences. Economic dependence in this field leads inevitably to a cultural colonialism' that was felt particularly acutely by 'Toronto producers.'[7] As a result, the increasing foreign ownership and control of the Canadian economy represented the 'most perplexing dilemna [sic] with which Canada is faced.'[8]

Unlike Spencer or Firestone, for whom the internationalization of feature film production provided not just a rationale for the establishment of a Canadian feature film industry but also the genres its films should emulate, the APC viewed the process more negatively. Internationalization of U.S. capital, as it was currently affecting European film production, only further compounded the problem. The March 1964 brief of the APC was titled 'Measures recommended by the Association professionnelle des cinéastes to the government of Canada to encourage the development of a feature film industry compatible with the country's economic and cultural interests,' and it outlined the 'vast international co-production system' that would likely be one of the 'unfortunate results' of the current American 'commercial offensive in the very heart of the European market':

It will almost be necessary for 'international' films to please the whole world. There will have to be a little of everything put in them. Subjects will have to be absolutely safe. Moral or political attitudes will have to be avoided. Stars from the four corners of the world will be used and they will often be unable even to understand one another. Voices will have to be dubbed in a multiplicity of foreign languages. The result will be hybrid works that no culture will be able to identify.[9]

Similarly, the establishment of Canadian feature-length cinematic production with American capital 'would ... bring with it Hollywood methods, a top-heavy super-structure patterned on the U.S. corporation, officialdom among technicians, the star system, high-pressure publicity, and the need to subject all films to the requirements of the American public.' For the APC, what distinguished the Canadian aspiration to making feature films – 'or at least [that of] its filmmakers' – was that it went against 'the winds of internationalization ... sweeping ... the western world.' Moreover, this defiant aspiration had paradoxically arisen in a country that did not have 'its own national film industry' and whose population 'falls short of 19 million' and, furthermore, was 'divided between two cultures and languages' and 'thinly scattered along the frontier which separates Canada from the colossus of our time.' In such a context, only the intervention of the state could provide the necessary measures required: 'The State must intervene.'[10]

For the APC, intervention by the state in the matter of the feature film could take two possible forms. One was that the 'government should just take over, *en bloc*, the fledgling Canadian cinema in order to put it on its feet.' But this would be tantamount to 'dabbling in totalitarianism,' since 'the actions that government takes are not intended to replace those of private investment but rather to open new fields of action and to increase its efficiency.'[11]

However, in Canada the cinema provided a particularly cogent example of a sector in which private industry had been unable to establish itself because of economic obstacles that it could not, by itself, overcome. These obstacles included too small an internal market, exhibition space that was controlled by foreign capital, the lack of Canadian risk capital, the absence of language barriers against competition by films from the United States, France, and Britain, and competition from television. In this context, the role of the state was to effectuate 'a new understanding between the public and private sectors of the economy,'[12] in particular, to limit the further extension of film production by the NFB and the CBC and to redirect resources towards the development of a competitive private industry. Such an industry, with the backing of economic measures undertaken by the state on its behalf, would then be better positioned to overcome competitively whatever obstacles remained.

Yet the discourse of the APC in 1964, despite greater emphasis on cinema's cultural characteristics,[13] and so on the feature film in particular as a dialogical communicative form, was substantially identical to that of emergent private sector in film production in Toronto. And with the one notable difference that the APC recommended a legislated minimum of 75 per cent ownership by Canadian capital of motion picture theatres in Canada, its policy recommendations were similar to those coming from Toronto as well. In substantial agreement as to the delimitative role of the state in the development of a Canadian, privately owned, commercially driven, feature film industry, the briefs prepared by the APC in 1964 were an integral part of the new private sector discourse to which the state responded and, after its own fashion, gave institutional form. Resistance within the Canadian industry was to the APC discourse on the feature film, not the other way around.

Resistance to the Feature within the Film Industry, 1964

Given their cohabitation with French Production, English-speaking filmmakers at the NFB could not but be affected by the ferment among their colleagues. Like them, they formed in December 1963 their own professional association of 'film craftsmen and artists,' the Society of Film Makers (SFM), an equivalent to the APC, 'that very dynamic and militant sister organization,' 'to bring some weight to bear on the development of the Canadian industry from the creative individual's point of view.'[14] With eighty-seven members by 1964, the great majority of whom worked at the NFB, the SFM also submitted a brief to the Interdepartmental Committee and later claimed to have been 'instrumental in aiding' both the drafting and the legislative passage of the CFDC Act. The SFM, by its emphasis on an *auteurist* cultural politics of creative individuality especially as it was manifested in the feature form, can be taken as the English-language equivalent to the APC in its discourse.[15]

The resistance such a discourse aroused within the English Production units at the Board is worth noting. That of management was perhaps predictably to be expected, though not sufficiently so as to be dismissed outright. Grant McLean, then director of English Production, in a June 1964 memorandum to Film Commissioner Guy Roberge, attributed the increasing preoccupation of the filmmakers with the development of a Canadian feature film industry to a generation gap on the one hand but also, as part of that gap, to a changing aesthetic that the NFB could only oppose. It had increasingly in recent years had found itself 'obliged to justify th[e] limitations' of filmmaking in the public service, 'particularly to the younger generation of film-makers':

That generation is inclined to the view, shared by the younger practitioners in all the arts, that the only restraints that are creatively relevant are those self-imposed by the artist himself and that all others are intolerable and destructive.[16]

While McLean felt the NFB had to live with these views, it also had to maintain '*firmly*' against them its own institutional aesthetic – 'namely that the discipline of public service is consonant with authentic film-making and ... can compare favourably with any other film-making experience, if not on economic grounds, then ... on creative and moral grounds.'[17] If this was unacceptable to filmmakers 'intent on making a name in the entertainment field, [they] should leave the Board rather than blithely attempting to ignore the fact that at the Board they are dealing with public funds.' It followed from this, McLean continued, 'that the Board does not have a major role to play in feature films.' And if it 'continue[d] to think in much larger terms regarding feature films (and I think this is the case with at least part of our French language production),' this could only end by weakening, if not destroying, its principal, documentary program. 'I believe also that the private sector will attack the Board's extensive development in this field and will succeed in getting us out of features – perhaps completely. But by that time we will have lost more than the right to make even the occasional feature.'[18]

McLean's position was shared in a lengthy statement three documentarians sent Roberge late in 1964. Entitled 'NFB 1964 ... Some Observations,' it was co-signed by Nick Balla, Ron Dick, and Dan Fraser, who acknowledged that while 'they seek to represent only themselves [consider that] ... they form a broad cross-section [of opinion] within the institution.'[19] What concerned them above all was that the 'NFB ... has increasingly come to be influenced by the reflections of a narrow circle of critics, ciné-club enthusiasts, festival committees and brother filmmakers – rather than by ... the average viewer.' There was 'a distinct danger of the NFB becoming oriented predominantly to the will and caprice of some of its film-makers, rather than to the needs of its audiences.' Not only was this growing tendency reflected in NFB films whose subject matter was 'increasingly dictated by the priorities of the film-maker's private aesthetic adventure,' but the organizational life of the institution itself was fragmenting 'into internal pressure groups, factional in character' and 'pretend[ing] to ... *consensus omnium*.' By advocating policies 'presented under the attractive and, in part, legitimate slogans of aesthetic and national[ist] idealism,' the factions were attempting 'to create an environment of total licence for the film-maker,' which not only distorted the past role of the NFB in Canadian society but risked 'to reduce the NFB ... to ... an art-factory ... in a narrowly parochial film-world.'[20]

Two recent developments were particularly alarming to the three authors of the statement. First, that the discourse of professional creativity went side by side with 'a touching solicitude for Private Industry.'

It is constantly emphasized that nothing that is contemplated will hurt or harm them and almost everything is intended to help them. They are to be stimulated and strengthened. In fact, there should also be a high degree of fluidity between the NFB staff and private industry.[21]

Second, that the insistence on the artistic creativity of the filmmaker was at the expense of a notion of 'audience.' Indeed, that the very concept of audience was to be sacrificed upon the altar of the boundless narcissism of the filmmaker. 'Audiences are not to be studied, served, worked with – they are to be led, and if they prove to be intractable, they are to be replaced by specialized groups who are in on the game.'[22] For the authors of 'NFB 1964 ... Some Observations' what, above everything, had characterized the NFB from its inception was 'a remarkable and close relationship with audiences.' This relationship was 'the foundation of our program, the source of our inspiration, the basis of our "raison d'être" ... our justification, our guide, our mentor.' It was what the discourse of creativity threatened to sever – by substituting 'manner' for 'matter,' by inverting the relationship between subject and expression to concentrate solely upon self-expression, 'genuine communication is lost, [and] ... coteries are exchanged for real audiences.'[23]

The English-Canadian debate over the discourse of creativity and its expressive form, the feature, took place in 1964 not only within the NFB, it also surfaced, briefly, within the film 'industry' in Toronto. The March–April issue of *Canadian Cinematography*, the magazine published monthly (in good years) by the Canadian Society of Cinematographers (CSC) since November 1961, included an unsigned article entitled 'Do We Expect Too Much Too Soon From the Film Industry.'[24]

For the writer, what reputation Canada possessed in filmmaking had been established by the NFB in the documentary and experimental fields. Outside the NFB, one or two directors had won recognition at international festivals, but their work could not be adequately judged until ('according to Truffault' [sic]) their third film. Beyond this, the 'national scene is made up primarily of television films and it is in this

field [that] we stand or fall as an industry.'[25] It was television production and the 'Madison Avenue oriented TV commercial' in particular
that constituted 'the foundation that makes up the industry.'

Is this level ... high enough from which to expect miracles? Are we expecting *too
much, too soon*, in dreaming of a feature industry? With the length and scope of
some television films now being made, are we downgrading them unjustly as
films, just because *they don't have* theatrical release? Perhaps all this talk ... is just
wishful thinking?[26]

In response, *Canadian Cinematography* published over the next two issues
the text of the speech given by APC president Guy L. Côté at the 9 May
1964 annual general meeting of the CSC in Toronto. The title the magazine
gave to the speech was 'Selling Job Must Be Done on Feature Films.'[27]
    Côté's half-hour speech reviewed recent developments, particularly
as seen from Montreal. His aim was to inform the CSC membership 'of
certain ideas that have been evolving and taking root.' If the notion of
'the feature film industry' evoked 'big finance ... huge investments ...
staggering sums of money,' then in Canada 'we have never *had* a film
industry.' The history of the Canadian feature 'is one of many hopes and
as many failures.' Côté summarily reviewed a 'history' that consisted of:
(1) exporting to Hollywood 'some of its most famous film people,' from
Marie Dressler to Jack Warner; (2) the Canadian Cooperation Project,
which 'sold the potential Canadian post-war film industry down the
river'; (3) French Canada's post-war 'Hollywood in Canada' features,
such as *Séraphin* (1949) and *La Petite Aurore* ... (1951); (4) sporadic
attempts to make features in Toronto between 1954 and 1960; and (5) the
shift back to Montreal with production by the students' association of
the Université de Montréal of *Seul ou avec d'autres* (1961), which marked
'the beginnings of a new era in the French-Canadian feature-length cinema.'[28] The importance of the latter film for Côté was entirely symbolic:
it had been made by committed 'young people,' not professionals; it had
been made in 'a new, free style of film-making,' using inexpensive
equipment; and it had been produced not to make money for investors
'but out of a strong, inner compulsion to create a feature length motion
picture.' The same compulsion, he continued, had led to Claude Jutra's
À tout prendre (1963) and Pierre Patry's *Trouble-fête* (1964); 'the dogged
determination of the film-makers themselves, who accepted considerable risk and personal sacrifice to complete their respective movies.'
    However, the production by the NFB of *Drylanders* (1963) and *Pour la*

suite du monde (1963) 'marked a turning point in Film Board policy, and indeed in the history of Canadian cinema,' just as Crawley's production of *Amenita Pestilensis* (1963) was 'a symbol of the risks which Canadian entrepreneurs must run in order to make films under present conditions.' This new stage of Canadian film history could be termed 'professionalization' given that Côté included the creation of the APC as a manifestation of professionalization. The work of the organization had taken its characteristic orientation as a result of circumstances in which two members 'had the opportunity of studying ... the structure of the film industry':

What we discovered literally horrified us. The facts, accessible to all, may be old hat to some of you. But these facts grieved and angered us, for we could not understand how any country aspiring to ... cultural integrity, could tolerate ... the situations we came across.[29]

Indignation, then, formed much of the basis for the briefs the APC produced in 1964 'to bring our case before the public.' The APC's findings were two-fold: that Canada was one of the few industrial countries in the world with no film legislation to support a national feature film industry, and that film distribution and exploitation in Canada was controlled by foreign interests and constituted a structure with all the characteristics of a monopoly. But the broader conclusion the APC came to was 'that public taste is something which can be formed, or deformed, according to circumstances.'[30] And in Canada, public taste had clearly been deformed by the American monopoly in feature distribution and exhibition: 'We have called the result cultural colonialism ... hard words, I know, and they will not please those who, in this country, earn their living in the film business. But, possibly, they too are victims of the same economic stranglehold' and of its tragic cultural consequences:

Nations have died ... from the moment that they began to dream the dreams of others, from the moment that they have proved themselves unable to create their own mythology ... We, in Canada, have often been ashamed of our own mythology, of our own domestic heroes, and we have been quick to mimic the fads of other lands. And so, with the cinema, we have lived by proxy, for the last sixty years.[31]

Despite Côté's undeniable eloquence, resistance to the discourse on feature films illustrated both the force and the limitations of the emerging economy of talk. Within the NFB, the discourse, which was perceived as the spectre of an increasingly vocal and vindictive private industry, was felt to threaten the very foundations of the institution. The self-protective retreat of the NFB from features, except on an occasional basis, thus entailed the abandonment of attempted further defining the Canadian feature film to an 'industry' discourse in which the feature film and the film industry itself were inseparably confused and intertwined. Even to question the *reality* of either the Canadian feature or the Canadian 'industry' was sufficient to unleash a torrent of abuse that underscored not just the fragility of the discourse, but its source in a murky dream of overcoming cultural frustration and wounded nationalist self-esteem.[32] However problematic, this discourse was increasingly and exclusively the preserve of a private 'industry' that was constituted as an alliance between small groups of film professionals in Montreal and Toronto, two groups bridged to some extent by the APC discourse on the feature film. Forged by its common hostility to the NFB and by its dependence on the state for the measures that would permit the 'industry' to develop further, the Montreal–Toronto alliance also constituted the other's Other. This allowed the APC (or more precisely Montreal francophone filmmakers already implicated in the beginnings of a complex, separatist process of differentiation in which, as Robert Boissonnault would put it in the early 1970s, 'one [wa]s not longer just a filmmaker; one [wa]s a Quebec film-maker'[33]) to construct Toronto as the site of the nightmare of cultural annihilation that gave its own discursive efforts their meaning as a dream to be realized. Conversely, for the Toronto 'industry' the APC discourse meant Quebec was the model of cultural authenticity that it required as the 'real' of its own obscure dream of participation in the institutions of an imaginary national culture. As we have seen, the singularity of the English Canadian 'industry' was its drive to seek institutionalization in the form of an English-language 'economistic' discourse of export-led development. Its exactly symmetrical French-language equivalent was to seek institutionalization of a 'cultural' discourse that differentiated Québécois from Canadian cinema within the economy of talk of the Canadian feature as the 'différance' (in Derrida's sense) of the same. It is this cultural difference and its institutional sites that are examined next.

Cultural 'Difference': Institutions of Display and Canon Formation, 1960–6

The critical acclaim earned outside of Canada by the NFB's French-speaking filmmakers of direct shorts, such as Michel Brault and Claude Jutra for their presentation of *Les Raquetteurs* (1958; directed by Michel Brault and Gilles Groulx) at the Flaherty Seminar at the University of California in Los Angeles in 1958, led to two crucial discoveries. First, that life for a francophone filmmaker was possible outside the NFB. Claude Fournier, one of the first filmmakers to make the jump to private industry, leaving the NFB in 1961 to join Drew Associates in New York and returning to Montreal in 1963 to found his own production company, said this was nothing short of a 'revelation.'

For the first time in our lives, we found ourselves in a different cinematic world from that of the Film Board. We encountered ... Americans, Frenchmen, Indians, all of whom were grappling with the problems of a private film industry. They did not live in a uterus as we did ... All those people ... were guys ... who had to make do, they weren't suckled on the breasts of government. This was extremely revelatory to us.[34]

From this revelation it was but a step to the conclusion that to remain at the NFB was to be neither fully a filmmaker – nor fully a man! – because one was choosing, in the Sartrian sense, to remain unfree. This conclusion would be made explicit most notably in the film criticism of Jean Pierre Lefebvre.[34]

Even more important was the second revelation to be derived from greater contact with international peers, namely that *their* opinion mattered more than that of the illiterates at home. Again, as Claude Fournier stated it, 'to position oneself on the same level as the natives is not much of an accomplishment. But to relate to one's peers in an international business, that at least allows for a more accurate perspective ... [In such a perspective] we find that if we are not the worst in the world, neither are we the best.'[36]

That such positive critical feedback fed the creative ferment of the young direct *cinéastes* was undeniable. As Jacques Bobet recalls:

They were in seventh heaven. I can still see Michel Brault coming out of an editing room, dancing – he must have been then 26 or 27 – another masterpiece! Every film we did made us feel that it was a masterpiece. And I remember that Pierre Juneau organized the first international meeting of filmmakers here [at the Board]: there was Truffaut, Kobayashi, many people, the whole French New Wave was there. And in the middle of it someone said, 'Let's go see Gilles Groulx's film,' the test print was ready of *Golden Gloves* [1961]. Everyone rushed off, Truffaut, Polanski, the whole gang. And it was just impossible, it was too beautiful – at one stroke Canadian film had come to life. From one day to the next. André Bazin of the *Cahiers du cinéma* sent me a little note through somebody, saying: 'That's it! You've got it! You've done it!' Six months before, while he was passing through, Bazin had asked me, 'Are you [the NFB] still doing the same insignificant shit?'[37]

But, as the three signatories of 'NFB 1964 ... Some Observations,' had feared, the growing influence of the 'narrow circle of critics, ciné-club enthusiasts, festival committees and brother film-makers' entailed not only an inordinate say in the critical direction of the inflation from shorts to feature-length productions.[38] More importantly, it risked substituting coteries of selected admirers for the possibility of engaging with audiences. This was one thing when limited to the confines of the NFB; it became another, as of 1960, with the institution of the Montreal International Film Festival (MIFF).

Initially non-competitive, the MIFF, whose organizers included Pierre Juneau, Fernand Cadieux, and Guy L. Côté, hoped to influence local distributor and exhibitor programming taste towards a more internationally oriented cinema. Building on the proliferation of ciné-clubs (some 345 in Quebec between 1960 and 1965), the festival, according to Yves Lever, 'served as the most official and the most efficient agent of the internationalization of our distribution [exchanges], the commercial ones as much as the alternative ones.'[39] Passing through Montreal on his way to New York, the French film critic Louis Marcorelles, soon to champion in *Le Monde* the Quebec direct feature, notably the films of Pierre Perrault, would write of his '[s]urprise ... to find European films projected ... in a gigantic, very American cinema ... More surprise on hearing everybody speaking an often incomprehensible French,' although nobody except for Claude Jutra at the time was seriously thinking of making features yet.[40]

By screening films that had just been awarded prizes at the principal European festivals, the Montreal festival, historian Yves Lever observes, privileged particularly the star filmmakers of the moment, such as Godard, Antonioni, Satyajit Ray, Truffaut, and Kaneto Shindo. But also by its orientation towards the most dynamic forms of emerging new cinema – the French New Wave, the young national cinemas of Eastern Europe – the festival helped foster the emergence locally of similarly oriented productions, especially after 1963.[41]

As of the fall of 1963 a competitive Festival du cinéma canadien was established within the structures of the larger Festival. It became the principal site for public exhibition of the feature-length productions of the Quebec direct filmmakers. The grand prize in 1963 went to Jutra's À tout prendre and a special jury prize went to the other entry in the feature category that year, Pour la suite du monde by Brault and Perrault. In 1964 the grand prize went to Gilles Groulx's Le Chat dans le sac, and a mention was given to Patry's Trouble-fête; in 1965 Gilles Carle's La Vie heureuse de Léopold Z received the grand prize and a mention went to Larry Kent's Sweet Substitute (1964) for 'translating the documentary form to fiction.' A member of the SFM who wistfully wished English-speaking Montrealers displayed the same enthusiasm, recalled that the Festival du film canadien

is patronised mainly by French Canadians, usually young, and they turn out to applaud their folk heroes. In fact the Festival now has its claque which is at its most vociferous and uncritical during the showing of Canadian films. Was the audience at 'La Neige a fondu etc.' showing ... critical acumen ... when they cheered the film at last year's Festival? Or were they applauding it because it presented the voices and faces of ... 'their' film, something to be proud of because it had been made 'chez nous'? Imagine the scene, on that closing night of the 1964 Festival, had the jury chosen 'Nobody Waved Goodbye' as Best Film, instead of 'Le Chat dans le sac.'[42]

Yet such prize-givings, Lever writes, masked an illusion. While 'very satisfying for the egos of filmmakers who grew proud from the admiration of their peers ... they masked [their] ongoing divorce from both the general public and some of the local critics.'[43] The elitism and marginality of a new French Canadian feature cinema was proudly valorized by film critic Patrick Straram when, in 1964, the festival opted to attract more ordinary movie-going audiences in response to criticism in Canadian newspapers. Reporting in the prestigious Cahiers du cinéma on the fifth Montreal festival of August 1964, Straram situated the importance of the festival precisely in its elitist role in the context of 'a backward feudal society.'[44] By its avant-garde function within such a society, the festival had made it possible, 'in Montreal at least,' to see current, quality films. The very creation of the festival in 1960 came about because 'the elite had alerted public opinion [and] put pressure on the government and the monopolies that have distorted cinema here for fifty years.' But by modifying its raison d'être 'on the fallacious pretext of satisfying a larger audience, the Festival has considerably disappointed the "milieu" of professionals and cinephiles without which it would never have come into being in the first place and without which it can no longer exist,' having been turned into 'a depressing ... circus.'[45]

On the other hand, this same elitism made possible in 1964 the beginnings of the *canonization* of Canadian cinema as a filmmakers' medium. That year an organizing committee under the patronage of the four associations of filmmakers, the APC, the SFM, the DGC, and the CSC, began working on what became the first retrospective of Canadian cinema as a whole. Held initially from September 1966 to April 1967 at the NFB under the auspices of the Cinémathèque canadienne,[46] and with the institutional support of the NFB, the Centennial Commission, the Canada Council, the Greater Montreal Arts Council, and the CBC, the 'Canadian Film – Past and Present' retrospective consisted of sixty programs of public screenings of some 250 Canadian films.

Beyond the public propaganda purpose of exposing Canadian films to larger, non-paying audiences, and in the context of the 1967 Centennial celebrations, the retrospective, particularly in the quantity of printed material it generated,[47] provided a unique insight into the discourse of the attempt by professional creators to essentialize Canadian cinema. Essentialism, in the view of the retrospective organizing committee in a booklet published subsequently, was necessary because of the need to 'look at our production as a whole rather than as a collection of side issues.'[48] Oddly, this meant approaching the history of film in Canada in the form of a chronology: discrete and disconnected events marked in a linear continuum of time that began out of the blue in 1898 when Massey-Harris 'introduce[d] the world's first sponsored film, shot on an Ontario farm by the Edison Studios.' As the organizers recognized, there were alternative approaches; films could have been classified 'according to schools of thought or artistic styles,' for example, but these were rejected by the committee because it wanted to foreground a continuum of 'creativity.' Thus, the companion to a chronological approach emphasizing continuity was a list of 'one hundred essential films of Canadian cinema.' The list was determined by the unanimous vote by an unspecified number of 'consultants' the committee drew on in order to establish a consensual, evaluative basis for the list.[49] Finally, and consistent with the discourse of creativity, instead of 'learned essays by critics, social scientists, or even politicians,' the committee included in a retrospective booklet, *How to Make or Not to Make a Canadian Film*, nineteen articles by filmmakers.

Most striking perhaps was the diversity of views of the filmmakers themselves, particularly as regarded the production of feature films. Claude Fournier, for one, remarked sagely that since Canadian film-makers were completely divorced from the dominant economic systems and their production imperatives, what they sought most of all was the 'institutionalization of their craft.'[50] On the other hand, for Patrick Watson 'the difficult part *has* been done and the remaining components of the solution are simple': injection of a little money, more resolute collusion for production and distribution between the CBC and the NFB, and 'a firm governmental stand' with commercial distributors. But, for Jacques Godbout the 'establishment of a feature film industry is a mirage in our desert,' and it was a mirage in large part because of the contradictory discourses of 'film-makers demanding a film industry while repudiating one of its essential elements, the script':

For the last five years they have all been clamouring and working for a traditional feature film industry, in which they will never participate themselves and against which, in fact, they have made their films. It is an avant-garde determined to create its own rear-garde – which is a very ironic situation indeed.[51]

Irony, not surprisingly, was the predominant tone taken by the film-makers. The articles covered a wide range: clever codifications of the practices of the generation of young (aged twenty-five to thirty) direct feature filmmakers by Guy Glover, who in his 'How To Make A Canadian Film' writes that 'there are no bad films; only bad audiences'; Claude Jutra, who in 'How Not To Make A Canadian Film' counsels filmmakers to '[c]hoose an uncommercial subject so intimate as to be indecent, uninteresting, futile'; George Roberston's wistful account of scripting *Waiting for Caroline* (1967), a particularly disastrous attempt by CBC and NFB to co-produce a feature; a hard-nosed piece on the economics of low budget feature production by cinematographer Reginald Morris; and a poetic statement by Pierre Perrault, as well as a denunciation of filmmaking technique by Jean Pierre Lefebvre.

The fourth entry in the booklet, 'Speaking of Canadian Cinema,' by Denys Arcand, consisted of three brief paragraphs that bluntly addressed all the talk about Canadian cinema:[52]

Too much is written about our cinema. Basically, we don't have cinema, we have film literature ... [I]f you were to collect all the articles, dossiers, briefs, etc. that have already been written on our films, it would take longer to read than to look at the films themselves ... [T]here is something unwholesome about it all.

To be sure, Arcand was specifically referring to the immediate, festering context of mid-1960s Quebec culture: 'let us admit, so as not to be too hard on the filmmakers, that wholesomeness is rare in Quebec.' But within that context, he was also commenting about the discourse of creativity:

Nowadays, we can scarcely read a newspaper or magazine without having some fashionable film-maker in an endless interview deliver himself of the creative tortures he goes through ... his reproaching us for having misunderstood his film ... his going on about being a victim ... his announcing to us his magnificent projects, all the while insisting ... on our unquestioning love ... [and] boundless admiration.[53]

Arcand, in other words, was addressing the institution of film criticism, and in particular its dissemination of what Steve Neale has termed an art cinema discourse. For Neale, such a discourse possesses a politically conservative function as 'a mechanism of discrimination ... producing and sustaining a division within the field of cinema overall.' Such a discourse does not challenge the economic, ideological, or aesthetic bases of the cinematic institution; on the contrary, it functions 'so as to carve out a space, a sector *within* it, one which can be inhabited, so to speak, by national industries and national film-makers whose existence would otherwise be threatened by the domination of Hollywood.'[54]

Canadian Film Criticism and the Problem of Voice in the 1950s and 1960s

The irony in the Canadian context is that this art cinema discourse had to be elaborated by the filmmakers themselves, outside the institutions of criticism. As historian Peter Morris has pointed out, what characterized English Canadian film criticism in mainstream newspapers and magazines in the post-war years was that 'most English-Canadian critics should have been so negative towards Canadian films in the '60s.'[55] For Morris, what is of interest to the historian is why film critics on the one hand and filmmakers on the other expressed such opposite sensibilities at the identical time:

Indeed, one could argue that critics and filmmakers stood at radically opposite poles not only of what made cinema 'art,' but also on what kind of cinema Canadian cinema should be. Out of that opposition, it was, arguably, the critics' views that prevailed and encouraged government policies and filmmaking itself towards the industrialized model of production that dominated Canadian film.[56]

The polarity between filmmakers and film critics meant that 'English-Canadian critics ... found it impossible to discuss a Canadian film in the same terms as a French, Italian or Czechoslovakian film.' The divergence stemmed from different critical assumptions as to what constituted the 'art' of cinema. But more importantly, what for Morris made such a polarity distinctive of English Canadian criticism was his own assumption that, in their inability to discuss Canadian films on the same terms as other 'national cinemas,' 'they stood in clear contrast to their colleagues in Quebec.'[57]

In Quebec just as much as in English Canada, as was noted above, the 'critical' discovery of the direct feature filmmakers by a largely European film criticism through the Montreal festival masked the divorce of the filmmakers not only from the general public but also from the local institutions of film criticism. Yet a content analysis of one of the two principal Quebec film publications of the 1960s, *Objectif*, published from 1960 to 1967, reveals that, with respect to Canadian cinema (the phrase 'cinéma québécois' only became generalized after 1968),

not only is it given less coverage than foreign cinema, but it is generally classified in a separate category, the object of special or documentary issues. Paradoxically, when the journal did cover Canadian film, the tone of the discussion was *less critical* and more anecdotal. As if one did not take terribly seriously what was being said.[58]

And of Catholic film criticism in Quebec (the second major film publication in the 1960s was *Séquences*, which started in 1955), it will have to suffice to recall its predominant tendency 'to use the feature film as an occasion for apologetics,' as a 1962 ciné-club committee put it in a brief to the Parent Commission on education.[59]

There were, to be sure, exceptions. The film criticism of Jean Pierre Lefebvre in *Objectif* remained at times outstanding both for its candour and for the sharpness of its assessments. For instance, on *Seul ou avec d'autres* he wrote: 'a student gag that dragged Michel Brault and Gilles Groulx into the worst [forms] of amateurism'; on Gilles Carle: 'an authentic *metteur en scène*, the first of the French Unit'; and on *À tout prendre*: 'what might have been an extraordinary film is instead a botched, lazy, weak and oh-so pretentious work.'[60] But, as Lever remarks, 'how can Pierre Perrault go on reading [a film critic like] Alain Pontaut of *Le Devoir*, who does not overly appreciate his filmic work, whereas Louis Marcorelles of *Le Monde* sees in it the summum of film art? How can Gilles Groulx take seriously the reservations of *Séquences* [about his films] when Cannes offers him a "triumph"?'[61]

The predominant negativity, then, of film criticism vis-à-vis an emergent Canadian cinema was less, as Morris argues, distinctive of English Canadian criticism in particular, than of the institutions of criticism in Canada, especially newspapers. As he remarks, 'the critics wanted Canadian films to be *better* than Hollywood films yet also wanted them produced according to the industrialized model of Hollywood and to be as popular as a Hollywood box-office hit.' This, he argues, rested on assumptions about cinema that 'the filmmakers ... and the younger critics did not share ... Their nationalism was more assertive ... Film for them demanded more than the recycling of plots and characters and themes ... Nor ... was film primarily an industrialized mass medium. Such rules as there were might be broken.'[62]

As Morris also points out, 'Canadian filmmakers of the '60s, both in Quebec and English Canada, embraced wholeheartedly the notion of "voice,"' but the problem was less one of voice than of the difficulties in its articulation. One of the assumptions that crystallized around *la politique des auteurs* debate, especially in the *Cahiers du cinéma*, was the belief that to understand a film one had to understand the 'voice' of its author rather than the ostensible subject matter, and, in addition, the correlative extension of this idea, especially as of the 1960s, which was that the form of cinemas of collective authorship was based on national, cultural, and other differences. It was, therefore, 'a cinema, one might say, based on "voice."'[63]

In the Canadian context, however, the notion of a cinema based on a distinctive inflection of voice challenged the long-standing assumption shared not just by film critics but also, as we have seen, by the state that film was above all an international 'language.' Furthermore, the question of voice became enormously problematic within a Canadian cinema profoundly marked by the complex, aesthetic strategies of the self-protective renunciation of language. And this renunciation had been a discernible practice, as Feldman has suggestively argued,[64] in various disguises since the films of the 1920s. It may be worth emphasizing once again that the collapse of an indigenous Canadian film 'industry' and its subsequent displacement from feature film making was related to its inability, in part for lack of capital, to negotiate the transition to the technology of voice. And *the* voice that was institutionalized as of 1939 within the NFB was the English-speaking voice of the state as a discourse of power in a cinema which, as Jean Pierre Lefebvre puts it emphatically, was '*the* property of the state, *its* political, social, and cultural mode of communication by which *to act* on Canadians and Quebecers.'[65] This was *the* voice which, furthermore, maintained institutional control over its filmmakers, through scripts among other means.

The institutional rupture that the direct film represented, it should also be remembered, was a *rejection of voice*, not only of the institutional voice-over, but also, with far more ominous consequences, of voice as a technique of written expression, filmic or otherwise. As Jacques Bobet puts it, as delicately as possible:

There was something else that was fundamental. Many of the filmmakers then and I've got to say it in quotes so as not to insult anybody – were culturally 'illiterate.' If there was one thing they had in common, except for people like Jacques Godbout, it was that they loathed writing. They hated writing and most of them couldn't write. A guy like Gilles Carle always had a good pen, Claude Fournier too, Godbout obviously; but for the others to have to take a pen and write half-a-page, they'd first get down on their knees: 'Listen, you write it, I'll sign it.' They hated the idea.[66]

This could be – and was, for a while – turned to advantage in making, for instance, *Le Chat dans le sac* and *La Vie heureuse de Léopold Z*, for which 'a lot of footage was shot, and with very little attempt at scripting, the absolute minimum scribbled on a desk corner, just enough to get the approval of an English production head [Grant McLean] who himself couldn't read French.' Bobet adds: 'So it wasn't really as stupid as it may seem ... The fact remains that the first two feature films we made in French ... were decided upon on the basis of a page-and-a-half synopsis.'[67]

On the other hand, this abhorrence of writing all too readily became a crippling limitation. The issue became particularly poignant when the Quebec direct films (first shorts, then features) were discovered by film critics in France. What struck them as significant about this new cinema was precisely the paradox of its renunciation of voice, its inability to speak, that betrayed a desperate hunger for the 'word.' As Dominique Noguez put it, Quebec cinema was 'a cinema of autodidacts,' 'a bulimia of the eye that compensates for, that *translates* provisionally [into images] the hunger for speech of the new Quebec.'[68] This was the very opposite of a cinema based on voice; rather, it was a cinema *aspiring* to voice via a 'language' of the eyes, an *inarticulate* visual 'language' whose subtleties of meaning required decoding by the specialized techniques of criticism, hermeneutics, or semiology. For, as cultural historian Sande Cohen perceptively remarks, 'the visual channel is independent of language unless reduced by the latter through intellectual/cognitive operations to verbal signals ... the most "showable" telling is also *the most silent* about how it shows.'[69] In Noguez's own subtle, yet highly eloquent, interpretation:

I would see here a fundamental, indeed existential, inclination: it's as if in a country where the possibility of speaking one's own language and of living in harmony with it is disputed daily by the facts of everyday life, in a country rustling with the invasive and thunderous sounds of another language, in a country that is *parasitized* linguistically, it's as if these people to whom speech is *prohibited* had decided to speak nevertheless, even by remaining silent, by beginning to act by means of the image in order to win the right to shout out their own or any words. As a matter of fact, *Les Raquetteurs* (1958) by Brault and Groulx, the first important Québécois film, is almost a silent film, but it is a film that says a lot by its silence: it is ... a way of shouting without opening one's mouth.[70]

It is hardly surprising, then, that for the critics at the *Cahiers du cinéma* what was seductive about such a cinema was its extreme alterity – the cinematic equivalent to the ontological status of the proletariat in Marxist metaphysics. Within the material cornucopia of an undifferentiated North and South America there had suddenly developed 'a cinema of dispossession,' of almost unspeakable alienation. Like Brazil's Cinema Novo, which the journal discovered at the same time and with which Quebec's cinema of dispossession shared, 'aside from its novelty, the fact of having emerged from a desert, of having come out of nowhere,' there was conferred on this cinema of the ineffable the onerous ontological burden 'of finding itself at the birth of a struggle that is not only artistic, but also concerns society, ethics, civilization itself: and this is [the birth of] revolutionary cinema.'[71]

Of course, it might be objected that Pierre Perrault's films, by their prolix discursiveness, contradict the fundamental mutism of this emergent cinema's inarticulate desire for speech.[72] But Perrault is not the exception to the discourse of creativity; on the contrary, he is, in many respects, the outstanding manipulator of its limitations. For, as David Clandfield intelligently points out, Perrault works by the 'creation of a hierarchy of discourse [which] has passed from the autochthonous control of the local communities or individuals into the hands of the privileged individual or elite of individuals who have access to the technology of print and film.' Notwithstanding the bonds of solidarity Perrault forged in the acquisition of the ethnographic data that inform his writings and films, the continuity of cultural transmission has been radically ruptured by his recourse to modern communications technology. Perrault's work is still firmly inscribed within the manipulation of codes of expression controlled by distant elites.[73]

A cinema based on voice? Rather, the Canadian feature-length cinema that emerged was a cinema based on voice's disarticulation within a discourse of power. This is, as Franklin puts it, an atrophied form of discourse, a *pre-discourse* reduced to its most elementary forms of expression. Such a pre-discourse corresponds to discursive conditions in which power oppresses but does not have to justify itself. Rather, the pre-discourse simply imposes itself as already legitimized by the intimacy it entertains with the earthly powers of which it represents the absolute will and arbitrariness. 'This is a moment without words in which the sacred that envelops power is its own sufficient speech; its eloquence is its silence. Concision, allusiveness are the style of such speech. Its laconicism guarantees the mystery that power feeds upon – it is also its irony.'[74]

Conclusion

It was, as Jacques Godbout observed, a most ironic situation indeed. And particularly so by 1967, centenary of Canada's difficult existence as a communicative community. That year, in which the Canadian Film Development Corporation Act passed into law, was especially ironic for the makers of feature films who had emerged from within institutions that had no place for them. In the process, they had invented an aesthetic of uncoded, refractory visual experience which, outside the films they had made, also had no place. But because they could not put that experience into words, and with few exceptions neither could the established critics, the entire enterprise was to be handed over to the controlling gaze of the more experienced outside observer. Ironically, too, the filmmakers themselves had all the while clamoured for the establishment of a traditional film industry that would only reinstitute the tyranny of the conventional script from which, a decade earlier, they had broken free. They were caught – and well caught – within the paradoxes and contradictions not only of their own discourse, such as it was, but also within an economy of talk, in whose articulation they had played a major part, without even realizing how much of a part. But by 1967–8 that economy had achieved its full extension. *All* the conflictual, consensual, and paradoxical terms within which the Canadian feature film would be discussed and rediscussed for the next twenty-five years were in position, only thereafter to repeat themselves over and over again, endlessly.

7

Discoursing about Canadian Cinema

The preceding chapters have described in some detail the formation of the economy of talk within which the Canadian feature film emerged in the 1950s and early 1960s as an object of policy discourse. A verbal universe was established in which a Canadian film industry was conceived, argued, and legislated, and then put into public circulation. However, rather than the processes of development being the differentiation of respective objects of talk – say, the feature film as an aesthetic object or the industry as an economic object in both its Canadian and Québécois variants – what emerged was a still largely undifferentiated discursive field across which were dispersed conflations of ongoing ideological polemics that were reinforced by the environing social and political organization of Canada as a cultural duality. Not only, then, did dualism bear upon the contextual organizing structures of the film industry, it applied as well to the political economy of language, particularly in the politicization of language in Quebec in the 1960s and 1970s from an instrument of communication to a symbol of membership in an increasingly self-conscious collectivity that by the 1970s distinguished itself from the rest of Canada by the use of the descriptor 'québécois.' Feature films emerged in the Canadian context diachronically in not one but two languages at a time of rising contestation and renegotiation of the political, economic, and cultural relations between Canada's two founding language groups. In this sense, the Canadian feature film was not only an overdetermined and fetishized object, but additionally the designator of a range of still unresolved constitutional, ideological, and cultural contestations that attempted to define the historical sedimentation of existentially contrived values and norms in search of an institutional dénouement. The economy of talk that had appeared by the late 1960s was itself dualistic in the sense of being both discourse and economy; its emergence meant the possibility of more 'talk' about an object-field. This did not, and could not, guarantee that the resulting talk would be particularly coherent.

Nevertheless, developments after the 1960s readily lend themselves to periodization by decade. If the 1960s witnessed an 'economy' in which a commercial discourse was the predominant form of talk, the first half of the 1970s saw the furtherance of a counter-discourse in which the Canadian feature was mainly conceived of in art cinema terms. (As we saw in chapters 1 and 2, the late 1970s was the period in which academic talk about Canadian cinema took shape.) In part, the counter-discourse was a reaction to the perceived failures in the attempt to develop a commercial cinema. But because the art cinema discourse was internally divided among marginal academics as well as by the increasingly vocal claim to différance articulated by Quebec filmmakers, it remained itself marginal to the dominant discourse of commerciality. In turn, the latter discourse was to be substantially reinforced in the mid-1970s by two crucial developments: (1) the entry of the Quebec state in 1975 into the economy of talk but, like the federal state before it, as the coordinator of a replicated economy of talk about the cinema under *its* control; and (2) also as of 1975 the 'industrialization' of feature film capitalization that resulted from modifications to federal income tax legislation (the capital cost allowance). If the result of the latter was to lead to an extraordinary boom in Canadian feature film production (from one to two features annually in 1963 to close to one hundred by the late 1970s), that boom collapsed by the early 1980s largely as a result of greed, the ineptitude of producers, and incompetent policies.

The failure of strategies based on production support then led to an increased focus on mechanisms to support distribution, although it was also clear that these could not include, contrary to the demands of nationalist factions, the nationalization of American-owned distribution facilities or, though there were serious discussions in this direction, the nationalization of the principal foreign-owned exhibition chain.[1] Instead, 'nationalization' occurred by other means. Following the collapse of private capitalization, the 1980s witnessed the incorporation of the *one* publicly owned channel of distribution of audiovisual production, the CBC, into the economy of talk surrounding the production of no longer just feature films, but now of an entirely new discursive entity, the 'film and video industry.' The transition from feature films to telefilms was formalized by the renaming of the CFDC in 1982 to Telefilm Canada. It should be emphasized, the dominant discourse remained throughout a commercial discourse that was constant in its demands for the creation of a private industry oriented towards world markets.[2]

In order to emphasize that we are dealing here with a general failure of policy formation, this concluding chapter, therefore, offers further illustrations of the logic of governmentality in the context of Canadian film policy development, instead of a discussion, one that would be insufficient in any case, on this or that particularity of a problem of policy. The first instance concerns the continuing debate within the Canadian state over the orientation of feature film policy into the mid-1970s, and a second the commission headed by the ubiquitous Pierre Juneau that re-examined in 1996 the mandates of federal agencies in film and broadcasting production with a view to projecting these into the 21st century. The study will conclude with some reflections on the relations between academic and policy knowledge, particularly in contexts of increased transnationalization of information flows.

1976: 'Why Does the Minister Want a Film Industry in Canada?'

The formation of the economy of talk with the passage of the act creating the CFDC in 1967 meant that a space had been established for discourse about 'the Canadian feature' and that at least the principal terms for talk about it had been elaborated. As filmmaker Jacques Godbout said of the establishment of the CFDC: 'If it works out, thank God, and if it doesn't at least we will know who to blame. Now there's someone we can present our case to.'[3] Thus, as of early 1968 when a Board of Directors was appointed and the administrative structures were finally set up, there was henceforth an institutionalized space, within the state, for the further production of discourse about 'the Canadian feature.' In the CFDC's first three years, production of Canadian-made feature-length films increased by 300 per cent,[4] although the basis of production in private industry remained anarchic, as companies 'came and went, merged, vanished, or rose from their own ashes according to the vicissitudes of production contracts' in an incessant, confusing movement in which 'nobody can keep track of what's really going on.'[5]

Outside this space and the discursive organs of the 'industry' immediately concerned, the economy of talk in what filmmaker Patrick Watson termed 'the demi-monde of filmmaking in Canada'[6] of the Canadian feature remained marginal relative to the availability of public space for the circulation of discourse. Within that space the mainstream press remained sceptical as to the ability of Canadian film producers to overcome internal divisions and external obstacles.[7] In English Canada particularly, the CBC blithely continued to be a negligible factor in the circulation of Canadian film production: for instance, of the two thousand feature films CBLT-TV (CBC Toronto) aired between 1967 and 1974, only two were Canadian-made.[8] And what was the case for the mainstream popular media was equally the case for the media of education. As Peter Harcourt has observed, educators who began to turn their attention to the study of Canadian film fared no better. In the rapidly expanding system of higher education that extended as of the mid-1960s to such new disciplines as media studies, 'the people responsible for setting up film programs in Canadian universities failed ... not just in relationship to Canadian film but also in relationship to the particularities of the Canadian situation.'[9]

Within the federal state, however, and in particular, in Pierre Trudeau's Ottawa beginning in late 1968, the universe was unfolding as it should. In regard to film this took the form of attempting to elaborate what was termed a 'global film policy,' consisting of restructuring the entire public sector involvement in the 'industry' to make it possible for the private sector 'to take the place of government agencies as the dominant force in Canadian film production.'[10] But, other than various 'interim measures,' the so-called global film policy had still not been worked out by the fall of 1976. And, as then Secretary of State John Roberts said in a memorandum to Cabinet, he did not expect it would be sorted out before the end of the decade and not be implemented before the early 1980s.[11] His timing was fairly accurate, although the global film policy itself never saw the light of day. Instead, in May 1984 Francis Fox, the federal minister of communications, released an insubstantial booklet ponderously entitled *The National Film and Video Policy* that described itself as 'a synchronized policy response' to the new technologies of the emerging information society. Warning of 'a cultural crisis of undetermined proportions,' which was also 'an economic challenge of unmeasured magnitude,' the booklet said the crisis could be met by a 'financially confident and economically viable Canadian film and video industry.'[12]

The attempt to formulate policy to provide a developmental *telos* by which to coordinate public-sector cultural production agencies (e.g., NFB, CBC, Canada Council, and, as of 1968, CFDC) had begun in the Department of the Secretary of State under Lamontagne. In 1965 special assistant Gordon Sheppard, formerly a CBC producer and Toronto independent filmmaker who had been secretary of the Interdepartmental Committee on the Possible Development of Canadian Feature Film Production, had concluded in a special report that the 'Government must decide whether it wants Canada to have a strong public film industry or a strong private film industry. We can't have both.'[13] Sheppard's report was shelved in the ministerial transition from Lamontagne to LaMarsh.[14] Between 1967 and 1971, the Department of the Secretary of State commissioned four more studies specifically of the Canadian film industry.[15] However, they did not produce the expected findings, prompting Wendy Porteous, director of the Arts and Culture Branch of the department, to write the assistant under-secretary of state exasperatedly seeking ministerial direction:

Is the report to reflect merely the status of the industry as it presently is? Or should it reflect an industry which is desirable for Canada? What is the nature of the industry which the Minister would like to see develop in Canada? Is it big-time commercial motion picture making? Is it film making for culture's sake? Is it film making for the sake of social animation between ethnic and other Canadian cultural groups? In other words, why does the Minister want a film-making industry in Canada! To what end? To involve whom? To go where?[16]

The economic situation of the film 'industry' was reviewed in 1971 and again in 1972; subsequently, committees were again established to study and report upon various aspects of it. Between 1974 and 1977 numerous briefs and proposals by the private film sector advocated that the government take steps to strengthen the private film industry The review process culminated in the April 1976 report of the Bureau of Management Consulting, the research division of the department, which had signalled at the outset of its consultations in July 1975 that the 'government is entertaining a possible change of direction on film matters.' While the specific purpose of the report was to analyse the composition of the labour force within the film industry, its principal recommendation was that the private sector replace government agencies as the 'dominant force' in the production of Canadian features.[17] The recommendation was all the more remarkable given the discussion in the report of the 'amorphous' composition of an 'industry' whose outstanding industrial trait was that it was 'unique ... in its dependence on government intervention.'[18]

The difficulty was, as the policy director in the department, Warren Langford, wrote in a memorandum to the minister, that *'a feature film industry did not exist'* until the establishment of the CFDC in 1968. And still, after eight years of feature film production and of investments of $21 million by the CFDC, and with annual losses averaging 86 per cent over the period, 'it remains questionable whether we have yet achieved what can properly be termed a feature film industry.'[19]

Langford was not the only technocrat to come to the conclusion that there was something amiss about the Canadian film industry. At the NFB, Film Commissioner André Lamy concluded, summarizing the Board's own decade-long contribution to 'global film policy,' that the entire enterprise was founded upon a catastrophic illusion: 'With the exception of the governmental economic systems ... the problem of the film industry in Canada is that it is precisely not an industry in the classical sense of the term. *Any policy solution based on the belief that such an industry exists will only lead to catastrophic results.'*[20]

The Paper World of the Administrative State

Undeterred by any of this uncertainty, the work of policy formation pressed on. By the mid-1970s the administrative state faced four options in terms of its continued involvement in attempting to bring the film industry into being: (1) the status quo; (2) dissolution; (3) retreat by transferring 'industry' responsibility either to the Department of Industry, Trade, and Commerce or to the NFB); or (4) an expansion of its role. After an agonizing consideration of the alternatives, the only valid option was to expand further the role of the CFDC.

The discussion of the dissolution option most clearly established the polarities of the governmentality within which the economy of talk of Canadian feature production 'worked,' and would continue to do so. On the one hand, around the pole of the governmental fiction of a futurable industry (probably best stated a decade later by then communications minister Flora MacDonald: 'Although our ultimate goal is the development of a Canadian film culture, it is obvious this goal will be best assured if the industry has a sound industrial base'[21]), discourse could form that was ostensibly economic and in which the economic problems of the industry could be identified in reasonably coherent terms. Thus Langford, for instance, identified these terms as follows:

The Canadian film industry is relatively young; it is seriously under-financed; it is regarded as high risk by investors and by banks and other lending institutions; it is trying to cope with foreign domination of the distribution system; it has to compete with a heavy volume of imported products laid down in Canada at prices which the Canadian filmmaker has difficulty in matching; it is lacking in business acumen and management expertise compared with its foreign competition; it has difficulty producing scripts that give reasonable assurance of box-office success; it has the task of trying to instil a Canadian spirit or character into its films without, at the same time, risking their universal appeal and acceptance in markets outside Canada; and it is trying to counterbalance deeply ingrained preferences of Canadians for American or other foreign films.[22]

Such an 'economic' discourse, preoccupied with establishing the film 'industry' on more solid footing within the capitalist economy, generated countless studies from within the planning instances of the state apparatus, federal as well as provincial. On the other hand, and as one proceeded from planning to the executive, the polarities within governmentality reversed themselves, as intra-state governmentalization turned into state-to-state *raison d'état*. The resulting shift, from an economistic discourse to a discourse of dependency, only reaffirmed the interior dependency of the film industry on the state with the exterior dependency of the Canadian state, in particular vis-à-vis the United States. The resulting discourse of dependency took the explicit form of the policy of 'moral suasion,' the long-standing conviction of the Canadian state since at least the mid-1940s that a rational, negotiated agreement between it and the American film industry could be arrived at with respect to the production and distribution problems of Canadian films. As an instrument of governance, the use of suasion, as political scientists Stanbury and Fulton remark, has been 'largely overlooked' by policy analysts, precisely because 'suasion offers enormous opportunities for deception, reversibility, redirection and selective use of information. These characteristics make suasion ... an attractive governing instrument from the point of view of politicians.'[23] From the point of view of the economy of talk of the Canadian feature, structured around the dualities within governmentality, the result was an intensification of the unreality of its discursive circulation within a paper world.

In this paper world, the only reality-principle was that the talk itself continued to grow – but as discourse more than economy. As Langford, who was only the latest voice in a chorus going back to Firestone, put it: 'The dearth of reliable facts and figures has been one of the main obstacles in the way of formulating ... policy on film.'[24] In the paper world, the

numbers could be changed at the stroke of a key – they did not mean anything much anyway. Thus a 20 August 1976 memorandum by Roberts to
Cabinet announced that 'some $60 million, by way of rental of films, is
siphoned out of the country.'[25] Two weeks later, in a memorandum on
7 September, the figure had mysteriously shrunk by half: '$30 million or
more is siphoned out of the country through rentals.'[26] And this insouci-
ance in regard to the most elementary facts about the putative industry
on whose behalf policy was being formulated was chronic. By the late
1980s Flora MacDonald, although claiming in the House of Commons
that the government in which she was minister of communications was
finally 'doing what no [Canadian] government has done in the last 50
years: setting the stage for a viable, dynamic, profitable Canadian film
industry,' did not even know the correct number of U.S.-owned theatre
chains dominating theatrical exhibition in Canada.[27]

1996: Return to the *Massey Report*

As a point of comparison, the report, 'Making Our Voices Heard: Canadian Broadcasting and Film for the 21st Century,' produced in 1996 by
the committee formed to review the mandates of the CBC, the NFB, and
Telefilm Canada and chaired by Pierre Juneau, came full circle, back to
the premises of the *Massey Report*. After leaving the NFB in the 1960s
Juneau had gone on to establish and then chair the CRTC, Canada's
broadcasting regulatory agency, and he subsequently became deputy
minister of the federal Department of Communications and later president of the CBC.

In its chapters on Telefilm Canada, the committee report observed
that of the three federal institutions they were asked to examine, 'Telefilm Canada is the least visible and the least understood.' Despite the
lack of knowledge surrounding Telefilm's workings, the report opined
that its significance as 'a cultural corporation' over the last ten years had
been 'nothing short of dramatic,' and would likely become even more
important given the onus of Information Highway policies to contribute
to 'the fragile Canadian cultural dialogue within our borders.'[28]

How Telefilm worked and what it did was little known because 'it
plays its role in a quiet way.' Rapidly reviewing the 'decades of frustration' that had preceded the setting up of the CFDC 'to foster a feature
film industry in Canada,' the report reviewed as well the limited financial resources available to the CFDC and to Telefilm until the establishment of the Broadcast Fund in 1983, which Telefilm administered.

Initially allocated a minimum $60 million a year, by 1989–90 Telefilm had become the 'second largest cultural institution' after the CBC.

The Government decided to underwrite the cost and the risks to a degree that would permit Canadian television productions to be financed domestically – and to give Canadian producers and broadcasters a chance to get around the economic disincentives of the marketplace. It was a leap of faith, but it succeeded to a remarkable degree.[29]

If the 'phenomenal expansion' of the independent television industry in Canada had grown to some $923 million by 1994, it was because the existence of the national broadcaster could offset the limitations of a domestic market in film that remained American-controlled. Even so, the report said of the increase in independent television production, in film and TV co-production, and 'made for export' products, that while economically important as a source of employment, 'very little of it ha[d] much to with reflecting Canada.' In fact, the 'resources intended to be used to develop a distinctive Canadian cinema' had inexplicably been over the years diverted away from that objective and Telefilm's successes had to a great extent been responsible for this industrial *détournement*.

Originally, the CFDC was given both an industrial and a cultural mandate: there was virtually no Canadian film industry at the time and assistance was needed to develop one ... Twenty-seven years later, not only is there a powerful independent production industry in Canada, but more and more of the production it carries no longer requires direct Government assistance.[30]

In other words, Telefilm had so successfully accomplished the tasks of *industrial* development that there was now an even greater need for this 'extraordinarly important instrument' to turn its energies back to the initial tasks of *cultural* development: 'the need has never been greater for all of Telefilm's resources to be used to assist films and television programs ... made primarily for Canada; that reflect the creativity of Canadian script-writers, directors and performers; that explore Canadian realities, tell Canadian stories, and address Canadian interests and needs.'[31]

As one disgruntled journalist put it in one example of the largely negative press response to the report: 'We are told that we need "Canadian culture" to protect ourselves from the wicked Americans, a claim which only proves the old adage: patriotism is the last refuge of a bureaucrat.'[32]

Grammars of Exchange in the Transition to Capitalism

As has been seen throughout this study, governmentality is a process of the limitless practices of administrative rationality. Even though the stated objective of Canadian policy beginning in the 1950s was always clothed in the discourse of cultural development, the result saw some three decades of attempts to establish an industrial production entity, a Canadian film industry, and later, given its distribution problems, a film *and* a television industry. The objective of creating a domestic market for local audiovisual production apparently having been reached (to the limits of the pump-priming capacities of the state), the discourse of administrative rationality, as exemplified in the two examples twenty years apart in this chapter, simply swerves unblinkingly back to its own initial premises in search of further practices to colonize. From the perspective of the discourses of administrative rationality, the point is not the object of policy, it is that the 'talk' of policy be able to continue unabated.

The problem, however, with such a strategy of discursive continuity is that the process, precisely because it consists of practices, is not *just* talk; certain things do get accomplished: institutions are created, and some people even *believe* in the talk and attempt to take it seriously. But, however much the enterprise of establishing a Canadian film industry may have been cloaked in the language of cultural development, it was in practice an attempt to effectuate the beginnings of a complex process of communicative transformation. In other words, what was being attempted, although it was never articulated as such, was nothing less than negotiating the passage from *the pre-capitalist artisanal economy of film production*, as it had developed either within or on the margins of the audiovisual production institutions of the state, to greater or lesser degrees of integration into the circuits of exchange of the international capitalist economy of audiovisual production or, as it has also been termed, entertainment software.

As signified by the feature film (an extraordinarily complex entity with intricate backlinks to the monopolization of capital that required a highly developed and differentiated division of labour), effecting such a transition in the Canadian context was bound to be wrenching and complicated. Furthermore, and contrary to the overly optimistic projections of its planners, this was not something that could be accomplished rapidly; it would involve decades to work itself out.

Given these complexities, it was not incorrect in and of itself to envisage the development of a Canadian film industry as an exporting industry. In the still early phases of what would later come to be termed 'cultural industries,' the Canadian attempt might even have been evidence of a prescient anticipation of the increasingly global scale of economic or cultural production as the twentieth century drew to a close. Firestone's proposal in the mid-1960s to integrate the Canadian film production economy into the continental economy not only mirrored agreements between Canada and the United States in shared control of continental waterways and automobile production; it also anticipated many aspects of the Free-Trade Agreement of 1989 and the later North American Free-Trade Agreement. The irony here is that, when the time did finally come, Canada's cultural industries would be exempted from the agreements, as a concession to the continuity of the discourse of cultural development. But if we look at the Canadian feature films produced in the 1960s in particular, *even* those with American distribution in Canada did not come close to recovering their costs in the Canadian or in any other market.[33] There was, in other words, and quite contrary to the discourse on cultural development's fears of the risks of imminent contamination from mass culture, a very long way to go before Canadian cinema seriously risked the taint of commodification.

The emergence of the Canadian feature film in the 1950s and 1960s was thus part of a complex transformation of practices in the transition to an increasingly globalized economy of generalized cultural exchange. The transition would also be accompanied by conjunctural transformations in the realms of subjectivity, of aesthetic practices, and of their discursive articulation. In this context, one might want to take another look at the consistency of the Canadian discourses on national identity. Not in the form of their self-definition as 'essential' dimensions of statecraft, but rather as experimental forms of 'currency,' that is, as nodes of sociability that attempt as part of the larger processes of transformation to establish a civil economy of symbolic exchange. Such an approach would make it possible to understand better the variety of shifting grammars (or knowledge effects) that come into play in the transition to commodity exchange in the political economies of culture. We will examine one such example, by way of conclusion.

Policy Knowledge versus Academic Knowledge

This study has repeatedly emphasized the extent to which understanding Canadian film history, and the emergence of the feature film in particular, has pitted different configurations of knowledge against one another. On the one hand, the considerable role played throughout this study by state secrecy (not to call it state ignorance) as concerns fundamental data with respect to the Canadian film industry has strongly been stressed, as have the often ludicrous misconceptions of basic facts that played key roles in the making of policy decisions. On the other hand, the repeated difficulties faced either by scholars in attempting to obtain basic economic information from the institutions of the state, or even by the state itself to establish adequate mechanisms of film industry data collection, have also been emphasized. In the face of these difficulties, Canadian scholarship in particular has dealt with these problems by a pronounced tendency to idealize its object of study, which has been costly because it dissimulated the extent to which the emergence of the Canadian feature was primarily conceived as an economic affair, however bizarre the underlying notions of 'economy.' Furthermore, because Canadian film scholarship restricted the study of Canadian cinema to predictable topics, and thus avoided messy entanglements with the real implications of Canada sharing the continent with the United States in so many fields, including those of knowledge, it has closed itself off to the study of 'safe' areas only.

The French sociologist Henri Lefebvre, in making the argument for new modes of intellectual production resulting from the increasing globalization of capitalist economies, has termed one such mode of intellectual production 'the state mode of production.'[34] In his perspective the national state, given the globalization of the modern state, finds itself increasingly reduced to 'policing a national territory.'[35] In doing so the state mode of production is distinguished by a specific articulation of knowledge:

State knowledge – that is, knowledge at the service of power, intermingled with the exercise of power – does not consist in the recognition of contradictions in economic or social life. It ignores them; it denies them ... State knowledge proceeds by a reductive process, at the limit by a process of [the] destruction [of knowledge].[36]

This study has shown the decisive role that state knowledge, or governmentality, has played in the emergence of Canadian feature film policy. As Richard Gaskins has argued, the powerful discursive strategy of 'arguments-from-ignorance' plays a crucial, but largely unheralded, role in contemporary public debates, either in public policy or within the academy, that stems in part from certain endemic features resulting from the divisions of intellectual labour within late modern culture.[37] Making public policy on the basis of arguments-from-ignorance is not beneficial for either policy, policy-makers, or those on the receiving end of policies. Conversely, the adoption of similar discursive strategies by scholars is neither a credit to scholarship nor helpful to knowledge. The present work has, it is hoped, contributed towards reorienting both policy and scholarship in the study of Canadian film history and cultural policies. After all, as Gertrude Stein once put it, history teaches that history teaches.

Notes

Introduction

1 Susan Sontag, 'The Decay of Cinema,' *New York Times Magazine*, 25 Feb. 1996; see also Seth Feldman, 'What Was Cinema?,' *Canadian Journal of Film Studies* 5, no. 1 (Spring 1996), 3–22.
2 Feldman, 'What Was Cinema?,' 8.
3 See D.J. Turner, *Canadian Feature Film Index 1913–1985* (Ottawa: Public Archives of Canada 1987).

1: Problems of Writing Canadian Film History

1 See especially James Curran and Vincent Porter, eds., *British Cinema History* (London: Weidenfeld & Nicolson 1983); D. Petrie, ed., *New Questions of British Cinema* (London: British Film Institute 1992); Pierre Sorlin, *European Cinemas, European Societies* (New York and London: Routledge 1991); Dana Polan, *Power and Paranoia: History, Narrative and the American Cinema 1940–1950* (New York: Columbia University Press 1987); Thomas Elsaesser, *The New German Cinema, a History* (London: BFI 1989); François Garçon, *De Blum à Pétain: cinéma et société française 1936–1947* (Paris: Cerf 1984); Robert C. Allen and Douglas Gomery, *Film History: Theory and Practice* (New York: Knopf 1985); Michèle Lagny, *De l'histoire du cinéma: méthodes historiques et histoire du cinéma* (Paris: A. Collin 1992); Zuzana M. Pick, *The New Latin American Cinema: A Continental Project* (Austin: University of Texas Press 1993); and Alberto Ruy Sanchez, *Mitologia de un ciné en crisis* (Mexico City: La Red de Jonas 1981).
2 Society for Cinema Studies, 'Cinema(s) in Canada' (call for papers for May 1997 annual conference, n.d.).

3 See Peter Harcourt, 'The Education We Need: Canadian Film Studies and Canadian Film,' *Cinema Canada* 150 (1988), 19–26.

4 See Peter Morris, *Canadian Feature Films, 1913–1940* (Ottawa: Canadian Film Institute 1970).

5 See Seth Feldman and Joyce Nelson, eds., *The Canadian Film Reader* (Toronto: Peter Martin Associates 1977); Peter Harcourt, 'Introduction: The Invisible Cinema,' *Cine-Tracts* (Spring–Summer 1978), 48–9; Piers Handling and Pierre Véronneau, eds., *Self Portrait: Essays on the Canadian and Quebec Cinema* (Ottawa: Canadian Film Institute 1980).

6 See Peter Morris, *Embattled Shadows: A History of Canadian Cinema 1895–1939* (Montreal and Kingston: McGill-Queen's University Press 1978).

7 See, for example, Dudley Andrew, *The Major Film Theories* (New York: Oxford University Press 1976), and *Concepts in Film Theory* (New York: Oxford University Press 1984). For a powerful critique of the theoretical moment in film, see Noel Carroll, *Mystifying Movies: Fads and Fallacies in Contemporary Film Theory* (New York: Columbia University Press 1985).

8 See Carl Berger, *The Writing of Canadian History: Aspects of English-Canadian Historical Writing, 1900–1970* (Toronto: Oxford University Press 1976); and Carl F. Klink, ed., *Literary History of Canada*, vol. 3 (Toronto: University of Toronto Press 1976), esp. 'Canadian History,' 63–83.

9 Handling and Véronneau, eds., *Self Portrait*, viii.

10 Ibid., xii–xiii.

11 Feldman and Nelson, eds., *The Canadian Film Reader*, vii–ix.

12 Ibid., emphasis added.

13 That the cinema and its study is 'an idealistic phenomenon' is very clearly articulated by Feldman's Martin Walsh Lecture given in 1996 to the annual meeting of the Film Studies Association of Canada. The lecture offers an interesting perspective on the underlying assumptions that motivated the beginnings of film scholarship in Canada, with the benefit of twenty years of hindsight. See Feldman, 'What Was Cinema?'

14 The point is powerfully made in Bart Testa's two-part 1994 review of recent Canadian film scholarship. See his 'In Grierson's Shadow,' and 'The Escape From Docu-Drama,' in *Literary Review of Canada* (November 1994), 9–12, and (December 1994), 17–22, respectively.

15 See the so-called 'Cinema We Need' debate in Douglas Fetherling, ed., *Documents in Canadian Film* (Peterborough: Broadview Press 1988), 260–336. The remark is by Professor Testa.

16 See Peter Harcourt, '1964: The Beginning of a Beginning,' in Handling and Véronneau, *Self-Portrait*, 64–76.

17 See, for example, Ina Bertrand and Diane Collins, *Government and Film in*

Australia (Sydney: Currency 1981). See also Michael Dorland, 'Policy Rhetorics of an Imaginary Cinema: The Discursive Economy of the Emergence of the Australian and the Canadian Feature Film,' in Albert Moran, ed., *Film Policy: International, National and Regional Perspectives* (London and New York: Routledge 1996), 114–27.

18 Graeme Turner, '"It Works For Me": British Cultural Studies, Australian Cultural Studies, Australian Film,' in Lawrence Grossberg et al., eds., *Cultural Studies* (Routledge: New York and London 1992), 640–50; see also his *National Fictions: Literature, Film and the Construction of Australian Narrative* (Sydney: Allen and Unwin 1986).

19 Susan Dermody and Elizabeth Jacka, *The Screening of Australia: Anatomy of a Film Industry* (Sydney: Currency 1987), 140.

20 Dermody and Jacka, *The Screening of Australia: Anatomy of a National Cinema* (Sydney: Currency 1988), 37.

21 Stephen Crofts, 'Reconceptualizing National Cinema/s,' *Quarterly Review of Film and Video* 14, no. 3 (1993), 49–67.

22 See, for example, Robert Fothergill's classic enumeration of some of these themes in 'Coward, Bully, or Clown: The Dream-Life of a Younger Brother,' in Feldman and Nelson, *The Canadian Film Reader*, 234–50, or more recently, Peter Harcourt, 'The Canadian Nation – an Unfinished Text,' *Canadian Journal of Film Studies* 2, nos. 2–3 (1993), 5–26, and in the same issue Christine Ramsay, 'Canadian Narrative Cinema from the Margins: "The Nation" and Masculinity in *Goin' Down The Road*,' 27–49.

23 Dermody and Jacka, *The Screening of Australia* (1988).

24 See among others Andrew Higson, 'The Concept of National Cinema,' *Screen* 30, no. 4 (Autumn 1987), 36–47. The studies published by Dermody and Jacka in 1987 and 1988 of Australian national cinema remain a model of critical analysis of the difficulties of such a conceptualization.

25 Crofts, 'Reconceptualizing National Cinema/s,' 63.

26 Royal Commission on National Development in the Arts, Letters, and Sciences, *Report* (Ottawa: King's Printer 1951), hereafter *Massey Report*.

27 See for example, Charles Backhouse, *The Canadian Government Motion Picture Bureau, 1917–1941* (Ottawa: Canadian Film Institute 1974); Mary O. Hill, *Canada's Salesman to the World: The Department of Trade and Commerce, 1852–1939* (Montreal and Kingston: McGill-Queen's University Press 1977); Morris, *Embattled Shadows*; Gary Evans, *John Grierson and the National Film Board: The Politics of Wartime Propaganda* (Toronto: University of Toronto Press 1984).

28 Gary Evans has produced an authorized history of the National Film Board in the post-war period. See his *In the National Interest: A Chronicle of the*

National Film Board of Canada from 1949 to 1989 (Toronto: University of Toronto Press 1991).

29 See Joyce Nelson, *The Colonized Eye: Rethinking the Grierson Legend* (Toronto: Between the Lines 1988), for a polemical rendition of some of these problems. For a more nuanced, scholarly account, see Peter Morris, 'Backwards to the Future: John Grierson's Film Policy for Canada,' in Gene Walz, ed., *Flashback: People and Institutions in Canadian Film History* (Montreal: Mediatexte 1986), 17–36. See also J.L. Granatstein, *How Britain's Weakness Forced Canada into the Arms of the United States* (Toronto: University of Toronto Press 1989); Reg Whitaker and Greg Marcuse, *Cold War Canada: The Making of a National Insecurity State, 1945–1957* (Toronto: University of Toronto Press 1994). For the British context, see Margaret Dickinson and Sarah Street, *Cinema and State* (London: British Film Institute 1985.

30 Dermody and Jacka, *The Screening of Australia* (1987), 26, emphasis added.

31 'Report of the Subcommittee of the Interdepartmental Committee on the Possible Development of a Canadian Film Industry' (24 Feb. 1964), 1, a copy of which is held by the Cinémathèque québécoise in Montreal.

32 Or, in his own words, 'la même petite merde.' Related to the author by NFB producer Jacques Bobet.

33 The best historical account produced to date of the North Atlantic feature film and policy triangle is Ian K. Jarvie, *Hollywood's Overseas Campaign: The North Atlantic Movie Trade 1920–1950* (Cambridge, Eng.: Cambridge University Press 1992).

34 *Massey Report*, 50. See also the discussion in Ted Magder, *Canada's Hollywood: The Canadian State and Feature Films* (Toronto: University of Toronto Press 1993), 81–5. The most thorough scholarly account of the Massey Commission is provided by Paul Litt, *The Muses, the Masses, and the Massey Commission* (Toronto: University of Toronto Press 1992).

35 For claims that Canada was being overwhelmed by 'a vast and disproportionate amount of [cultural] material coming from a single alien source' and that although '[w]e are now spending millions to maintain a national independence which would be nothing but an empty shell without a vigorous and distinctive cultural life,' '[w]e must not be blind ... to the very present danger of permanent dependence,' see *Massey Report*, 18.

36 Ibid., 59; Magder, *Canada's Hollywood*, 84.

37 *Massey Report*, 42.

38 Ibid., 283–4. For the full background, see Marc Raboy, *Missed Opportunities: The Story of Canada's Broadcasting Policy* (Montreal and Kingston: McGill-Queen's University Press 1990), especially 95–108 dealing with the Massey Commission.

39 Raboy, *Missed Opportunities*, 98, emphasis added.
40 André J. Bélanger, 'Les Idéologies politiques dans les années 50,' in Jean-François Léonard, ed., *Georges-Émile Lapalme* (Sillery: Presses de l'Université du Québec 1988), 121–32.
41 Pierre Véronneau, 'Résistance et affirmation: la production francophone à l'ONF, 1939–1964,' PhD dissertation, Université du Québec à Montréal, 1987.
42 See Michel Brunet, *La Présence anglaise et les Canadiens* (Montreal: Beauchemin 1964), 113–66.
43 Gérard Laurence, 'Le Début des affaires publiques à la télévision québécoise,' *Revue d'histoire de l'Amérique française* 36, no. 2 (1982), 215–39; and Véronneau, 'Résistance et affirmation.'
44 See Michael Dorland, ed., *The Cultural Industries in Canada: Policies, Problems and Prospects* (Toronto: Lorimer 1996), especially Michael Dorland, 'Cultural Industries and the Canadian Experience: Reflections on the Emergence of a Field,' 347–65, and Kevin Dowler, 'The Cultural Industries Policy Apparatus,' 328–46.
45 See Ted Magder, 'A "Featureless" Film Policy: Culture and the Canadian State,' *Studies in Political Economy*, 16 (1985).

2: The Canadian State and the Problem of Knowledge Formation

1 Jakob Burckhardt, *The Civilization of the Renaissance in Italy* (New York: New American Library 1960), part 1.
2 The term is that of Canadian philosopher George Grant in his contribution to one of the Massey Commission's background studies. See *Royal Commission Studies: A Selection of Essays Prepared for the Royal Commission on National Development in the Arts, Letters and Sciences* (Ottawa: King's Printer 1951), 119–34.
3 See their *The Shaping of Quebec Politics and Society: Colonialism, Power and the Transition to Capitalism in the 19th Century* (Washington: Crane Russak 1992), especially Chapter 3 on 'The Theory and Practice of *Ancien Régime* Domination,' 65–98.
4 See Philip Resnick, *The Masks of Proteus: Canadian Reflections on the State* (Montreal and Kingston: McGill-Queen's University Press 1990), 152.
5 See especially Graham Burchell, Colin Gordon, and Peter Miller, eds., *The Foucault Effect: Studies in Governmentality* (Chicago: University of Chicago Press 1991), and more recently Andrew Barry, Thomas Osborne, and Nikolas Rose, eds., *Foucault and Political Reason: Liberalism, Neo-Liberalism, and Rationalities of Government* (Chicago: University of Chicago Press 1996).
6 See for example, Burchell et al., *The Foucault Effect*; also M. Foucault, *Résumé des cours 1970–1982* (Paris: Julliard 1989).

7 Foucault, *Résumé*, 99, 101.
8 See Martin Allor and Michelle Gagnon, *L'État de culture: généalogie discursive des politiques culturelles québécoises* (Montreal: GRECC and Concordia University 1994), 27–34.
9 See Michael Dorland, '"The Expected Tradition": Innis, State Rationality and the Governmentalization of Communication,' *Topia* 1, no. 1 (Spring 1997), 1–16.
10 See Allan Smith, *Canada – An American Nation? Essays on Continentalism, Identity and the Canadian Frame of Mind* (Montreal and Kingston: McGill-Queen's University Press 1994), 57–8, emphasis added.
11 See Paul Audley, *Canada's Cultural Industries: Broadcasting, Publishing, Records, and Film* (Toronto: Canadian Institute for Economic Policy and Lorimer 1983).
12 See Morris, *Embattled Shadows*, 238. Because the book was out of print, McGill-Queen's reprinted it in the early 1990s, but for reasons of economy the text remains unchanged from the first edition.
13 Ibid.
14 In subsequent essays Morris has begun a powerful rethinking of the premises of early Canadian film historical studies. See especially his 'Backwards to the Future: John Grierson's Film Policy for Canada,' in Gene Walz, ed., *Flashback: People and Institutions in Canadian Film History* (Montreal: Mediatexte 1986), 17–36, and his 'Rethinking Grierson: The Ideology of John Grierson,' in P. Véronneau et al., *Dialogue: cinéma canadien et québécois* (Montreal: Éditions Médiatexte and La Cinémathèque québécoise 1987).
15 Morris, *Embattled Shadows*, 238–42. Here he is drawing heavily upon the then considerable influence of literary critics such as Margaret Atwood in *Survival* (Toronto: Anansi 1972), itself powerfully beholden to Northrop Frye's *The Bush Garden: Essay in the Canadian Imagination* (Toronto: Anansi 1971).
16 For example, Gaile McGregor, *The Wacousta Syndrome: Explorations in the Canadian Langscape* (Toronto: University of Toronto Press 1985).
17 Yvan Lamonde and Pierre-François Hébert, *Le Cinéma au Québec: essai de statistique historique* (Quebec: Institut de recherche sur la culture 1981), 132.
18 Véronneau, *Résistance et affirmation*, 128.
19 The claim was made by the late film critic Patrick Straram in a short-lived film journal. See his 'Fragments/citations à propos d'un génocide,' *Cinécrits* 3 (n.d.), 37–40.
20 See, for example, the special issue of the French journal *CinémAction*, edited by Louise Carrière et al., 'Aujourd'hui le cinéma québecois' 40 (1986); Fernand Dansereau, 'Le Cinéma québécois: un cinéma colonisé,' *Cinéma/Québec* 3 (1974), 9–10, 81–3; Pierre Maheu, 'L'ONF ou un cinéma québécois,'

Parti pris 7 (April 1964), 2–5. More generally, see Yves Lever, *Histoire générale du cinéma au québécois* (Montreal: Boréal 1988).

21 See, for example, Jacques Bobet, 'Cinéma si,' *Liberté* 8, no. 2 (1966), and, in the same issue, his 'Lettre ouverte au commissaire du gouvernement,' 104–11. See also Véronneau, 'Résistance et affirmation,' 49–53.

22 See Leo Panitch, ed., *The Canadian State: Political Economy and Political Power* (Toronto: University of Toronto Press 1977); Gordon Laxer, 'The Political Economy of Aborted Development: The Canadian Case,' in Robert J. Brym, ed., *The Structure of the Canadian Capitalist Class* (Toronto: Garamond 1985), 67–102; Glen Williams, *Not For Export: The Case of Canada's Arrested Industrialization* (Toronto: McClelland and Stewart 1986).

23 For a brief account, see for example Robert J. Brym and Bonnie J. Fox, *From Culture to Power: The Sociology of English Canada* (Toronto: Oxford University Press 1989).

24 Dallas Smythe, *Dependency Road: Communications, Capitalism, Consciousness and Canada* (Norwood, N.J.: Ablex Publishing 1981). It is significant and indeed perhaps illustrative of the problem he was analysing that Smythe was unable to find a Canadian publisher for this book.

25 Ibid., xi.

26 Ibid., 270.

27 See for example, ibid., 159–60.

28 Ibid., xii–xiii.

29 Ibid., xii, 51.

30 Manjunath Pendakur, *Canadian Dreams & American Control: The Political Economy of the Canadian Feature Film Industry* (Garamond Press: Toronto 1990). Pendakur's study compares interestingly with Paul Audley's more nationalistic approach in *Canada's Cultural Industries*.

31 Ibid., 32–4.

32 Ibid., 39.

33 Ibid., 42–4.

34 Ibid., 276.

35 Gordon Laxer, 'The Schizophrenic Character of Canadian Political Economy,' *Canadian Review of Sociology and Anthropology* 26, no. 1 (February 1989), 178–92; and, in a similar vein, Michal Y. Bodemann, 'Elitism, Fragility and Commoditism: Three Themes in the Canadian Sociological Mythology,' in S.D. Berkowitz, ed., *Models and Myths in Canadian Sociology* (Toronto: Butterworths 1984), 210–28.

36 Magder, *Canada's Hollywood*, published by the University of Toronto Press as part of a series of studies entitled 'The State and Economic Life,' whose general editors were political economists Mel Watkins and Leo Panitch.

37 Ibid., 4.
38 Ibid., 17–18.
39 Jarvie, *Hollywood's Overseas Campaign*, 12, 41, 45.
40 Ibid., 41–2.
41 Ibid., 27, 98–9.
42 Ibid., 27.
43 Richard Collins, 'The Metaphor of Dependency and Canadian Comunications: The Legacy of Harold Innis,' *Canadian Journal of Communication* 12, no. 1 (Winter 1986), 1–19.
44 See Richard Collins, *Culture, Communication and National Identity: The Case of Canadian Television* (Toronto: University of Toronto Press 1990).
45 See Susan M. Crean, *Who's Afraid of Canadian Culture?* (Toronto: General Publishing 1976); and Véronneau's address to an American audience, in 'Canadian Film: An Unexpected Emergence,' *Massachussetts Review* 31, nos. 1–2 (Spring–Summer), 213–26.
46 Jarvie, *Hollywood's Overseas Campaign*, 3.

3: A New Policy Field, Television, and Changing Production Practices

1 Reginald Whitaker, *The Government Party: Organizing and Financing the Liberal Party of Canada 1930–58* (Toronto: University of Toronto Press 1977), 420.
2 Ibid.
3 Philip Resnick, *The Land of Cain: Class and Nationalism in English Canada 1945–1975* (Vancouver: New Star Press 1977).
4 Maria Tippett, *Making Culture: English-Canadian Institutions and the Arts before the Massey Commission* (Toronto: University of Toronto Press 1990), 184–5.
5 Donald Creighton, *The Forked Road: Canada 1939–1957* (Toronto: McClelland and Stewart 1976), 249, emphasis added.
6 Bernard Ostry, *The Cultural Connection: An Essay on Culture and Government Policy in Canada* (Toronto: McClelland & Stewart 1978), 69.
7 Peter C. Newman, *The Distemper of Our Times: Canadian Politics in Transition 1963–1968* (Toronto: McClelland & Stewart 1968), 248.
8 See the text of the speech in Claude Bissell, ed., *Canada's Crisis in Higher Education: Proceedings of a Conference held by the National Conference of Canadian University at Ottawa, Nov. 12–14, 1956* (Toronto: University of Toronto Press 1957), 249–57.
9 Ibid., 249.
10 Ibid.
11 Ibid., 250–1, emphasis added.
12 Ibid.

13 Ibid., 254, emphasis added.
14 See National Film Board Archives, Minutes of the Board of Governors, 71st meeting, appendix 9a.
15 Paul Rutherford, *When Television Was Young: Primetime Canada 1952–1967* (Toronto: University of Toronto Press 1990), 41.
16 Ibid., 385.
17 Until the development of television, the output of the NFB was 'a cinema devoted only to the idea of social development,' according to Pierre Juneau (interview with the author, 4 April 1990).
18 NFB Archives, Minutes of the Board, 43rd meeting, appendix 9, 2–3.
19 NFB Archives, Briefs, box A-183, file 1070.
20 See Gerald Pratley, 'Point to Stress: Canada Is "Rural,"' *Variety*, 29 April 1964, 29–32.
21 D.B. Jones, *Movies and Memoranda: An Interpretive History of the National Film Board of Canada* (Ottawa: Canadian Film Institute 1981), 58.
22 Bobet, 'Lettre ouverte,' 109.
23 Distribution of NFB films abroad by the late 1950s was considered by the Department of External Affairs to be 'the most important' of Canada's information programs; it was assured through diplomatic posts and missions and yielded an estimated audience of '18 million annually.' See Mulholland, confidential memorandum, NFB Archives, Minutes of the Board, 43rd meeting, appendix 9, 3–5.
24 NFB Archives, Marjorie McKay, 'History of the National Film Board of Canada' (unpublished ms, 1964), 102.
25 Rutherford, *When Television Was Young*, 47–9.
26 NFB Archives, Minutes of the Board, 34th meeting, 4.
27 Kirwan Cox, 'A Chronological Review of the National Film Board and Television from 1950 to 1984' (24 Aug. 1986), an unpublished document prepared for the NFB from its archives and the minutes of the meetings of the Board of Governors.
28 Ibid., 1.
29 See Véronneau, 'Résistance et affirmation,' 25–6. See also NFB Archives, Minutes of the Board, 43rd meeting, appendix 10, 3.
30 See NFB Archives, Minutes of the Board, 43rd meeting, appendix 10, 1–2.
31 National Archives of Canada, RG 41, vol. 343, file 15-6, part 3, 'Relations with National Film Board.'
32 See communication from NFB commissioner Guy Roberge to the chair of the Board of Broadcast Governors, Andrew Stewart, in NFB Archives, Minutes of the Board, 43rd meeting, 3.
33 Véronneau, 'Résistance et affirmation,' 28.

34 Cited in ibid., 34.
35 See André Lafrance and Gilles Marsolais, *Cinéma d'ici* (Montreal: Léméac 1973), 129.
36 In the sense given to the phrase by dependency theory; see chapter 2, endnote 22 above. Filmmaker Arthur Lamothe complained not long before quitting the NFB that working there was like training lawyers only to plead parking tickets. See Lamothe, 'Alors, le cinéma canadien, ça vient?,' *La Presse*, 20 July 1963, in NFB Archives, press clippings, box P-13, file 3082.
37 See Michel Houle and Alain Julien, eds., *Dictionnaire du cinéma québécois* (Montreal: Fides 1978), 233.
38 Ibid.
39 Ibid., 226.
40 Production costs given in Véronneau, 'Résistance et affirmation,' 33.
41 See ibid., 34 ff. In an interview, Pierre Juneau commented on the lack of support for narrative fictions that permeated 'our entire distribution system: the people in the system worked with agricultural movements, with tradeunions and schools, and so they said: "What do you want us to do with these? Our people don't want stories, they want to know how to set up cooperatives"' (interview with the author, 4 April 1990). While this was true of the early series, by narrowcasting its distribution the NFB 'fairly quickly moved into a choice of subject areas which did provide useful 16mm films ... on topics ... in high demand for special interest group programs.' See Mulholland, memorandum to the Board of Governors, September 1959, NFB Archives, Minutes of the Board, 43rd meeting, appendix 9.
42 Cited in Véronneau, 'Résistance et affirmation,' 35.
43 Ibid., 36.
44 See Dansereau, 'Le Cinéma québécois: un cinéma colonisé,' 82.
45 Lever, *Histoire générale*, 149–50.
46 Cited in Gilles Marsolais, *L'Aventure du cinéma direct* (Paris: Seghers 1974), 129.
47 Lever, *Histoire générale*, 149.
48 Marsolais, *L'Aventure*, 129.
49 Véronneau, 'Résistance et affirmation,' 38; Marsolais, *L'Aventure*, 122–30.
50 Pierre Véronneau, 'La Transgression des normes télévisuelles dans un certain cinéma québécois,' in Cécile Cloutier and Calvin Seerveld, eds., *Opuscula Aesthetica Nostra: Essays on Aesthetics and the Arts in Canada* (Edmonton: Academic Printing and Publishing 1984), 169–72.
51 Rutherford, *When Television Was Young*, 77, 116.
52 Ibid., 80.
53 NFB Archives, Minutes of the Board, 72nd meeting, appendix 7. See also

O.J. Firestone, 'Problèmes particuliers au Québec en matière de distribution cinématographique,' *Sociologie et sociétés* 8, no. 1 (April 1976), 43–70.

54 Rutherford, *When Television Was Young*, 86.

55 See ibid., 130–1.

56 Michelle Hilmes, *Hollywood and Broadcasting: From Radio to Cable* (Urbana and Chicago: University of Illinois Press 1990), 148–9. See also Tino Balio, ed., *Hollywood in the Age of Television* (Boston: Unwin Hyman 1990).

57 See Austin E. Weir, *The Struggle for National Broadcasting in Canada* (Toronto: McClelland & Stewart 1965), 381.

58 The same pattern occurred with the establishment of the CTV network. See 'US Sees Canada Coin Potential,' *Variety* 26 July 1961. For the Motion Picture Export Association of America, the export lobby of the Hollywood film Majors, the establishment of second, i.e., non-state, television networks, particularly in Europe as of the early 1960s, provided the opportunity to realize 'the principal objective [of] an increase in the planned proportion of film to live programming during the early stages of operation.' Such an increase would establish a precedent 'likely to influence programming patterns for years to come.' See MPEA, *Interim Report on Television* (21 Oct. 1960), cited in Thomas Guback, 'Shaping the Film Business in Postwar Germany: The Role of the US Film Industry and the US State,' in Paul Kerr, ed., *The Hollywood Film Industry* (London: RKP and BFI 1986), 245–75.

59 Dean Walker, 'TV series gives big boost to Canada's filmmakers,' *Saturday Night*, 7 Dec. 1957, 12–13, 42–3.

60 Peter Morris, *Canadian Feature Films, 1913–1969: Part 2: 1941–1963* (Ottawa: Canadian Film Institute 1974), 7–8.

61 See *Canadian Film Weekly* 23, no. 3 (15 Jan. 1958). In a lengthy unpublished interview on 15 February 1985 with Professor Peter Morris of York University, Davidson commented that the impetus for feature film production in Toronto in the mid-1950s came from the margins of the industry: 'Almost everybody was interested in some way in film drama but mostly it was those other people who weren't involved in film; the majority of film people tended to be extremely cautious.'

62 See Ron Johnson, 'Despite Flop, Plenty of Enthusiasm,' *Toronto Daily Star*, 12 August 1959.

63 Morris, *Canadian Feature Films, 1913–1940*, 10.

64 Johnson, 'Despite Flop,' *Toronto Daily Star*, emphasis added.

65 *Canadian Film Weekly* 23, no. 10 (5 March 1958).

66 Ibid., 23, no. 1 (1 Jan. 1958).

67 Ibid., emphasis added.

68 See Rutherford, *When Television Was Young*, 375.

69 Production company Crawley Films of Ottawa was described as 'this Canadian motion picture enterprise which has done more than any other Dominion company to develop production for industry and education' *Canadian Film Weekly* 23, no. 34 (3 Sept. 1958). Capitalization for the series was provided by Montreal newspaper publisher J.R. McConnell.

70 See NFB Archives, Minutes of the Board, 43rd meeting, appendix 10, 5, emphasis added.

71 Rutherford, *When Television Was Young*, 379.

72 Ibid., 378.

73 *Canadian Film Weekly* 25, no. 11 (16 March 1960).

74 Ibid., 23, no. 19 (7 May 1958).

75 Ibid., 26, no. 2 (11 Jan. 1961). Three years earlier, Crawley Films Ltd president F.R. 'Budge' Crawley, speaking over CBC's Trans-Canada network, had stated that a Canadian feature film industry was not foreseeable in the near future. See 'Can't See Canadian Feature Industry,' *Canadian Film Weekly* 23, no. 24 (11 June 1958).

75 James W. Carey, 'Time, Space and the Telegraph,' in David Crowley and Paul Heyer, eds., *Communication in History: Technology, Culture and Society* (New York and London: Longman 1991), 132–7.

77 NFB Archives, Minutes of the Board, 44th meeting, appendix 2, 25 (item 4), emphasis added.

78 See *Canadian Film Weekly* 23, no. 5 (29 Jan. 1958).

79 NFB Archives, Memorandum, Foster to Juneau, 29 Aug. 1958, Briefs, box A-183, file 1070.

80 The NFB kept a sharp eye for critical articles appearing in the Canadian press or policy resolutions by business organizations (such as the Canadian Chamber of Commerce). For a number of attacks and the NFB's detailed responses, see NFB Archives, AMPPLC, box B-77, file 5-A.

81 NFB Archives, box P-13, file 3082, 'Notes,' 25 Aug. 1958.

82 NFB Archives, Memorandum, Foster to Juneau, 29 Aug.

83 NFB Archives, Mulholland to Coristine, 23 December 1958, AMPPLC, box B-77, file 5-A, vol. 1 (May 1957–May 1959).

84 NFB Archives, Rekert to Roberge, 7 July 1958, Briefs, box A-183, file 1030.

85 NFB Archives, box B-77, file 5-A, statistical file no. 1-3-23. Juneau, as secretary to the Board of Governors, reported in a 28 Oct. 1959 note on a meeting with N.A. Taylor, who put the size of the Canadian domestic market at 6 per cent of the total U.S. world market. See NFB Archives, 'Note au dossier AMPPLC,' box B-77, file 5-A.

86 Ibid., NFB Archives, box P-13, file 3082, 'Notes.'

87 Juneau to Roberge, 4 Sept. 1958 (the date is wrongly typed '1953'), NFB

Archives, Briefs, box A-183, file 1070, Film Commissioner, Survey of Foreign Legislation, 1953–62.

88 According to the 'Notes,' 'The basic principle of coproduction arrangements is as follows: to surrender all rights in the other participating country and part of the rights on all exterior markets in return for participation in the financing of the production.' NFB Archives, box P-13, file 3082. For a study of the Canadian experience with co-productions from 1963 to 1983, see Michael Dorland, 'Quest for Equality: Canada and Coproductions: A Retrospective 1963–1983,' *Cinema Canada* no. 100 (October 1983), 13–19.

89 For a summary of these transformations, see Magder, *Canada's Hollywood*, 177–8; also Balio, ed., *Hollywood in the Age of Television*.

90 See *Canadian Film Weekly* 26, no. 17 (26 April 1961).

91 Ibid.

92 François Baby, 'Le Cinéma post-industriel,' *Cinécrits* 3 (n.d.), 5–14.

4: Reconfiguring the Public Sphere

1 See Chapter 2, note 5.

2 Robert S. Fortner, 'The System of Relevances and the Politics of Language in Canadian Public Policy Formation: The Case of Broadcasting,' *Canadian Journal of Communication*, 12, nos. 3–4 (1986), 19–35.

3 NFB Archives, Film Commissioner, AMPPLC, box B-77, file 5-A, vol. 1.

4 NFB Archives, AMPPLC, box B-77, file 5-A, 3–5, AMPPLC draft brief.

5 NFB Archives, Minutes of the Board, 43rd meeting, agenda item 11.

6 NFB Archives, AMPPLC draft brief, 3–16.

7 'Producers Plan Appeal to Ottawa,' *Canadian Film Weekly* 23, no. 45 (14 Nov. 1958), emphasis added.

8 'Producers' Brief Coming Along,' *Canadian Film Weekly* 24, no. 24 (17 June 1959).

9 National Archives of Canada, RG 41, vol. 343, file 15-6, part 3, 'Relations with National Film Board' (undated), 39–41.

10 NFB Archives, Mulholland to Young, 17 June 1959, box B-77, file A-5, 'Materials re NFB Study of Brief,' 1959–60.

11 NFB Archives, AMPPLC, box B-77, file 5-A, AMPPLC revised brief, 2.

12 Ibid., 1–2, emphasis added.

13 Ibid., AMPPLC draft brief, 14.

14 Ibid., 1, emphasis in original.

15 Ibid., 3, 5.

16 Ibid., 1–2, 6–7.

17 Ibid., AMPPLC revised brief, ii, 5.

18 Ibid., 10.
19 For parallels between Canada and Britain in television production, see 'World Imitating Our TV Pattern,' *Canadian Film Weekly* 24, no. 11 (18 March 1959).
20 NFB Archives, AMPPLC, box B-77, file A-5, vol. 1. This was literally a reiteration of the Canadian strategy vis-à-vis feature production in the 1920s with respect to the 1927 British film quota. See Morris, *Embattled Shadows*, 177–82.
21 NFB Archives, AMPPLC revised brief, 10.
22 Ibid., 22.
23 Ibid., AMPPLC draft brief, 4.
24 Ibid., 13. The Theatres and Cinematographs Act was amended in 1919 to require that applicants for theatre licences, producers, and distributors be British subjects. See Malcolm Dean, *Censored! Only in Canada* (Toronto: Virgo Press 1981).
25 NFB Archives, AMPPLC draft brief, 13. At a very general level, such a view was consistent with that of British film historian Rachel Low. See her *The History of the British Film 1929–1939: Film Making in 1930s Britain* (London: Geo. Allen and Unwin 1985), xiv, 33, 115. See also Dickinson and Street, *Cinema and State*, 40–1.
26 NFB Archives, AMPPLC brief, 13.
27 Ibid., 22.
28 That is, the non-distinguished object ambiguously constituted from the confusion of (1) the foreign controlled branches in exhibiting, distribution, and services; (2) Canadian independent exhibition, distribution, production, and services; and (3) the state-administered production, distribution, and service sector, but in whose name any of these components could speak.
29 *Canadian Film Weekly*, 21 Oct. 1959, 3.
30 Robert E. Babe, *Canadian Television Broadcasting Structure, Performance and Regulation* (Ottawa: Economic Council of Canada 1979), 19.
31 Cited in Raboy, *Missed Opportunities*, 134.
32 Ibid.
33 Fortner, 'The System of Relevances and the Politics of Language in Canadian Policy Formation.'
34 Ibid.
35 'Taylor's Showbiz "Global Concept,"' *Canadian Film Weekly* 24, no. 38 (7 Oct. 1959), 1, 6.
36 Ibid.
37 'Taylor-Roffman, Others in Prod'n,' *Canadian Film Weekly*, 25, no. 22 (1 June 1960), 1, 19.

38 'Toronto Interational and Meridian join forces,' *Canadian Film Weekly* 25, no. 22 (1 June 1960).

39 Ibid.

40 'Film Trade TV Holdings Growing In Number,' *Canadian Film Weekly*, 25, no. 29 (20 July 1960), 1, 3.

41 See Rutherford, *When Television Was Young*, 114.

42 For a discussion, see Weir, *The Struggle for National Broadcasting*, 372–5. For an unfavourable comparison to the Australian experience, see Bertrand and Collins, *Government and Film in Australia*, 124–7. For an economic critique, see Babe, *Canadian Television Broadcasting*, 309–10.

43 'Canada's First Visual Quotas,' *Canadian Film Weekly*, 12 Jan. 1960, 5.

44 Ibid.

45 'BBG's 55% Big Boost for Canadian Prod'n,' *Canadian Film Weekly* 24, no. 31, (19 Aug. 1959), 1, 9.

46 Rutherford, *When Television Was Young*.

47 *Canadian Film Weekly*, 12 Jan. 1960, 5.

48 See Rutherford, *When Television Was Young*, 113.

49 'MP's Given Quota Pitch by IA Union,' *Canadian Film Weekly* 26, no. 16 (19 April 1961); for a copy of the letter by William F. White, 23 Feb. 1961, see NFB Archives, AMPPLC, box B-77, file 5-A, vol. 2 (January 1959–December 1960).

50 NFB Archives, letter by William F. White. The figure was contested in the *Canadian Film Weekly* article reporting on the IATSE letter and reduced downwards to 'perhaps' $20 million. See *Canadian Film Weekly* 26, no. 16 (19 April 1961).

51 *Canadian Film Weekly* 26, no. 17 (26 April 1961). Note that Taylor had earlier argued before the NFB Board of Governors that Canada represented 6 per cent of the U.S. world earnings; see chapter 3, note 85. Using the *Canadian Film Weekly*'s own estimates of the size of the U.S. world market by 1960, 3 per cent still gave the average non-Canadian film a gross potential of nearly $7 million.

52 'Our Business,' *Canadian Film Weekly* 26, no. 20 (17 May 1961). See also 'What's The Best Way to Help?' 26, no. 21 (24 May 1961), for a summary of the quota vs. subsidy debate.

53 See NFB Archives, Minutes of the Board, 44th meeting; see also AMPPLC, box B-77, file 5-A, vols. 1 and 2, Commissioner's Office, 'Materials re NFB study of Brief.'

54 NFB Archives, AMPPLC, box B-77, file 5-A, black books, refutation point 7. A statement in the brief to be refuted was numbered and the NFB's response given under the appropriate number.

55 Ibid., point 13-2, 9.
56 See NFB Archives, Minutes of the Board of Governors, 35th meeting.
57 NFB Archives, AMPPLC, black book, point 13-3.
58 Ibid., point 11, 6.
60 Ibid., point 3, 2; point 11, 2, 1; emphasis added.
61 Ibid.
62 Ibid., revised 28 Jan. 1963.
63 Not only were the NFB's interests increasingly divergent from those of private producers, they diverged as well from those of private Canadian producers. See its cold-shouldered rejection of the proposal by Astral Films of Montreal in 1966 to distribute NFB films theatrically, because Astral could not, in the NFB's view, match the 'long-standing arrangement' it had developed with Columbia Pictures and its 'international connections.' See NFB Archives, Minutes of the Board of Governors, 79th meeting, 8–9.
64 Granatstein, *How Britain's Weakness*, 50–1.
65 Pierre Véronneau, *Cinéma de l'époque duplessiste*, Dossiers de la Cinémathèque 7 (Montreal: Cinémathèque québécoise 1979), annexe 1: 'Un projet de coopération Canada-USA,' 141–51, is still the best account of the Canadian Cooperation Project.
66 Ibid., 150. See also Pierre Berton, *Hollywood's Canada: The Americanization of Our National Image* (Toronto: McClelland & Stewart 1975); Maynard Collins, 'Cooperation, Hollywood and Howe,' *Cinema Canada* 56 (June–July 1979), 34–6; and Michael Spencer, 'Inside the Wagon Train: A Cautionary Tale – U.S.–Canada film relations 1920–1986,' *Cinema Canada* 131 (June 1986), 10–17.
67 NFB Archives, AMPPLC, box B-77, file 5-A, 'Materials ... Canadian Cooperation Project' (no page numbering).
68 Ibid.
69 Ibid. For a fuller account, see Véronneau, 'Un projet de coopération.'
70 NFB Archives, Minutes of the Board of Governors, 22 March 1949. By late 1950 the project was transferred to the administrative responsibility of the Interdepartmental Committee for Canadian Information Abroad; by 1959 it was no longer subject 'to continuous or even intermittent review.' See NFB Archives, 'Materials ... Canadian Cooperation Project,' emphasis added.
71 Morris, 'Backwards to the Future: John Grierson's Film Policy for Canada,' 28–30, emphasis added.
72 Producer Paul l'Anglais of the AMPPLC in an April 1960 letter to the MPAA representative in Canada. See NFB Archives, 'Materials ... Canadian Cooperation Project.'
73 NFB Archives, 'Summary of Comments,' Minutes of the Board of Governors, 44th meeting, appendix 2, 1–5.

74 The phrase is Rutherford's in *When Television Was Young*, 113.
75 See NFB Archives, AMPPLC, box B-77, file 5-A, vol. 2, 'Notes prepared by the Board for Minister's use ...'
76 Ibid.
77 'Withholding tax from 5 to 15%,' *Canadian Film Weekly* 26, no. 1 (4 Jan. 1961).
78 See NFB Archives, Minutes of the Board of Governors, 43rd meeting.
79 Ibid., 46th meeting.
80 Ibid., 49th meeting.
81 NFB Archives, Roberge to Minister, 13 March 1961, AMPPLC, box B-77, file 5-A, vol. 3, (November 1960–8), emphasis added.
82 In interviews with the author, both Roberge and Juneau claimed 'paternity' for the use of co-production as the developmental mechanism for a Canadian feature film industry. Roberge interview 14 May 1990; Juneau interviews, 4 and 18 April 1990.
83 NFB Archives, Minutes of the Board of Governors 55th meeting, text in appendix 9.
84 Ibid., emphasis added.
85 Ibid.
86 Ibid., 56th meeting, 5–7.

5: Discoursing on Cinema within the State

1 See Jean Franklin, *Le Discours du pouvoir* (Paris: UGE 1975).
2 NFB Archives, Minutes of the Board of Governors, 55th meeting, appendix 9.
3 For this and other contemporary press clippings, see NFB Archives, Direction de la Production française, 1962–72, box P-153, file 4101.
4 For the controversies surrounding the release of *Drylanders*, originally planned as three half-hour shows for television, see NFB Archives, 'Report of the CBC Representatives (NFB-CBC Working Committee)' (11 May 1963). For the NFB's wildly exaggerated figures on the film's theatrical release, see Minutes of the Board of Governors, 64th meeting, 5.
5 Clipping in NFB Archives, box P-153, file 4101.
6 For disgruntled commentary on early Canada-France co-productions, see Houle and Julien, *Dictionnaire du cinéma québécois*, 29–30.
7 NFB Archives, box P-153, file 4101.
8 Les Wedman, 'At the Movies,' *Vancouver Sun*, 11 Oct. 1963.
9 Ibid.
10 NFB Archives, Minutes of the Board of Governors, 65th meeting, 4.
11 Ibid., 63rd meeting, appendix 9, 2.
12 Ibid., 4.

13 Roberge, interview with the author, 14 May 1990; Juneau, interviews, 4 and 18 April 1990.
14 Bobet, 'Lettre ouverte,' 104.
15 Ibid., 108.
16 Ibid., 109–11, emphasis added.
17 National Archives of Canada, Pickersgill Memorandum, 9 Dec. 1963; Privy Council Office, Record of Cabinet Decision, 12 Dec. 1963. RG 6, vol. 848, file 5020-1.
18 For some discussion, see Magder, *Canada's Hollywood*, 121–6.
19 For the NFB's subsequent floundering in attempting to develop an 'integrated' or 'global' approach to Canadian government film policy, see NFB Archives, Film Policy black books, box 262.
20 See National Archives of Canada, RG 41, vol. 337, file 14-4-4.
21 NFB Archives, Interdepartmental Committee, Minutes, box A-460, file 4365, emphasis added. (Copies of the minutes are also to be found in the National Archives of Canada, RG 6, Secretary of State, vol. 824.)
22 Ibid., 2nd meeting, 3–4, emphasis added.
23 Franklin, *Le Discours du pouvoir*, 129.
24 NFB Archives, A-460, Interdepartmental Committee, Minutes, 2nd meeting, 4.
25 Cinémathèque québécoise Archives, 'Report of the Subcommittee on the Possible Development of a Canadian Film Industry,' 24 Feb. 1964, 1. As Roberge's right-hand as the NFB's representative, Michael Spencer drafted the committee's reports.
26 Ibid., 2, emphasis added.
27 Ibid., 2–3.
28 Ibid., 3–4.
29 Ibid., 6.
30 Ibid., 10.
31 Except for René Bonnière, who had worked for Radio-Canada, and Roffman, who had left the NFB just after the Second World War, the others were recent 'graduates' of the NFB, having for the most part left in disgust for private industry.
32 Cinémathèque québécoise Archives, 'Report,' 10–11.
33 NFB Archives, 'Addendum to the Report ... ' 13 March 1964, box A-460, file 4365, 4–5, emphasis added.
34 National Archives of Canada, RG 6, vol. 848, file 5020-1, Privy Council Office, Record of Cabinet Decision, 4 Aug. 1964.
35 NFB Archives, Interdepartmental Committee, Minutes, 11th meeting.
36 Franklin, *Le Discours du pouvoir*, 128.

37 NFB Archives, 'Terms of Reference' 19 Jan. 1965, box A-416, file 4159.
38 Michael Spencer, 'Canadian Feature Film Production ... ,' 1–2, 2, 4, 17, in NFB Archives, box A-416, file 4159.
39 Ibid., 4–5, 12.
40 Ibid., 5.
41 NFB Archives, Interdepartmental Committee, Minutes, 18th meeting.
42 Ibid.
43 For the desperate appeals by Montreal company Cooperatio from August 1965 through May 1966 for a $75,000 grant to allow it to remain in business, see National Archives of Canada, RG 6, vol. 851, file 5040-195/C2.
44 NFB Archives, Fernand Cadieux, 'The Feature-Length Film Production Industry in French-Speaking Canada' (n.d.), box A-416, file 4159, 1.
45 Ibid., 3/2, 7.
46 Ibid., 28.
47 Ibid.
48 Ibid., 39.
49. Ibid.
50 Of German background, Firestone was interned in Canada during the Second World War. He later became economic adviser to the Central Mortgage and Housing Corporation as head of its economic department, and came to the attention of post-war Liberal 'Minister of Everything' C.D. Howe. Firestone subsequently became head of the Economics Department at the University of Ottawa and assistant dean of Social Sciences. In 1966 he published a study on broadcast advertising in Canada. He was also noted as an art collector and established a substantial collection of works by the Group of Seven.
51 See NFB Archives, Firestone report, box A-460, file 4125, pt 1, vol. 1, R-S-35.
52 NFB Archives, Interdepartmental Committee, Minutes, 19th meeting.
53 NFB Archives, Firestone report, part 1, vol. 1, 2–25.
54 Ibid., 1-23-4.
55 Ibid., 1-24.
56 Ibid., 1-25. See also Firestone's article, 'Problèmes particuliers au Québec en matière de distribution cinématographique,' in Sociologie et sociétés in 1976.
57 NFB Archives, Firestone report, 1–24; S-24, 10–12.
58 Ibid., Interdepartmental Committee, Minutes, 19th meeting.
59 NFB Archives, Firestone, 1-25.
60 Ibid., R-S-25; R-5-40.
61 Ibid., R-5-29a–30.
62 Ibid., R-S-33.
63 Ibid., 7-38–9.

64 Ibid., 7-3; see also vol. 2, S-18.
65 See Michael Spencer's account, 'Inside the Wagon Train,' 13.
66 NFB Archives, Interdepartmental Committee, Minutes, 19th meeting.
67 NFB Archives, Firestone report, part 2, S-22. Spencer, in 'Inside the Wagon Train,' 13, writes that the Americans 'really couldn't understand our enthusiasm for Canadian production. One of them remarked that the prospect scared the hell out of him.'
68 NFB Archives, Firestone report, part 2, S-19; 5-23-5. For the American arguments for rejecting the proposed Film Agreement, see part 2, S-19–20.
69 Ibid., 5-25.
70 Ibid., 7-24-5.
71 Ibid., 9-S-31.
72 Ibid., 9-14.
73 Spencer, 'Inside the Wagon Train,' 13.
74 Batz's subtle warnings regarding the role of the state in the feature film economy, in a paper written in French for the committee, seem to have been largely ignored, particularly his point about the risks of substituting 'la raison d'Etat' for 'motivations lucratives.' NFB Archives, A-460, 4365, 'Note au sujet de la production cinématographique de long métrage au Canada' (6 June 1965).
75 NFB Archives, 'Second Report,' 3–8, box A-416, file 4159.
76 Ibid., 9–13.
77 NFB Archives, Secretary to the Board, Allocutions, Hon. Maurice Lamontagne, 1964–5, box A-183, file 3005.
78 Ibid., Allocution, 5 Aug. 1964, 3.
79 Ibid., 3–4.
80 Ibid.
81 Ibid., Allocution, 13 Oct. 1965, 3.
82 Ibid.
83 See National Archives of Canada, RG 6, vol. 848, file 5020-1, memorandum Steele to secretary of state, 2 Sept. 1965.
84 Lamontagne was forced to resign in the wake of a scandal involving fringe characters of the Quebec underworld; he was replaced as secretary of state by Judy LaMarsh.
85 National Archives of Canada, RG 6, vol. 848, file 5020-1, Spencer to Steele, draft memorandum to the minister, 20 Feb. 1976.

6: Filmmakers, Critics, and the Problem of Critical Voice

1 Pierre Véronneau, 'L'Association professionnelle des cinéastes,' Le Cinéma:

théorie et discours, Dossiers de la Cinémathèque 12 (Montreal: Cinémathèque québécoise 1984), 21–5.

2 Ibid., 22.

3 For an enumeration of the dates and titles of the briefs, see ibid.; for APC president Guy. Côté's speech on 9 May 1964 to the annual general meeting of the Canadian Society of Cinematographers summarizing the briefs, see NFB Archives, box P-170, file 4297.

4 For the brief submitted to Quebec, see Cinémathèque québécoise Archives, APC, 'Mémoire présenté au premier ministre du Québec: mesures d'ensemble que l'APC recommande au gouvernement du Québec pour favoriser le développement d'une industrie du cinéma de long métrage conformément aux intérêts économiques et culturels de la population' (March 1964), 5–6.

5 Cinémathèque québécoise Archives, APC, 'Mémoire présenté au secrétaire d'État du Canada: vingt-deux raisons pour lesquelles le gouvernement du Canada doit favoriser la création d'une industrie de long métrage au Canada et s'inquiéter des conséquences économiques et culturelles de l'état actuel de la distribution et de l'exploitation des films' (February 1964), point 20.

6 Ibid., point 19.

7 Ibid., points 17, 20, 21.

8 Cinémathèque québécoise Archives, APC, 'Mesures' (March 1964), 3.

9 Ibid., 6.

10 Ibid., 3, 6.

11 Ibid., 3, 7.

12 Ibid., 3.

13 However, by 1965–6, the cultural emphasis became stronger as cinema was increasingly defined linguistically, ranking second after language as a tool for the cultural differentiation of collectivities, in effect as a major sense organ, that of vision for 'le peuple.' On the APC's exhaustion by 1965–6 in the face of institutional torpor and crises, see Véronneau, 'L'Association professionelle des cinéastes,' 24–5.

14 NFB Archives, box 5-S, file B-77, 'Aims and Achievements of the Society of Film Makers' (5 Oct. 1967).

15 See Bill Davies, 'Some Personal Prejudices about Films and Film-making from the Other Side of the Fence,' in Jacques Bobet, ed., 'Cinéma si,' special issue of *Liberté* 8, no. 2 (1966), 67–72.

16 See NFB Archives, McLean to Roberge, 4 June 1964, 3, box P-51, file 1122.

17 Ibid., 3–4.

18 Ibid., 3–4, 7.

19 See NFB Archives, 'NFB 1964 ... Some Observations' (n.d.), box A-392, file 1070.

20 Ibid., 1–4.
21 Ibid., 8.
22 Ibid., 11.
23 Ibid., 19.
24 *Canadian Cinematography* 3, no. 3 (March–April 1964), 8.
25 Ibod. Emphasis added.
26 Ibid.
27 *Canadian Cinematographer* 3, no. 4–5 (May/June–July/August 1964). For the text of Côté's speech as released by the APC, see NFB Archives, box P-170, file 4297.
28 NFB Archives, speech by Guy L. Côté, 2–7.
29 Ibid., 7–9. The reference is to the five-volume study carried out by Arthur Lamothe and Côté in 1963 for the Conseil d'orientation économique du Québec. The fifth volume envisaged the production of ten features a year. See a copy of the study in the Cinémathèque québécoise Archives.
30 Ibid., 13–14, 16.
31 Ibid.
32 For an analysis of the cultural roots of a wounded Canadian nationalism, see Michael Dorland, '"A Thoroughly Hidden Country": *Ressentiment*, Canadian Nationalism, Canadian Culture,' *Canadian Journal of Political and Social Theory* 12, nos. 1–2 (1988), 130–64.
33 Robert Boissonnault, 'Les Cinéastes québécois et l'Office national du film: la séquence du long métrage,' *Cinéma/Québec*, 2, no. 5 (January–February, 1973), 14–19.
34 Cited in Lafrance and Marsolais, *Cinéma d'ici*, 85.
35 See his 'Petite éloge des grandeurs et des misères de la colonie française de l'Office national du Film,' *Objectif* 28 (August–September 1964), 3–17.
36 In Lafrance and Marsolais, *Cinéma d'ici*, 118, emphasis added.
37 Quoted in Michael Dorland, 'The Creation Myth: Jacques Bobet and the Birth of a National Cinema,' *Cinema Canada* 106 (1984), 7–12.
38 Long-time NFB editor Werner Nold recalls the efforts made to stretch *La Vie heureuse de Léopold Z* to 90 minutes so it could qualify as a feature film in the Montreal Festival. Interview with the author, 8 March 1990.
39 Lever, *Histoire générale*, 194.
40 Louis Marcorelles, 'American Diary,' *Sight and Sound*, Winter 1962–3, 5.
41 Lever, *Histoire générale*, 198.
42 Davies, 'Some Personal Prejudices,' 72.
43 Lever, *Histoire générale*, 199–200.
44 Patrick Straram, 'Festival ou Foire?,' *Cahiers du cinéma*, no. 163 (Feb. 1965), 71–3.

45 Ibid., 72–3.
46 This institution became the Cinémathèque québécoise in 1971.
47 See NFB Archives, box A-414, file 3435.
48 André Pâquet, ed., *How to Make or Not to Make a Canadian Film* (Ciné-mathèque canadienne 1968) (unpaginated).
49 NFB Archives, Organizing committee letter, 29 July 1966, box A-414, file 3435.
50 NFB Archives, Retrospective Program Notes, 22 February screening, box A-414, file 3435.
51 Jacques Godbout, 'A Trap: The Script,' in Pâquet, ed., *How To Make or Not to Make a Canadian Film*.
52 See also his earlier equally sardonic article, 'Des évidences,' *Parti pris* 1, no. 7 (April 1964).
53 Denys Arcand, 'Speaking of Canadian Cinema,' in Pâquet, ed., *How to Make or Not to Make a Canadian Film*.
54 Steve Neale, 'Art Cinema as Institution,' *Screen* 22, no. 1 (1981), 11–39.
55 Peter Morris, 'Defining a (Canadian) Art Cinema in the Sixties,' *CinéAction* (Spring 1989), 7–13.
56 Ibid., 8.
57 Ibid., 8.
58 Yves Lever, 'La Revue *Objectif* (1960–1967),' in Pierre Véronneau, Michael Dorland, and Seth Feldman, eds., *Dialogue: cinéma canadien et québécois* (Montreal: Éditions Médiatexte and La Cinémathèque québécoise 1987), 71–82.
59 Pierre Véronneau, 'Préludes à l'enseignement du cinéma,' *CinémAction* (1991), special issue on film education, 12–14.
60 Jean Pierre Lefebvre, 'Petite éloge,' 3–17.
61 Lever, *Histoire générale*, 200.
62 Morris, 'Defining a (Canadian) Art Cinema,' 10–11, 13.
63 Ibid., 11–12, emphasis added.
64 Seth Feldman, 'The Silent Subject in English Canadian Film,' in Seth Feldman, ed., *Take Two: A Tribute to Film in Canada* (Toronto: Irwin 1984), 48–57.
65 Jean-Pierre Lefebvre, 'Le Concept de cinéma national,' in Veronneau, Dorland, and Feldman, eds., *Dialogue*, 83–96.
66 Quoted in Dorland, 'The Creation Myth,' 10.
67 Ibid.
68 Dominique Noguez, *Essais sur le cinéma québécois* (Montreal: Éditions du jour 1970), 19.
69 Sande Cohen, *Historical Culture: On the Recoding of an Academic Discipline* (Berkeley: University of California Press 1986), 80, emphasis added.

70 Noguez, *Essais*, 19.
71 Jean-Louis Comolli, 'Situation du nouveau cinéma: Brésil, Canada,' *Cahiers du cinéma*, no. 176 (March 1966), 5, 57–70. See also no. 194 (Oct. 1967), 56–8, where Comolli attempts to establish an ontological distinction between Anglo-Canadian cinema as 'ressemblance' (to Hollywood cinema), and Quebec cinema as 'différence.'
72 See also Maximilien Laroche, 'Pierre Perrault et la découverte d'un langage,' in Cahiers Sainte-Marie, *Le Cinéma québécois: tendances et prolongements* (Montreal: Éditions Sainte-Marie 1968), 25–48; Michel Brûlé, *Pierre Perrault ou un cinéma national* (Montreal: Presses de l'université de Montréal 1974); and Peter Ohlin, 'Film as Word: Questions of Language and Documentary Realism,' in Ron Burnett, ed., *Explorations in Film Theory: Selected Essays from 'Ciné-Tracts'* (Bloomington: Indiana University Press 1991), 127–35.
73 David Clandfield, 'Ritual and Recital: The Perrault Project,' in Feldman, ed, *Take Two*, 136–48.
74 Franklin, *Le Discours*, 150–1.

7: Discoursing about Canadian Cinema

1 The discussions that took place in the mid-1970s between the Department of the Secretary of State and the Canadian owners of Famous Players–Paramount remain to be examined by scholars. My source for this information is former filmmaker and director of the Canadian Council of Filmmakers, Peter Pearson.
2 For an extended discussion, see Magder, *Canada's Hollywood*, 149–215; Pendakur, *Canadian Dreams*, 169–251; Michael Dorland, Michel Saint-Laurent, and Gaëtan Tremblay, 'Téléfilm Canada et la production audio-visuelle indépendante: la longue érrance d'une politique gouvernementale,' *Communication* 14, no. 2 (Fall 1993), 101–37. For the best account of these developments from the perspective of filmmakers having to deal with concrete policy environments, see journalist Michael Posner's *Canadian Dreams: The Making and Marketing of Independent Films* (Vancouver: Douglas and McIntyre 1993).
3 Cited in Wendy Michener, 'Can There Ever Be a Canadian Film Industry?' *Globe and Mail*, 12 March 1968.
4 Data reported in *Cinéma/Québec* 1, no. 7 (1972), 15.
5 Ibid., 30.
6 Quoted in Pâquet, ed., *How to Make or Not to Make a Canadian Film*.
7 See Wendy Michener, 'Scene One, Take One for the Canadian Film Development Corporation,' *Globe and Mail*, 16 March 1968; Susan Kastner, 'Ottawa's

in the Movie Business,' *Toronto Daily Star*, 16 March 1968; Martin Knelman, 'What Kind of Scenario is Ottawa Writing for Canada's Film Future?' *Globe and Mail*, 21 Oct. 1972.

8 Canadian Radio-Television and Telecommunications Commission, *Radio Frequences Are Public Property* (31 March 1974), 64.

9 Peter Harcourt, 'The Education We Need,' 22–3.

10 NFB Archives, Film Policy, box 262 (1967–77). What follows relies in particular on the draft memorandum, 'Background Paper,' 22 April 1977, by the director of policy in the Department of the Secretary of State, Warren Langford, and on two secret cabinet memoranda by then secretary of state John Roberts, 'Further Development of the Canadian Film Industry,' 20 Aug. 1976, and 'Measures to Assist the Film Industry in Canada,' 7 Sept. 1976.

11 Ibid., Roberts, 'Measures to Assist.'

12 Canada, Department of Communications, *The National Film and Video Policy* (Ottawa: Supply and Services 1984), 3, 19.

13 'Special Report on Cultural Policy and Activities of the Government of Canada 1965–1966,' National Archives of Canada, RG 41, vol. 337, file 14-4-4, parts, 1–4, 9. See also NFB Archives, box A-279, file 2-S.

14 Douglas Fisher and Harry Crowe, 'The Case of the Sheppard Report,' *Toronto Telegram*, 5 January 1967.

15 See National Archives of Canada, RG 6, vol. 848, 5020-5, part 1, especially W. Porteous to A. Fortier, 31 Dec. 1971.

16 National Archives of Canada, RG 6, 5030-10-2, Porteous to Fortier, 18 May 1971.

17 NFB Archives, Langford draft memorandum, 2; also excerpt of the memorandum in *Cinema Canada* 31: 9–12.

18 NFB Archives, Langford draft memorandum.

19 Ibid., emphasis added.

20 NFB Archives, Film Policy, box 262, Lamy to Litwack, 13 April 1977, emphasis added.

21 Hon. Flora MacDonald, 'Notes for a Statement' (Department of Communication, release, 8 June 1988). The notion of the 'futurable' comes from cultural historian Sande Cohen's *Historical Culture*.

22 NFB Archives, Langford draft memorandum, 1.

23 William T. Stanbury and Jane Fulton, 'Suasion as a Governing Instrument,' in Allan M. Maslove, ed., *How Ottawa Spends 1984: The New Agenda* (Toronto: Methuen 1984), 282–324.

24 NFB Archives, Langford draft memorandum, 6.

25 NFB Archives, Roberts, 'Further Development,' 2.

26 Ibid., Roberts, 'Measures,' 7.
27 MacDonald, 'Notes' (1988), 2.
28 *Making Our Voices Heard: Canadian Broadcasting and Film for the 21st Century,* Report of the Mandate Review Committee (Ottawa: Supply and Services 1996), 193.
29 Ibid., 194–5, 198.
30 Ibid., 202–7, 213.
31 Ibid., 214.
32 See Brian Keppler, 'Stop Cultural Elites before They Tax Again,' *Gazette,* Montreal, 30 Jan. 1996, B3.
33 See detailed production and cost-recovery data in NFB Archives, box D-203, file 4159, Director of Distribution, features and one-hour films, 1967–71.
34 Henri Lefebvre, *De l'État,* 4 vols. (Paris: UGE 1976–8).
35 Ibid., 2: 82.
36 Ibid., 2: 51.
37 Richard H. Gaskins, *Burdens of Proof in Modern Discourse* (New Haven: Yale University Press 1992).

Bibliography

Archival Sources

Canadian Film Development Corporation, Montreal
Minutes of the Board (1968–1973).

Cinémathèque québécoise Archives, Montreal
Association professionnelle des cinéastes, 'Mémoire présenté au premier ministre du Québec: mesures d'ensemble que l'APC recommende au gouvernement du Québec pour favoriser le développement d'une industrie du cinéma
de long métrage conformément aux intérêts économiques de la population,'
March 1964
Conseil d'orientation économique du Québec, five-volume study of proposed
film industry, 1963
– 'Mémoire présenté au secrétaire d'État du Canada: vingt-deux raisons pour
lesquelles le gouvernement du Canada doit favoriser la création d'une industrie de long métrage au Canada et s'inquiéter des conséquences économiques
et culturelles de l'état actuel de la distribution et de l'exploitation des films,'
February 1964
'Report of the Subcommittee on the Possible Development of a Canadian Film
Industry,' 24 February 1964

National Archives of Canada, Ottawa
RG 6, Secretary of State, vols. 824, 848, 851
RG 41, Canadian Broadcasting Corporation, vols. 337, 343

National Film Board of Canada, Archives, Montreal
Allocutions, Hon. Maurice Lamontage, 1964–5, box A-183, file 3005.

Association of Motion Picture Producers and Laboratories of Canada, box B-77, file 5-A, vol. 1 (May 1957–May 1959) and vol. 2 (January 1959–December 1960), including Black books; 'Canadian Cooperation Project'; Pierre Juneau, 'Note au dossier AMPPLC,' 28 Oct. 1959; 'Materials re NFB Study of Brief' (1959–60); 'Notes prepared by the Board for Minister's use'; Statistical files

Jean-Claude Batz, 'Note au sujet de la production cinématographique au Canada,' 6 June 1965, box A-460, file 4365.

Board of Governors, Minutes, 1958–72.

Fernand Cadieux, 'The Feature-length film production industry in French-speaking Canada,' n.d., and Michael D. Spencer, 'Canadian Feature Film Production in the English language,' 6 April 1965, box A-416, file 4159

Film Commissioner, Survey of Foreign Legislation, 1953–62, box A-183, file 1170

Film industry associations, box P-170, file 4297; box B-77, file 5-S

Film Policy, Black Books, box 262, 1967–77, especially Warren Langford, draft memorandum, 'Background paper,' 22 April 1977; Memoranda, Secretary of State John Roberts, 'Further Development of the Canadian Film Industry,' 20 August 1976, and 'Measures to Assist the Film Industry in Canada,' 7 September 1976

O.J. Firestone report, box A-460, file 4125.

Interdepartmental Committee on the Possible Development of a Feature Film Industry in Canada, Minutes, box A-460, file 4365

'Notes on Government Legislation Related to the Development of a National Film Industry in Various Countries,' box P-13, file 3082, 25 Aug. 1958

Press clippings, box P-13, files 3082 and 4010, 1962–72

Press clippings, industry organizations and NFB responses, file B-77, box 5-A

Production data on NFB films, Director of Distribution, features and one-hour films, box D-203, file 4159, 1967–71

Other Unpublished Materials

Audley, Paul. 'Film and Television Production in Canada: Trends to 1989 and Projections to 1995.' Report, March 1991

Babe, Robert E. 'The Economics of the Canadian Cable Television Industry.' PhD dissertation, Michigan State University, 1972

Berland, Jody. 'Canadian Culture and the Discourse of Cultural Policy 1951–1981: Between the Devil and the Deep Blue C.' Unpublished paper, Trent University, 1985

Cox, Kirwan. 'A Chronological Review of the National Film Board and Television From 1950 to 1984.' Prepared from NFB archives and Board minutes, 24 Aug. 1986

Davidson, William. Unpublished interview with Professor Peter Morris. Typescript, 15 Feb. 1985

Juneau, Pierre. Personal interview. Montreal, 4 and 18 April 1990

MacDonald, Flora. 'Notes for a Statement.' 17 July 1986

– 'Notes for a Statement.' 8 June 1988

Magder, Ted. 'The Political Economy of Canadian Cultural Policy: The Canadian State and Feature Films, 1917–84.' PhD dissertation, York University, 1987

Masse, Marcel. 'The Canadian Film Industry in the North American Context.' Notes for a statement to representatives of the American film industry, Los Angeles, 17 June 1985

McKay, Marjorie. History of the National Film Board of Canada. 1964

Nold, Werner. Personal interview. Montreal, 8 March 1990

Roberge, Guy. Personal interview. Ottawa, 14 May 1990

Turner, Graeme. '"It Works for Me": British Cultural Studies, Australian Cultural Studies, Australian Film.' University of Queensland, 1990

Published Works

Adilman Sid. 'Our faceless giant stirs restlessly.' *Toronto Telegram*, 9 Nov. 1963

Allen, Robert C., and Douglas Gomery. *Film History: Theory and Practice*. New York: Knopf 1985

Allor, Martin, and Michelle Gagnon. *L'État de culture: genéalogie des politiques culturelles québécoises*. Montreal: GRECC and Concordia University, 1984

Andrew, Dudley. *The Major Film Theories*. New York: Oxford University Press 1976

– *Concepts in Film Theory*. New York: Oxford University Press 1984

Arcand, Denys. 'Des évidences.' *Parti pris* 7 (April 1964), 19–21

– 'Speaking of Canadian Cinema.' In André Pâquet, ed., *How to Make or Not to Make a Canadian Film*. Montreal: La Cinémathèque canadienne, 1968

Audley, Paul. *Canada's Cultural Industries: Broadcasting, Publishing, Records, and Film*. Toronto: Canadian Institute for Economic Policy and Lorimer, 1983

Babe, Robert E. *Canadian Television Broadcasting: Structure, Performance and Regulation*. Ottawa: Economic Council of Canada 1979

Baby, François. 'Le Cinéma post-industriel.' *Cinécrits* 3 (n.d.), 5–14

Backhouse, Charles. *The Canadian Government Motion Picture Bureau 1917–1941*. Ottawa: Canadian Film Institute 1974

Balio, Tino, ed. *Hollywood in the Age of Television*. Boston: Unwin Hyman 1990

Barry, Andrew, Thomas Osborne, and Nikolas, Rose, eds. *Foucault and Political Reason: Liberalism, Neo-Liberalism, and Rationalities of Government*. Chicago: University of Chicago Press 1996

Bélanger, André J. 'Les idéologies politiques dans les années 50.' In Jean-François Léonard ed., *Georges-Émile Lapalme*, 121–32. Sillery: Presses de l'université du Québec 1988

Berger, Carl. *The Writing of Canadian History: Aspects of English-Canadian Historical Writing, 1900–1970.* Toronto: Oxford University Press 1976

Bernier, Gérald. 'Le Cas québécois et les théories de développement et de la dépendance,' 19–54. In Edmond Orban et al., *La Modernisation politique du Québec.* Montreal: Éditions du Boréal Express 1976

Bernier, Gérald, and Daniel Salée. *The Shaping of Quebec Politics and society: Colonialism, Power and the Transition to Capitalism in the 19th Century.* Washington: Crane Russak 1992

Berton, Pierre. *Hollywood's Canada: The Americanization of Our National Image.* Toronto: McClelland & Stewart 1975

Bertrand, Ina, and Diane Collins. *Government and Film in Australia.* Sydney: Currency 1981

Bissell, Claude, ed. *Canada's Crisis in Higher Education: Proceedings of a Conference held by the National Conference of Canadian Universities at Ottawa, November 12–14, 1956.* Toronto: University of Toronto Press 1957

Bobet, Jacques. 'Lettre ouverte au commissaire du Gouvernement à la cinématographie.' In Bobet, ed., 'Cinéma si,' *Liberté* 8, no. 2 (1966) 104–11

– ed. 'Cinéma si.' Special issue of *Liberté* 8, no. 2 (1966)

Bodemann, Y. Michal. 'Elitism, Fragility and Commoditism: Three Themes in the Canadian Sociological Mythology.' In S. D. Berkowitz, ed., *Models and Myths in Canadian Sociology*, 210–28. Toronto: Butterworths 1984

Boissonnault, Robert. 'Les Cinéastes québécois et l'Office national du film: la séquence du long métrage,' *Cinéma/Québec* 2, no. 5 (January–February 1973), 14–19

Brûlé, Michel. *Pierre Perrault ou un cinéma national.* Montreal: Presses de l'université de Montréal 1974

Brunet, Michel. *La Présence anglaise et les canadiens.* Montreal: Beauchemin 1964

Brym, Robert J., and Bonnie J. Fox. *From Culture to Power: The Sociology of English Canada.* Toronto: Oxford University Press 1989

Burchell, Graham, Gordon Colin and Peter Miller, eds. *The Foucault Effect: Studies in Governmentality.* Chicago: University of Chicago Press 1991

Burckhardt, Jakob. *The Civilization of the Renaissance in Italy.* New York: New American Library 1960

Canada, Department of Communications. *The National Film and Video Policy.* Ottawa: Supply and Services 1984

Canadian Radio-Television and Telecommunications Commission. *Radio Frequencies Are Public Property.* Public announcement and decision of the

Commission on the applications for renewal of the Canadian Broadcasting
Corporation's television and radio licences, especially the joint presentation of
the Council of Canadian Filmmakers and the Society of Filmmakers. 31 March
1974

Carey, James W. 'Time, Space and the Telegraph.' In David Crowley and Paul
Hellyer, eds., *Communication in History: Technology, Culture, Society*, 132–7.
New York and London: Longman 1991

Carrière, Louise, et al., eds. 'Aujourd'hui le cinéma québécois.' *CinémAction* 40
(1986)

Carroll, Noel. *Mystifying Movies: Fads and Fallacies in Contemporary Film Theory.*
New York: Columbia University Press 1988

Clandfield, David. 'Ritual and Recital: The Perrault Project.' In Seth Feldman,
ed., *Take Two: A Tribute to Film in Canada*, 136–48. Toronto: Irwin 1984

Cohen, Sande. *Historical Culture: On the Recoding of an Academic Discipline.* Berkeley: University of California Press 1986

Collins, Maynard. 'Cooperation, Hollywood and Howe.' *Cinema Canada* 56
(June–July 1979), 34–6

Collins, Richard. 'The Metaphor of Dependency and Canadian Communications: The Legacy of Harold Innis,' *Canadian Journal of Communication* 12, no. 1
(Winter 1986), 1–19

– *Culture, Communication and National Identity: The Case of Canadian Television.*
Toronto: University of Toronto Press 1990

Coulombe, Michel, and Jean Marcel, eds. *Dictionnaire du cinéma québécois.* Montreal: Boréal 1988

Crean, Susan M. *Who's Afraid of Canadian Culture?* Don Mills: General Publishing
1976

Creighton, Donald. *The Forked Road, Canada 1939–1957.* Toronto: McClelland &
Stewart 1976

Crofts, Stephen. 'Reconceptualizing National Cinema/s.' *Quarterly Review of
Film and Video* 14, no. 3 (1993), 49–67

Curran, James and Vincent Porter, eds. *British Cinema History.* London: Weidenfeld and Nicolson 1983

Dansereau, Fernand. 'Le Cinéma québécois: un cinéma colonisé.' *Cinéma/Québec*,
3, nos. 9–10 (1974), 81–3

Davies, Bill. 'Some Personal Prejudices about Films and Film-making from the
other Side of the Fence.' In Jacques Bobet, ed., 'Cinéma si,' *Liberté* 8, no. 2
(1966), 67–72

Dean, Malcolm. *Censored! Only in Canada.* Toronto: Virgo Press 1981

Dermody, Susan, and Elizabeth Jacka. *The Screening of Australia: Anatomy of a
Film Industry.* Sydney: Currency 1987

- *The Screening of Australia: Anatomy of a National Cinema.* Sydney: Currency 1988
Dickinson, Margaret, and Sarah Street. *Cinema and State.* London: British Film Institute 1985
Dorland, Michael. 'Quest for Equality: Canada and Coproductions: A Retrospective 1963–1983.' *Cinema Canada* 100 (1983), 13–19
- 'The Creation Myth: Jacques Bobet and the Birth of a National Cinema.' *Cinema Canada* 106 (1984), 7–12
- '"A Thoroughly Hidden Country": *Ressentiment,* Canadian Nationalism, Canadian Culture.' *Canadian Journal of Political and Social Theory* 12, nos. 1–2 (1988), 130–64
- 'Policy Rhetorics of an Imaginary Cinema: The Discursive Economy of the Emergence of the Australian and Canadian Feature Film.' In Albert Moran, ed., *Film Policy: International, National and Regional Perspectives,* 114–27. London and New York: Routledge 1996
- '"The Expected Tradition": Innis, State Rationality and the Governmentalization of Communication.' *Topia* 1, no. 1 (Spring 1997), 1–16
- ed. *The Cultural Industries in Canada: Policies, Problems and Prospects.* Toronto: Lorimer 1996
Dorland, Michael, Michel Saint-Laurent, and Gaëtan Tremblay. 'Téléfilm Canada et la production audiovisuelle indépendante: la longue errance d'une politique gouvernementale.' *Communication* 14, no. 2 (Fall 1993), 101–37
Evans, Gary. *John Grierson and the National Film Board: The Politics of Wartime Propaganda.* Toronto: University of Toronto Press 1984
- *In the National Interest: A Chronicle of the National Film Board of Canada from 1949 to 1989.* Toronto: University of Toronto Press 1991
Feldman, Seth. 'The Silent Subject in English Canadian Film.' In Seth Feldman, ed., *Take Two: A Tribute to Film in Canada,* 48–57. Toronto: Irwin 1984
- 'What Was Cinema?' *Canadian Journal of Film Studies* 5, no. 1 (Spring 1996), 3–22
Feldman, Seth, and Joyce Nelson. eds. *The Canadian Film Reader.* Toronto: Peter Martin Associates 1977
Fetherling, Douglas, ed. *Documents in Canadian Film.* Peterborough: Broadview Press 1988
Firestone, O.J. 'Problèmes particuliers au Québec en matière de distribution cinématographique.' *Sociologie et sociétés* 8, no. 1 (April 1976), 43–70
Fisher, Douglas, and Harry Crowe. 'The case of the Sheppard Report.' *Toronto Telegram,* 5 Jan. 1967
Fortner, Robert S. 'The System of Relevances and the Politics of Language in Canadian Public Policy Formation: The Case of Broadcasting,' *Canadian Journal of Communication* 12, nos. 3–4 (1986), 19–35

Foucault, Michel. *Résumé des cours 1970–1982*. Paris: Julliard 1989
– 'Governmentality.' In Graham Burchell, Colin Gordon, and Peter Miller, eds., *The Foucault Effect: Studies in Governmentality*, 87–104. Chicago: University of Chicago Press 1991
Franklin, Jean. *Le Discours du pouvoir*. Paris: UGE 1975
Frye, Northrop. *The Bush Garden: Essays on the Canadian Imagination*. Toronto: Anansi 1971
Gaskins, Richard H. *Burdens of Proof in Modern Discourse*. New Haven: Yale University Press 1992
Godbout, Jacques. 'A Trap: The Script.' In André Pâquet, ed., *How to Make or Not to Make a Canadian Film*. Montreal: La Cinémathèque Canadienne 1968
– 'Pour un cinéma québécois.' *Cinéma/Québec* 1, no. 7, January–February 1972, 5–8
Granatstein, J.L. *How Britain's Weakness Forced Canada into the Arms of the United States*. Toronto: University of Toronto Press 1989
Guback, Thomas. 'Shaping the Film Business in Postwar Germany: The Role of the U.S. Film Industry and the U.S. State.' In Paul Kerr, ed., *The Hollywood Film Industry*, 245–75. London: RKP and BFI 1986
Handling, Piers, and Pierre Véronneau, eds. *Self-Portrait: Essays on the Canadian and Quebec Cinema*. Ottawa: Canadian Film Institute 1980
Harcourt, Peter. 'Introduction: The Invisible Cinema.' *Cine-Tracts*, Spring–Summer 1978, 48–9
– 'The Education We Need: Canadian Film Studies and Canadian Film.' *Cinema Canada* 150 (1988), 19–26
Higson, Andrew. 'The Concept of National Cinema.' *Screen* 30, no. 4 (1987), 36–47
Hill Mary O. *Canada's Salesman to the World: The Department of Trade and Commerce 1852–1939*. Montreal and Kingston, McGill-Queen's University Press 1977
Hilmes, Michelle. *Hollywood and Broadcasting: From Radio to Cable*. Urbana and Chicago: University of Illinois Press 1990
Houle, Michel, and Alain Julien, eds. *Dictionnaire du cinéma québécois*. Montreal: Fides 1978
Jarvie, Ian K. *Hollywood's Overseas Campaign: The North Atlantic Movie Trade 1920–1950*. Cambridge, Eng.: Cambridge University Press 1992
Johnson, Ron. 'Despite Flop, Plenty of Enthusiasm.' *Toronto Daily Star*, 12 Aug. 1959
Jones D.B. *Movies and Memoranda: An Interpretive History of the National Film Board of Canada*. Ottawa: Canadian Film Institute 1981
Kastner, Susan. 'Ottawa's in the Movie Business.' *Toronto Daily Star*, 16 March 1968

Kerr, Paul, ed. *The Hollywood Film Industry.* London: RKP and BFI 1986

Klinck, Carl F., ed. *Literary History of Canada.* Toronto: University of Toronto Press 1976

Knelman, Martin. 'What Kind of Scenario is Ottawa Writing for Canada's Film Future?' *Globe and Mail,* 21 Oct. 1972

Lafrance, André, and Gilles Marsolais. *Cinéma d'ici,* Montreal: Léméac 1973

Lamonde, Yvan, and Pierre-François Hébert. *Le Cinéma au Québec: essai de statistique historique.* Quebec: Institut québécois de recherche sur la culture 1981

Lamothe, Arthur. 'Alors, le cinéma canadien, ça vient?' *La Presse,* 20 July 1963

Laroche, Maximilien. 'Pierre Perrault et la découverte d'un langage,' In *Le Cinéma québécois: tendances et prolongements,* Cahiers Sainte-Marie. 25–48. Montreal: Éditions Sainte-Marie 1968

Laxer, Gordon. 'The Political Economy of Aborted Development: The Canadian Case.' In Robert J. Brym, eds., *The Structure of the Canadian Capitalist Class,* 67–102. Toronto: Garamond 1985

– 'The Schizophrenic Character of Canadian Political Economy.' *Canadian Review of Sociology and Anthropology,* 26, no. 1. (February 1989), 178–92

Laxer, Robert M. *Canada Ltd.: The Political Economy of Dependency.* Toronto: McClelland & Stewart 1973

Lefebvre, Henri. *De l'État.* 4 vols. Paris: UGE 1976–8

Lefebvre, Jean Pierre. 'Petite éloge des grandeurs et des misères de la colonie française de l'Office National du Film.' *Objectif* 28 (August–September 1964), 3–17

– 'Le Concept de cinéma national.' In Pierre Véronneau, Michael Dorland, and Seth Feldman, eds. *Dialogue: cinéme canadien et québécois,* 83–96. Montreal: Éditions Médiatexte and la Cinémemathèque québécoise 1987

Lever, Yves.'La revue *Objectif* (1960–1967).' 71–82. In Pierre Véronneau, Michael Dorland, and Seth Feldman, eds., *Dialaogue: cinéma canadien et québécois,* 71–82. Montreal: Éditions Médiatexte and La Cinémathèque québécoise 1987

– *Histoire générale du cinéma québécois.* Montreal: Boréal 1988

Litt, Paul. 'The Massey Commission as Intellectual History: Matthew Arnold Meets Jack Kent Cook.' Proceedings of the annual conference of the Association for Canadian Studies, University of Windsor. *Canadian Issues* 12 (1990), 23–4

– *The Muses, the Masses, and the Massey Commission.* Toronto, University of Toronto Press 1992

Low, Rachel. *The History of the British Film 1929–1939: Film Making in 1930s Britain.* London: Geo. Allen & Unwin 1985

Magder, Ted. 'A "Featureless" Film Policy: Culture and the Canadian State.' *Studies in Political Economy,* 16 (1985)

- *Canada's Hollywood: The Canadian State and Feature Films*. Toronto: University of Toronto Press 1993
Maheu, Pierre. 'L'ONF ou un cinéma québécois,' *Parti pris* 7 (April 1964), 2–5
Making Our Voices Heard: Canadian Broadcasting and Film for the 21st Century. Report of the Mandate Review Committee. Ottawa: Supply and Services 1996.
Marcorelles, Louis. 'American Diary.' *Sight and Sound* (Winter 1962–63), 4–5
- 'Nothing But the Truth.' *Sight and Sound* 32, (1963), 114–17
Marsolais, Gilles. *L'Aventure du cinéma direct*. Paris: Seghers 1974
McGregor, Gaile. *The Wacousta Syndrome: Explorations in the Canadian Langscape*. Toronto: University of Toronto Press 1985
Michener, Wendy. 'Can There Ever Be a Canadian Film Industry?' *Globe and Mail*, 12 March 1968
- 'Scene One, Take One for the Canadian Film Development Corporation.' *Globe and Mail*, 16 March 1968
Morris, Peter. *Canadian Feature Films. Part 1: 1913–1940. Part 2: 1941–1963*. Ottawa: Canadian Film Institute 1970–4
- *Embattled Shadows: A History of Canadian Cinema 1895–1939*. Montreal and Kingston: McGill-Queen's University Press 1978
- *The Film Companion*. Toronto: Irwin Publishing 1984
- 'Backwards to the Future: John Grierson's Film Policy for Canada.' In Gene Walz, ed. *Flashback: People and Institutions in Canadian Film History*, 17–36. Montreal: Mediatexte Publications 1986
- 'Rethinking Grierson: The Ideology of John Grierson.' In Pierre Véronneau, Michael Dorland, and Seth Feldman, eds., *Dialogue: cinéma canadien et québécois*, 21–56. Montreal: Éditions Médiatexte and La Cinémathèque québécoise 1987
- 'Defining a (Canadian) Art Cinema in the Sixties.' *CinéAction*, Spring 1989, 7–13
Neale, Steve. 'Art Cinema as Institution.' *Screen* 22, no. 1, (1981), 11–39
Nelson, Joyce. *The Colonized Eye: Rethinking the Grierson Legend*. Toronto: Between the Lines 1988
Newman, Peter C. *The Distemper of Our Times: Canadian Politics in Transition 1963–1968*. Toronto: McClelland & Stewart 1968
Noguez, Dominique. *Essais sur le cinéma québécois*. Montreal: Éditions du jour 1970
Ohlin, Peter. 'Film as Word: Questions of Language and Documentary Realism.' In Ron Burnett, ed., *Explorations in Film Theory: Selected Essays from 'Ciné-Tracts,'* 127–35. Bloomington: Indiana University Press 1991
Ostry, Bernard. *The Cultural Connection: An Essay on Culture and Government Policy in Canada*. Toronto: McClelland & Stewart 1978

Panitch, Leo, ed. *The Canadian State: Political Economy and Political Power*. Toronto: University of Toronto Press 1977

Pâquet, André. 'Le Cinéma québécois se laisse aller à un glissement progressif de désir commercial ... et les maudits Français nous abandonnent.' In Louise Carrière et al., eds., 'Aujourd'hui le cinema québécois,' *CinéAction* 40 (1986), 110–16

– ed. *How to Make or Not to Make a Canadian Film*. Montreal: La Cinémathèque canadienne 1968. Unpaginated

Pendakur, Manjunath. 'Cultural Dependency in Canada's Feature Film Industry.' In Gorham Kindem, ed., *The American Movie Industry: The Business of Motion Pictures*, 351–60. Carbondale and Edwardsville: Southern Illinois University Press 1982

– *Canadian Dreams and American Control: The Political Economy of the Canadian Feature Film Industry*. Toronto: Garamond Press 1990

Posner, Michael. *Canadian Dreams: The Making and Marketing of Independent Films*. Vancouver: Douglas & McIntyre 1993

Pratley, Gerald. 'Point to Stress: Canada Is "Rural."' Interview with N.A. Taylor. *Variety*, 29 April 1964, 29–32

Raboy, Marc. *Missed Opportunities: The Story of Canada's Broadcasting Policy*. Montreal and Kingston: McGill-Queen's University Press 1990

Resnick, Philip. *The Land of Cain: Class and Nationalism in English Canada 1945–1975*. Vancouver: New Star Press 1977

– *The Masks of Proteus: Canadian Reflections on the State*. Montreal and Kingston: McGill-Queen's University Press 1990

Royal Commission on National Development in the Arts, Letters, and Sciences, 1949–1951. *Report*. Ottawa: King's Printer 1951

Rutherford, Paul. *When Television Was Young, Primetime Canada 1952–1967*. Toronto: University of Toronto Press 1990

Smith, Allan. *Canada – an American Nation? Essays on Continentalism, Identity and the Canadian Frame of Mind*. Montreal and Kingston, McGill-Queen's University Press 1994

Smythe, Dallas. *Dependency Road: Communications, Capitalism, Consciousness and Canada*. Norwood N.J.: Ablex 1981

'La Société de développement de l'industrie cinématographique canadienne.' *Cinéma/Québec* 1, no. 7 (January–February 1972), 14–15

Sontag, Susan. 'The Decay of Cinema.' *New York Times Magazine*, 25 Feb. 1996

Spencer, Michael. 'Inside the Wagon Train: A Cautionary Tale – U.S.–Canada Film Relations 1920–1986.' *Cinema Canada* 131 (June 1986), 10–17

Stanbury, William T., and Jane Fulton. 'Suasion as a Governing Instrument.' In Allan M. Maslove, ed. *How Ottawa Spends 1984: The New Agenda*, 282–324. Toronto: Methuen 1984

Straram, Patrick. 'Fragments/citations à propos d'un génocide.' *Cinécrits* 3
(n.d.), 37–40
Tadros, Connie. 'From Community to Commodity: Tracing the Path of the
Industry between 150 Covers.' *Cinema Canada* 150 (March 1988), 5–14
Tadros, Jean-Pierre. 'Redécouvrir le goût du cinéma québécois.' *Cinéma/Québec*
no. 45 (1976), 5
Testa, Bart. 'In Grierson's Shadow.' *Literary Review of Canada*, November 1994,
9–12
– 'The Escape from Docudrama.' *Literary Review of Canada*, December 1994,
17–22
Tippett, Maria. *Making Culture: English-Canadian Institutions and the Arts before
the Massey Commission.* Toronto: University of Toronto Press 1990
Turner, D.J. *Canadian Feature Film Index 1913–1985.* Ottawa: Public Archives of
Canada 1987
Véronneau, Pierre. *Cinéma de l'époque duplessiste.* Dossiers de la Cinémathèque 7.
Montreal: Cinémathèque québécoise, 1979. Annexe 1: 'Un projet de coopéra-
tion Canada–USA,' 141–51
– *L'Office national du film l'enfant martyr.* Dossiers de la Cinémathèque 5. Mont-
real: Cinémathèque québécoise 1979
– 'Introduction,' xi–xiv. In Piers Handling and Pierre Véronneau, eds. *Self-
Portrait: Essays on the Canadian and Quebec Cinema*, xi–xiv. Ottawa: Canadian
Film Institute 1980.
– 'L'Association professionnelle des cinéastes,' *Le Cinéma: théorie et discours*,
21–5. Dossiers de la Cinémathèque 12. Montreal: La Cinémathèque qué-
bécoise 1984
– 'La transgression des normes télévisuelles dans un certain cinéma direct
québécois.' In Cécile Cloutier and Calvin Seerveld, eds., *Opuscula Aesthetica
Nostra: Essays on Aesthetics and the Arts in Canada.* 169–172. Edmonton: Aca-
demic Printing and Publishing 1984
– 'Résistance et affirmation: la production francophone à l'ONF 1939–1964.'
PhD dissertation, Université du Québec à Montréal, 1987. Published in part as
Histoire du cinéma au Québec 3. Montreal: La Cinémathèque québécoise 1987
– 'Canadian Film: An Unexpected Emergence.' *Massachussetts Review* 31, nos.
1–2, (Spring–Summer 1990), 213–26
– 'Préludes à l'enseignement du cinéma.' *cinémAction*, special issue on film
education (1991)
Veronneau, Pierre, Michael Dorland, and Seth Feldman, eds. *Dialogue: cinéma
canadien et québécois.* Montreal: Éditions Médiatexte and La Cinémathèque
québécoise 1987
Walker, Dean. 'TV Series Gives Big Boost to Canada's Film-makers.' *Saturday
Night*, 7 Dec. 1957, 12–13, 42–3

Wedman, Les. 'At the Movies.' *Vancouver Sun*, 11 Oct. 1963, 6
Weir, E. Austin. *The Struggle for National Broadcasting in Canada*. Toronto:
    McClelland & Stewart 1965
Whitaker, Reginald. *The Government Party: Organizing and Financing the Liberal
    Party of Canada 1930–58*. Toronto: University of Toronto Press 1977
Whitaker, Reginald, and Greg Marcuse. *Cold War Canada: The Making of a
    National Insecurity State, 1945–1957*. Toronto: University of Toronto Press 1994

Journals

Cahiers du cinéma, 1955–67
Canadian Cinematography, 1961–7
Canadian Film Weekly, 1958–7
Cinema Canada, 1967–89
Cinéma/Québec, 1971–5
Objectif, 1964–7

Index

power, 9, 19–22, 147–9; scholarly, problems of, 29, 149; separate from the state, 22, 149; and state formation, 21

Lamontagne, Maurice, 37; and cultural development, 92, 110–14; as secretary of state, 37, 89
L'Anglais, Paul, 70
language, barriers, 6, 118; context, 6; in discussions of culture, 20; as economics, 94, 99; film as, 132, 134–5; politicization of, 137; visual, 134
Last of the Mohicans, The: making of, 48; sales, 48
Laxer, Gordon, 30
Lefebvre, Jean Pierre, 125; as film critic, 131–3
Lever, Yves, 126–7
Liberal Party of Canada, 36, 89
Luck of Ginger Coffey, The, 98
Lutte, La, 45

Magder, Ted, 15, 18, 31–2
Mains nettes, Les, 44
Maître du Pérou, Le, 44
marketing: scientific, 27; strategies for Canadian TV series and films, 50
Marxism. See theories
masculinity, in Canadian film, 9, 153n22
Massey Report, 14–16, 20, 36, 39–40, 59, 68, 144, 154n35
Massey, Vincent, 11
McKay, Marjorie, 41
McLuhan, H. Marshall, 27
media, mass: hegemony of, viii; policies, 27; rise of and domination by, 27; studies of, 140
Meridian Films, 49, 52, 69

modernization, critique of, 26
monopoly, vii; of cinema and moving images, 28, 33–4
Montreal, 33, 86; as site of cultural authenticity, 124
Montreal International Film Festival, 87, 126–8
Morris, Peter, 23, 80, 130–3, 156n14
Motion Picture Association of America, Inc., 66, 77–9, 104, 119
motion pictures: equipment, 49, 53–4; NFB films in, 39, 87; and product booking, 33; role in Canada, 40; and theatre-chain ownership, 7, 33
Mulholland, Donald, 53, 61
multinational firms, 12; and multinationalization, 56

national affirmation: in Canada, 59, 123; cinema's role in, 91, 123; grand narrative of, 6; in Quebec, 24
national chauvinism, 10–11
national cinema, 6; in Canada, birth of, 126; of France, 6; as ideal-type, 7; of Italy, 6, 23; as national styles, viii; national styles, differences in, 131; as questionable term, 6–9, 130; reconceptualizations of, 8–9; typology of, 8–9
National Film Board of Canada (NFB), x: administration of, 43, 119–20; and anglophone filmmakers, 119–21; and audiences, 41; and big-budget TV series, 50; Board of Governors, x, 89; and Canadian Cooperation Project, 79–80; and CBC, relations with, 40–51, 74; community circuits, 41, 44; contestation of, 17; and feature films, 86–92, 111–14, 119–21; films and Canadian identity, 39; films and telecasts, 39; films, as

Lightning Source UK Ltd.
Milton Keynes UK
UKHW021129080819
347609UK00018B/592/P